MADE TO COUNT

LIFE PLANNER

DISCOVERING WHAT TO DO WITH YOUR LIFE

BOB RECCORD
RANDY SINGER

with CLAUDE V. KING

LifeWay Press®
Nashville, Tennessee

ISBN 1-4158-2819-9

This book is a resource for course CG-1112 in the Personal Life category of the Christian Growth Study Plan.

Dewey Decimal Classification: 248.84
Subject Heading: CHRISTIAN LIFE \ GOD—WILL \ SELF-PERCEPTION

Photography: Cover Images © PhotoDisc, Inc.

The people interviewed for this study graciously gave us permission to include their stories.

Unless otherwise indicated, all Scripture quotations are taken from the Holy Bible, New International Version, copyright © 1973, 1978, 1984 by International Bible Society.

Scripture quotations marked NKJV are taken from the New King James Version. Copyright © 1979, 1980, 1982, Thomas Nelson, Inc., Publishers.

Scripture quotations marked AMP are taken from The Amplified Bible®, copyright © 1954, 1958, 1962, 1964, 1965, 1987 by The Lockman Foundation. Used by permission. (*www.lockman.org*)

Scripture quotations marked NLT are taken from the Holy Bible, New Living Translation, copyright © 1996. Used by permission of Tyndale House Publishers, Inc., Wheaton, IL 60189 USA. All rights reserved.

Scripture quotations marked MSG are from Eugene H. Peterson, The Message.

Scripture quotations marked KJV are taken from the King James Version of the Bible.

To order additional copies of this resource, WRITE to LifeWay Church Resources Customer Service; One LifeWay Plaza; Nashville, TN 37234-0113; FAX (615) 251-5933; PHONE toll free (800) 458-2772; E-MAIL *customerservice@lifeway.com;* ORDER online at *www.lifeway.com;* or VISIT the LifeWay Christian Store serving you.

Printed in the United States of America

Leadership and Adult Publishing
LifeWay Church Resources
One LifeWay Plaza
Nashville, TN 37234-0175

Contents

The Authors

BOB RECCORD

Before becoming the president of the North American Mission Board (NAMB), Bob served in a variety of ministry capacities, including church-staff member, senior pastor of two churches, and U.S. director of leadership training for Evangelism Explosion International. Bob led the major implementation of restructuring the Southern Baptist Convention for the 21st century. Bob has also been a business executive, working in a corporate environment and dealing with business issues ranging from renovating a manufacturing plant to doubling sales revenues during a recession.

In each role in his career, Bob was on mission with God, frequently sharing the way Christ found him, redeemed him, and called him away from a career path that at first seemed to be leading to medical school but then took him in a new direction of ministry. As the president of NAMB, Bob travels and speaks extensively.

Bob is the author of *Forged by Fire* and *Beneath the Surface*.

RANDY SINGER

Randy, the executive vice-president of NAMB, began his career by teaching and coaching in high school. After teaching for five years, he pursued his dream of attending law school. For 12 years Randy practiced law at a Virginia law firm, serving for two years as the head of a litigation section of 30 lawyers. During his tenure as a trial lawyer, Randy was also a law-school professor.

Recently, Randy became an award-winning fiction author, tapping into his courtroom experience to write legal thrillers designed to entertain readers while presenting biblical truths on controversial issues. The gospel is woven throughout *Directed Verdict, Irreparable Harm,* and *Dying Declaration*, confronting readers with the need for personal faith in the living God.

CLAUDE V. KING

Claude entered college with plans to become an archaeologist, but God called him to begin working with people. While he was studying to become a pastor, God led him to become trained to equip lay people for ministry. Claude's degrees in theology and adult education prepared him to work as a design editor of discipleship courses at LifeWay Christian Resources. In this role he worked with Henry Blackaby to develop *Experiencing God* and other discipleship studies. The widespread success of those works led to other writing opportunities. Claude has written or coauthored 20 books that have sold more than five million copies in aggregate. Today Claude serves with the North American Mission Board as the prayer-strategy coordinator in New York City for New Hope New York.

Using the Life Planner

Made to Count Life Planner was designed to help you experience the joy and excitement of being part of God's work to make a difference in your world.

Made to Count is the parent book for the *Life Planner*. Although the book is not required reading for completing this *Life Planner*, reading it will inspire you to seek God's plan and mission for your life. In it you'll meet incredible people who openly and honestly share how they discovered God's plan for making their lives count. They don't just relate the way they found their life's work, although many will tell you that story. And they don't just tell you how they overcame adversity, although you'll read those adventures too. You'll learn much more: how they advanced from just getting by to really making their lives count by fulfilling their God-given callings. You'll also be introduced to eight principles for a life that counts. Recommended readings from *Made to Count* are suggested at the beginning of each week in this *Life Planner*.

Made to Count Life Planner is the resource for this study. Like *Made to Count,* your *Life Planner* includes inspiring stories and discusses eight biblical principles for a life that counts. However, the *Life Planner* uses an educational approach that is intentionally designed to help you experience God's best as you respond to His calling in your life. We want to help you experience God's work through your life to make a difference, beginning right where you are. In this workbook we will help you gain a deeper understanding of the eight principles for a life that counts. You'll enter a closer relationship with Jesus Christ in which you'll hear His calling and direction for your life mission. You'll begin to realize how God is speaking to you to reveal His calling for your life. As you begin taking actions of obedience, God will bear fruit through your life that will make a difference for eternity!

The *Life Planner* may be different from many books you've read. In this workbook we, the authors, will interact with you to help you apply the truths to your life and in your workplace. We'll ask questions and dialogue with you.

We'll suggest activities for you to work through with other Christ-followers in your workplace, profession, or church. To gain the most from the *Life Planner*, you are asked to do two things:

Complete daily individual reading and application. This study consists of 10 weeks of study. Each week's material is divided into five daily segments so that you can use the *Life Planner* as a daily guide for your personal devotional life. Each daily segment includes a Bible passage called "Today's Word on Work" for meditation and a prayer of response that will help you turn your thoughts toward the Lord. Read one day's material at a time and complete the suggested learning activities as you read. You will need to complete your reading of the assigned week's material prior to each small-group session.

In each day's study you will encounter learning activities or application opportunities. Instructions will look like this:

Turn to page 10 and find the first learning activity in week 1, day 1. Check this box when you've done so: ❑

Did you complete the preceding activity? We know this one is very elementary, but please don't skip the learning activities. This process will make your journey more interesting and will help you apply truths while they are fresh on your mind. You not only want to know about God's calling for your life and workplace, but you also want to experience Him actively working through you to make your life count.

Attend weekly small-group sessions. To get the most help from the *Life Planner,* join a small group of one or more Christ-followers each week to discuss what God is saying to you about your life and work. Suggestions for starting and guiding a small group and for conducting each group session are provided on pages 209–22.

WEEK I

A Life That Counts

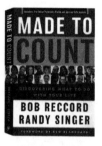

**THIS WEEK'S
SUPPLEMENTARY READING**

Chapter 1, *Made to Count*

During Vacation Bible School, Mike, age 10, committed his life to Jesus Christ. At 14 he became actively involved with a local Christian radio station. Later he began attending a Bible study for teenagers led by a bulldozer operator and his wife, a homemaker. Mike, greatly influenced by this couple, was amazed that they were not full-time Christian workers. Their faith was not relegated to Sundays; they lived it Monday through Saturday.

As Mike grew in his faith, he began to believe that God wanted him to do something special with his life. He thought that if a person answered God's call, he needed to go to seminary and become a preacher. "I never saw myself as a pastor," Mike said. "I saw myself as getting involved in Christian media or media related to evangelism." But people told me I ought to go to seminary because that's what people do when they sense God's call. So off I went to Southwestern Seminary."

During his seminary years Mike did free-lance radio spots for evangelist James Robison's areawide crusades. Later Mike was asked to be the head of the ad and media work. Confused about how this could fit with seminary and God's call, he talked to a wise professor, Oscar Thompson. When Mike explained the opportunity to Dr. Thompson, he expected to hear counsel to stay in school. Instead Dr. Thompson asked, "Why did you come to seminary, Mike?" Mike responded that he had come to prepare himself for a Christian vocation in media.

Dr. Thompson asked, "Then what have you been offered in this job?" Mike explained that it indeed was the fulfillment of everything he had hoped for. Dr. Thompson responded: "Then why are you asking me? God has given you the talent, combined with the passion that is now combined with an opportunity. I think you ought to take it!"

After four years in media Mike moved back to Arkansas, where he accepted a position as a full-time pastor. "Frankly, that was not even on my agenda; but I thought, *Well, I have nothing else to do.* So unlike most pastors, I sort of backed into pastoring."

During 12 years of pastoring, Mike developed a deep interest and love for politics and public policy.

He became a member of the Chamber of Commerce in Texarkana and was elected the president of the Arkansas Baptist Convention. In that position he found himself being consulted on religious and political issues by Governor Bill Clinton.

"The more I saw of politics in the state, the more I became frustrated about what government was doing—and sometimes not doing. My experience showed me that most Christians were willing to stand out on the Capitol steps trying to be a voice *to* government, but very few were willing to actually get inside the Capitol with a voice *in* government. I became convinced that one of the best ways to change things was not simply from the outside shouting inward but from the inside and working outward."

In 1992 Mike determined to run for a U.S. Senate seat and resigned his pastorate to begin a campaign. Many saw his move as leaving the ministry. Although Mike lost the election, Pastor H. D. McCarty commended him for trying to make a difference in the political arena.

Soon thereafter Bill Clinton moved into the White House, and the lieutenant governor, Jim Guy Tucker, stepped into the governor's mansion. That left the lieutenant governor's role open, and Mike was the only Republican with recent statewide experience in a political campaign. The Republican Party turned to Mike. In a surprising upset he beat Bill Clinton's hand-picked candidate!

"I really believe that my call to enter the political arena was as dramatic, as real, and as certain as was the call I felt when I was a teenager and thought God was calling me into some type of ministry. As lieutenant governor, I was seeing God clearly using each sequential step through the seminary, pastoring, and the failed U.S. Senate race to put me exactly where He wanted me. Now I was stepping into a platform in which I could truly be a witness in ways I never could have as a pastor."

On May 28, 1996, Governor Tucker was convicted on federal charges of fraud and conspiracy related to the Whitewater trial. On July 15, 1996, Mike Huckabee became the new governor of Arkansas. Today Mike is an advocate for young Christian men and women actively becoming involved in the political arena, where their lives can make a difference.[1]

Take a moment to pray that God will call others like Mike to engage our culture with a voice inside government. Thank God for Christ-followers who already serve there.

DAY 1
Making a Difference

TODAY'S WORD ON WORK

"We are God's workmanship, created in Christ Jesus to do good works, which God prepared in advance for us to do." Ephesians 2:10

RESPONDING PRAYER

Lord, You have created me for good works that will allow my life to reflect Your workmanship. Teach me how to live my life according to Your plan. Amen.

This study will help you—
• find your life's meaning;
• discover your life's purpose;
• live your life's passion.

> **Read and think about "Today's Word on Work" in the margin and respond to the Lord in prayer.**

Most people want to make a difference in this world. We want to leave an imprint—to leave things and people better than we found them. Yet we fear that the impact of our lives could resemble a fist in the water more than a handprint in cement. The handprint is there to stay. But the water ripples made by the fist soon settle and smooth as though the fist had never been there. Many dread the notion that, in the end, their lives might not count for much.

1 Suppose that your contributions to people and the world ended today. How would you describe the mark you would have left on the world? Check one or write your own.
❑ a. Like a building or a city—a large and lasting mark.
❑ b. Like a handprint in cement—a small but lasting mark.
❑ c. Like a fist in water—few, if any, will remember.
❑ d. Like: _____

For many people this is a great fear: to come to life's end without having made a significant difference. This study speaks directly to that fear. It will help you find your find your life's meaning, discover your life's purpose, and live your life's passion. That's quite a promise, but we hope we can help you experience what God wants to do through your life.

2 If God used this *Life Planner* to ensure that your life would count for eternity, how valuable would that be to you? Check all that apply.
❑ a. Not very much. I don't really care whether my life makes a difference for eternity.
❑ b. It would be worth my time and attention to study and apply these truths to my life and work.
❑ c. It would be worth the adjustments to put aside other less important activities and to focus my life on something lasting.
❑ d. I'm not sure yet, but I'll give this *Life Planner* a try.

We hope that you checked *b* and/or *c.* We'll even accept *d* as a positive response. If you checked *a,* stay with us anyway. We believe that God still speaks and moves in mysterious and wonderful ways. He created you to make a difference. He has plans for you—" 'plans to prosper you and not to harm you, plans to give you hope and a future' " (Jeremiah 29:11). God not only made you to count but also stands ready to work in and through you to ensure that His purposes come to pass.

③ **Read Philippians 2:13 in the margin and answer the following questions.**

a. Who is at work in you? _____

b. What is God causing you to do? Fill in the blanks:

He is causing me "to _____ and to _____."

c. Whose good purpose is the guideline for your actions?

❏ Mine   ❏ His

> "It is God who works in you to will and to act according to his good purpose."
> Philippians 2:13

Throughout the Bible you can see that God was at work in and through the lives of people like Moses, Joseph, David, and the disciples. He gave them a purpose for living. He was the One who caused them to want to do His will, and He was the One who enabled them to do it. God cares about your work too! He has a purpose for your life.

Every believer's vocation should be the result of a call by God. A believer's life belongs to Jesus Christ. All aspects of our lives, not just spiritual matters, belong under His care and direction. Because God is interested in healing, He calls some people to be doctors and nurses. Because He's the Mighty Counselor, He calls others into counseling. Because He created and established commerce, He calls still others into business as salt and light. God calls people wherever there's a sphere of influence, whether it be politics, writing, acting, medicine, or any other area. And there's no greater place to be than where you know God has called you to live your life for Him!

④ **Review today's summary ideas and respond to God in prayer.**
- God created you to make a difference.
- God not only made you to count but also stands ready to work in and through you to ensure that His purposes come to pass.
- God cares about your work.
- God has a purpose for your life.
- There's no greater place to be than where you know God has called you to live your life for Him!

DAY 2

Paul Turns His World Upside Down

Before meeting Jesus Christ, Saul of Tarsus was a Pharisee and a persecutor of Christ-followers. He consented to the stoning death of Stephen, an early martyr of the church. He wreaked havoc against the church, going from house to house arresting the Lord's disciples and dragging them off to prison. In the most literal sense of the word, Saul was a terrorist. But one day that all changed. Before we look at what God did with Saul ...

TODAY'S WORD ON WORK

"I can do all things through Christ who strengthens me."
Philippians 4:13, NKJV

RESPONDING PRAYER

Jesus, I need Your strength today. Without You I can do nothing of lasting value. I want my life to count for You. Be my strength today! Amen.

> **Read and think about "Today's Word on Work" in the margin and respond to the Lord in prayer.**

1. **Read the following Scripture and underline the assignment God had for Saul. What had God chosen Saul to do?**

Saul was still breathing out murderous threats against the Lord's disciples. He went to the high priest and asked him for letters to the synagogues in Damascus, so that if he found any there who belonged to the Way, whether men or women, he might take them as prisoners to Jerusalem. As he neared Damascus on his journey, suddenly a light from heaven flashed around him. He fell to the ground and heard a voice say to him, "Saul, Saul, why do you persecute me?"

"Who are you, Lord?" Saul asked.

"I am Jesus, whom you are persecuting," he replied. "Now get up and go into the city, and you will be told what you must do. ..."

When he opened his eyes he could see nothing. So they led him by the hand into Damascus. For three days he was blind, and did not eat or drink anything. ...

The Lord said to Ananias, "Go! This man is my chosen instrument to carry my name before the Gentiles and their kings and before the people of Israel. I will show him how much he must suffer for my name."

Then Ananias went to the house and entered it. Placing his hands on Saul, he said, "Brother Saul, the Lord—Jesus, who appeared to you on the road as you were coming here—has sent me so that you may see again and be filled with the Holy Spirit." Immediately, something like scales fell from Saul's eyes, and he could see again. He got up and was baptized. ...

Saul spent several days with the disciples in Damascus. At once he began to preach in the synagogues that Jesus is the Son of God. All those who heard him were astonished and asked, "Isn't he the man who raised havoc in Jerusalem among those who call on this name? And hasn't he come here to take them as prisoners to the chief priests?" Yet Saul grew more and more powerful and baffled the Jews living in Damascus by proving that Jesus is the Christ (Acts 9:1-22).

Jesus had chosen Saul to be an instrument to " 'carry [His] name before the Gentiles and their kings and before the people of Israel' " (Acts 9:15). Saul didn't become a more accomplished Pharisee or a more intimidating terrorist. His heart changed. His priorities changed. His mission changed. Even his name changed. Saul, the terrorist of the church, became "Paul, an apostle of Christ Jesus by the will of God" (Ephesians 1:1).

Paul's mission changed from destroying the church to building it. God called Paul to do things Paul could never have done on his own. Paul the apostle became an advocate for the faith rather than a persecutor of it. Don't you love the way God works? He took Saul, the worst of sinners, and turned him into Paul, the best of missionaries!

Then God called Paul to preach, although Paul wasn't particularly eloquent or wise. God did all this so that there would be no mistake about who got the glory or about how all this was possible in the first place: "My message and my preaching were not with wise and persuasive words," Paul said, "but with a demonstration of the Spirit's power, so that your faith might not rest on men's wisdom, but on God's power" (1 Corinthians 2:4-5).

2 **Read the list of Paul's accomplishments in the margin. Then circle the one that, in your opinion, seems to be the most significant.**

Fairly impressive list of accomplishments, isn't it? But you might be surprised to know how Paul made his living.

3 **Read the following Scripture and circle the word that describes the work Paul did to support himself.**

Paul went to see [Aquila and Priscilla], and because he was a tent-maker as they were, he stayed and worked with them. Every Sabbath he reasoned in the synagogue, trying to persuade Jews and Greeks (Acts 18:2-4).

PAUL'S ACCOMPLISHMENTS

• Paul led many Jews, Greeks, and people of high standing to faith in Christ.

• Paul started churches in cities throughout the regions of the northeastern Mediterranean.

• Paul healed many, including a crippled man in Lystra.

• Paul survived a stoning and continued preaching.

• Paul endured a flogging and later led the jailer and his family to faith in Christ.

• Paul trained young men like Timothy and Titus to be pastors and leaders.

• Paul collected an offering among the Gentile churches to assist the Jewish Christians in Judea during a famine.

• When a young boy fell out of a window and died while Paul was preaching, Paul prayed, and the boy was brought back to life.

• Paul cast evil spirits out of people.

• Paul witnessed about Jesus Christ to governors and kings and perhaps to Caesar too.

• Paul wrote 13 books of the New Testament.

Paul was a tentmaker by profession. Although he could have received his funding from the churches he served, Paul chose to earn his own living so that he could preach the gospel "free of charge" (1 Corinthians 9:18).

The Apostle Paul is considered the greatest Christian missionary of all time. He left a legacy through his New Testament writings that have had an impact on people for two thousand years. His jealous opponents in Thessalonica made this charge of Paul and Silas: " 'These who have turned the world upside down have come here too' " (Acts 17:6, NKJV). God had created Paul for a divine purpose. Paul's life is a wonderful illustration of what this book is all about. Paul was made to count.

Because Paul is a good example of someone whose life made a significant difference in his world, we will examine his story from time to time to discover what we can learn from his example. In addition, Paul had much to say in his 13 New Testament books about how Christ-followers should live their lives to make them count for Christ. His teachings will help you learn how you can allow your life to count for Christ also.

> God had created Paul for a divine purpose.

4 **Review today's summary ideas and respond to God in prayer. Ask the Lord to teach you through Paul's life and message how your life can count for Christ.**

- "I can do all things through Christ who strengthens me" (Philippians 4:13, NKJV).
- God called Paul to do things Paul could never have done on his own.
- Don't you love the way God works? He took Saul, the worst of sinners, and turned him into Paul, the best of missionaries!
- Paul chose to earn his own living so that he could preach the gospel "free of charge" (1 Corinthians 9:18).

DAY 3

Eight Principles

The stories of Mike Huckabee and Saul of Tarsus show that God can mold and shape someone into a life that makes a difference for Christ's kingdom. God can and will do that with your life if you are willing. In fact, He pursues that kind of relationship with you.

Read and think about "Today's Word on Work" in the margin and respond to the Lord in prayer.

If you want your life to count for Christ's kingdom, you must begin with a personal relationship with Jesus Christ. God comes in and prepares you for a life of significance in service to the Creator of the universe, Jesus Christ.

Today we will introduce you to eight biblical principles for a life that counts. These principles are set forth in Scripture, placed there for your benefit by the same God who created you for a special plan and life-changing purpose.

1 **Read the eight principles. Then write in the margin a title for each principle that encapsulates its key idea.**

EIGHT PRINCIPLES FOR A LIFE THAT COUNTS

1. God prepared a unique plan and calling for your life even before you were born.
2. God calls you to a life-changing relationship with Him through Jesus Christ.
3. God calls you to partner with Him in a mission that is bigger than you are.
4. God calls you to be on mission with Him right where you are—starting now.
5. God reveals His mission through His Word, His Spirit, wise counsel, and His work in circumstances around you.
6. God repeatedly brings you to a crossroads of choice as He forges you for His mission.
7. God guides and provides for your mission one step at a time.
8. When you answer God's call, you experience His pleasure and change your world.

TODAY'S WORD ON WORK

" 'Behold, I stand at the door and knock. If anyone hears My voice and opens the door, I will come in to him and dine with him, and he with Me.' "
Revelation 3:20, NKJV

RESPONDING PRAYER

Lord, come on in! I would love to experience this kind of fellowship with You. I want to count for Your kingdom. Amen.

YOUR TITLES

I. _____

2. _____

3. _____

4. _____

5. _____

6. _____

7. _____

8. _____

OUR TITLES

I. God's Unique Plan
2. Life-Changing Relationship
3. Called to a Mission
4. Called Now
5. God Reveals His Mission
6. Crossroads of Choice
7. God Guides and Provides
8. Changing Your World

Read in the margin the titles we gave the principles. You may have written different titles, and that's OK. We want to help you recognize and understand these eight principles so that you can apply them in your life. The principles are not applicable just to a subculture of "professional" ministers or missionaries. They apply equally to believers who are called to be on mission with God in their workplaces and in their daily life. They apply to you!

2 As you review the eight principles ...

- Which one are you most interested in learning more about?

  Number _____

- Which one, if any, seems to be the most difficult to believe?

  Number _____

- If these principles were on a time line for your life, which principle would apply to your life at the present time?

  Number _____ Why? _____

  _____

These principles are woven through the lives of people in a way that makes it impossible to organize everything into neat little categories. They should be viewed more as ingredients in a recipe than cookie-cutter solutions that force everyone into the same mold. Nevertheless, these eight God-centered principles will help make your life count for eternity. Keep reading to learn how.

3 Review the principles as today's summary. Then talk to the Lord about your greatest concern for your life and your place in His unique plan.

DAY 4

Three Stages in God's Process

> **Read and think about "Today's Word on Work" in the margin and respond to the Lord in prayer.**

TODAY'S WORD ON WORK

" 'If anyone would come after me, he must deny himself and take up his cross daily and follow me.' "
Luke 9:23

Did you ever run in a race in which the starter used these words: "Get ready; get set; go!"? Those words can describe three stages in God's process of making your life count.

RESPONDING PRAYER

Lord Jesus, I want to follow You. I want to experience life at its best. Would You help me understand what is required for me to deny myself, take up my cross, and follow You? Amen.

THREE STAGES IN GOD'S PROCESS

1. Get ready: Cultivate Your Relationship
2. Get set: Receive God's Assignments
3. Go: Fulfill Your Mission

As we study these three stages, we will learn how the eight principles for a life that counts, which we overviewed yesterday, relate to these three stages in God's process.

Stage I: Cultivate Your Relationship

Your relationship with God is the essential element in experiencing His best. Without it your life will have no eternal and lasting value, and you will be limited to what humans are capable of doing in their own power. But in a relationship with God you can experience Him working through you in a way that only God can work—accomplishing things that only God can do.

① **To see an example of someone who discovered a life-altering relationship with God, read Jonathan Aitken's story in "Finding God on the Way to Prison" on page 18.**

FINDING GOD ON THE WAY TO PRISON

Jonathan Aitken's political rise was as spectacular as his downfall. Educated at Eton and Oxford, Jonathan spent time as a political correspondent, an author, and a TV director. First elected as a Tory member of England's Parliament in 1974, he served as defense minister and then as chief secretary to the treasury.

"I was leading a life that was not pleasing in God's eyes," Jonathan explains. "Although I was paying Him lip service for an hour a week as a 'Sunday Christian,' I was not living a committed Christian life in my behavior, attitude, and commitment." In 1999 Jonathan was accused of lying in court. He was convicted of perjury and sentenced to 18 months in jail, a dramatic end to a glittering career.

Jonathan readily admits that he came to know Christ in the depths of personal adversity. Two years passed between his indictment and his sentencing, and God was at work in Jonathan's life during that time. He says: "Those two years were a very painful but also very fruitful period of my life. Painful in the sense that my whole world was falling apart in a very short period of time. I went through defeat, disgrace, divorce, bankruptcy, and jail; that's a pretty good crush of crises by anybody's standards. But at the same time, thanks to Chuck Colson, a group of Christian friends created by him gathered around me in a small fellowship group that sort of steered me and mentored me. Before I went to prison, I definitely arrived in the new country of committed faith, committed belief, and total commitment to Jesus."

When Jonathan left prison, God had a plan to call him to be on mission with Him. "When I came out of prison, I said to myself, *What I most want to do with the rest of my life is to serve God.* What I didn't know was how." Jonathan determined that in order to serve God, he needed to know Him better. So he applied to Wycliffe Hall, a theological college in Oxford. He spent two years there and at age 57 found himself taking tests, learning Greek, and passing the university's theological exam.

Many of the other students had given up successful careers to become ministers. But God had other plans for Jonathan. "I could have been called to be an ordained minister of the gospel, but I never felt that call." Instead he got involved in mission trips around the world, during which he sharpened his evangelism skills.

"I suppose God had given me two talents. One was the ability to write coherent English, and the other was to go and talk and address an audience. But now I was on a totally different wavelength of spiritual service preaching the gospel of Christ. I started to feel called to do missions through my pen and my public-speaking activities."

At the time of our interview with Jonathan, he was writing a biography of Charles Colson—another politician who met Christ after his political downfall.[2]

2. **If God evaluated your relationship with Him right now, how would you measure up? Check one.**

❑ a. I'm like the person Jonathan used to be: a "Sunday Christian" who is living a lie by paying only lip service to God.

❑ b. I'm in "the new country of committed faith, committed belief, and total commitment to Jesus."

❑ c. I'm somewhere between *a* and *b*.

❑ d. I'm already on mission with God in exciting ways.

The first stage in a life that counts is to enter and cultivate a personal relationship with Jesus Christ. Think about the eight principles for a life that counts, which you studied yesterday. The first two of those principles relate to stage 1, Cultivate Your Relationship with God. Each principle requires that you make a response to God.

STAGE I: CULTIVATE YOUR RELATIONSHIP

Principle 1: God prepared a unique plan and calling for your life even before you were born.

Your response: Seek to recognize, understand, and participate in God's plan.

Principle 2: God calls you to a life-changing relationship with Him through Jesus Christ.

Your response: Enter the relationship and submit to God's transforming work in your life.

Stage 2: Receive God's Assignments

In the second stage of God's process to make your life count, you receive God's assignments. The next three of the eight principles describe the second stage.

STAGE 2: RECEIVE GOD'S ASSIGNMENTS

Principle 3: God calls you to partner with Him in a mission that is bigger than you are.

Principle 4: God calls you to be on mission with Him right where you are—starting now.

Principle 5: God reveals His mission through His Word, His Spirit, wise counsel, and His work in circumstances around you.

Your response: Receive God's assignments and begin obeying by faith.

Your response in this second stage is similar for all three principles. You receive God's assignments. You clarify what God is asking you to do and where He wants you to do it. Then you begin obeying by faith.

EIGHT PRINCIPLES FOR A LIFE THAT COUNTS

I. God prepared a unique plan and calling for your life even before you were born.

2. God calls you to a life-changing relationship with Him through Jesus Christ.

3. God calls you to partner with Him in a mission that is bigger than you are.

4. God calls you to be on mission with Him right where you are—starting now.

5. God reveals His mission through His Word, His Spirit, wise counsel, and His work in circumstances around you.

6. God repeatedly brings you to a crossroads of choice as He forges you for His mission.

7. God guides and provides for your mission one step at a time.

8. When you answer God's call, you experience His pleasure and change your world.

3 **Fill in the blanks to complete your responses in the first two stages of God's process to make your life count. You can look back to find the answers if you need to.**

1. Seek to recognize, understand, and participate in God's _____.
2. Enter the _____ and _____ to God's transforming work in your life.
3. Receive God's _____ and begin obeying by _____.

We'll look more deeply into these stages, the principles, and your responses in later weeks of study. Before we move to the third stage, we want to begin alerting you to the nature of the mission to which God may call you. He may give many assignments that are both large and small. But the mission or ministry to which God may call you will have more significant dimensions to it. The lists below are not exhaustive but may help you begin to understand what God has in store for you.

4 **As you read the following lists describing what a mission is and what it is not, underline statements that seem to be especially meaningful or applicable to you. If you have questions, write them in the margin.**

QUESTIONS

_____
_____
_____
_____
_____
_____
_____
_____
_____
_____
_____
_____
_____
_____

A mission or ministry is—
- a ministry to which God has called you, one He has assigned you to accomplish;
- a specific ministry in which you work with intention to participate in God's redemptive plan for the world;
- a ministry for which God provides a spiritual gift to bring forth fruit;
- a ministry for which He provides the necessary human and material resources;
- a significant ministry—one that has worth because of the God-sized dimensions, one that makes a difference for God's redemptive work in the lives of people, or one that requires significant effort and time;
- a ministry that penetrates spiritually dark areas of our world, society, or culture with spiritual light.

A mission or ministry is not—
- quietly living a moral life with the hope that someone might guess that Jesus is the reason for your lifestyle;
- participating in religious activities primarily for your personal knowledge or development;
- giving money to the church primarily so that someone else can do ministry on your behalf;
- spontaneously performing an isolated act of service because of guilt,

an emotional appeal, or a desire to appear right or good in the eyes of observers.

5 **Review today's summary ideas and respond to God in prayer. Ask Him to open your mind to recognize the mission He has in store for you when He calls you.**

- In a relationship with God you can experience Him working through you in a way that only God can work—accomplishing things that only God can do.
- Seek to recognize, understand, and participate in God's plan.
- Enter the relationship and submit to God's transforming work in your life.
- Receive God's assignments and begin obeying by faith.

DAY 5

Fulfill Your Mission

God has a mission assignment and a purpose for every member of His kingdom. Even when God was carrying out judgment on His people in captivity in Babylon, He sent them word through Jeremiah that He had good plans for them.

> **Read and think about "Today's Word on Work" in the margin and respond to the Lord in prayer.**

Because God is perfect love, He always seeks our best. That is what love is all about. Sometimes God's love requires Him to discipline and correct us so that we can be the kind of people who will receive His best. As with the exiles in Babylon, God has plans for us that include prosperity, hope, and a future.

1 **In Jeremiah 29:11-13 God promised that His people would find Him when they seek Him in a particular way. How should we seek God?**

With all _____

TODAY'S WORD ON WORK

"I know the plans I have for you," declares the Lord, "plans to prosper you and not to harm you, plans to give you hope and a future. Then you will call upon me and come and pray to me, and I will listen to you. You will seek me and find me when you seek me with all your heart."
Jeremiah 29:11-13

RESPONDING PRAYER

God, I trust that You have plans for my life, plans that are good for me and not harmful. I want to be the kind of person who will cooperate with Your plans. I want the kind of prayer relationship with You in which I will find You. Show me the way to experience Your best. Amen.

Yesterday we introduced you to three stages in God's process of making your life count.

2 **Review the three stages by filling in the blanks below. If you need to review, look back at page 17.**

THREE STAGES IN GOD'S PROCESS
1. Get ready: Cultivate Your _____
2. Get set: Receive God's _____
3. Go: Fulfill Your _____

Stage 2 is a place where many people over the years have missed God's best because of a lack of understanding. People have often assumed that God calls only professional clergy to the mission assignments in His kingdom. The rest miss the pleasures of experiencing God's power at work through them to accomplish His purposes. The wonderful truth is that when God brings you into a relationship with Himself through Jesus Christ, He already has a plan for your life that will count for eternity. He wants you to be a part of that exciting and fulfilling mission more than you do, because this is His work at stake, not yours.

Even when people have understood that God has a mission for everyone in His kingdom, they have sometimes missed God's best because they limited their thinking only to ministries inside the organized church. God's influence for good is as big as the universe. At the beginning of your quest, we want to expand your thinking to include the vast scope in which God works. God is not limited to the inside of a church building or an organization.

SEVEN ARENAS FOR MISSION ASSIGNMENTS

l. The structures of culture and society

2. Your daily workplace

3. The platform of your profession or career

4. The needy people of society or the world

5. Your home and extended family

6. Your other circles of influence or relationships

7. The organizational life of the church

3 **Read in the margin the list of arenas in which God may give you a mission assignment or ministry. Then answer the questions that follow.**

a. Which of these seven arenas is the most typical place for Christ-followers to participate in a ministry or mission? Number _____

b. In which of these seven arenas do think Christ-followers would have the greatest difficulty making a significant impact? Number _____
Why? _____

_____

c. If God called you to it, in which of these seven arenas do you think you would have the greatest pleasure making a difference? Number _____
Also write the name of the arena: _____

d. Can you think of other arenas in which God might call a person to be on mission? If so, write them below.

_____

_____

_____

_____

_____

For many years the most typical place for Christ-followers to participate in a mission or ministry was inside the organized church. Another typical area was among the needy. You may have chosen a different response for question *b*, but the structures of culture and society are often the least likely places for Christ-followers to pursue mission and ministry. Yet government, higher education, media, and law are the places where Christ's salt and light are needed the most. These are the places where our society and culture will be shaped for evil or good.

> Government, higher education, media, and law are the places where Christ's salt and light are needed the most.

4 **Take a moment to pray about where God may want to call you to be on mission with Him.**
  - Ask Him to call people to serve in every aspect of our society and culture where change is needed.
  - Ask Him to guide and enable you to serve in the places where He has placed you to have an influence for His kingdom.

5 **Write one of your prayers about God's calling for your life or your mission.**

_____

_____

_____

_____

_____

_____

Yesterday we began looking at three stages in God's process of making your life count.

THREE STAGES IN GOD'S PROCESS
1. Get ready: Cultivate Your Relationship
2. Get set: Receive God's Assignments
3. Go: Fulfill Your Mission

First, you get ready by cultivating your relationship with Jesus Christ. Second, you get set by receiving God's assignments and beginning to obey in faith. Third, you go by fulfilling your mission in the place to which God sends you.

Stage 3: Fulfill Your Mission

Stage 3 encompasses the final three of the eight principles for a life that counts. Each principle has a corresponding response.

STAGE 3: FULFILL YOUR MISSION

Principle 6: God repeatedly brings you to a crossroads of choice as He forges you for His mission.

Your response: Seek His directions at every crossroads and pay the price for the adjustments required.

Principle 7: God guides and provides for your mission one step at a time.

Your response: Depend on God for guidance and provision as you continue your walk of faith.

Principle 8. When you answer God's call, you experience His pleasure and change your world.

Your response: Obey Him and give Him glory when He accomplishes His work through you.

A MISSION ACCOMPLISHED

You will probably always remember where you were on that Saturday morning in February 2003 when the space shuttle Columbia disintegrated over Texas. All of our hearts stood still as we watched the sequence in stunned silence. Hurtling through space on reentry at more than 18 times the speed of sound and experiencing temperatures in excess of 3,000 degrees at more than 200,000 feet in altitude, the Columbia began to break apart. Shortly afterward, President George W. Bush spoke to the nation to confirm the tragedy. Somberly, our president told us that all seven astronauts had been killed.

Rick Husband, the commander of the Columbia, was a close friend of contemporary Christian singer Steve Green. In an interview Green said: "Rick recognized his calling absolutely to be an astronaut. Rick was a shining example of someone who understood his calling. He'd been gifted and called into an arena of service as an astronaut. He did it with everything inside of him. He was the best he could possibly be, and he did it to the glory of God."[3]

Rick Husband saw himself as on mission but not just for NASA. He had an even higher calling. During his time at NASA Rick invited other astronauts and aspiring astronauts into his home for Bible study. He wanted those gifted and talented people to know the Creator into whose heavens they would soar. That was Rick's mission field, his platform for making a difference for the Savior he knew. Will you also fulfill your mission?

6 **Read "A Mission Accomplished" on page 24 to see an example of someone who fulfilled God's mission for him.**

7 **Review today's summary ideas and respond to God in prayer about your calling and mission.**

- God has a mission assignment and a purpose for every member of His kingdom.
- Because God is perfect love, He always seeks our best.
- When God brings you into a relationship with Himself through Jesus Christ, He already has a plan for your life that will count for eternity.
- God is not limited to the inside of a church building or an organization.
- Government, higher education, media, and law are the places where Christ's salt and light are needed the most.

---

[1]Authors' interview, 12 May 2003.
[2]Authors' interview, 19 June 2003.
[3]Interview with Baptist Press, 11 February 2003.

WEEK 2

God's Unique Plan

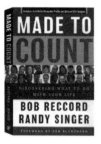

THIS WEEK'S SUPPLEMENTARY READING

Chapters 2–4, *Made to Count*

Jay was born in Brooklyn, New York, on June 10, 1956. Later his family moved to Long Island, where Jay attended a Hebrew school, although religion was never a very important part of his life. As a teenager Jay moved with his family to Atlanta, where he finished high school.

After graduation Jay enrolled in Mercer University, a Baptist college, so that he could stay close to home and study law. Determined to outstudy and outsmart the Christians, Jay especially looked forward to Bible class, where he would be able to prove that Jesus was not the Messiah.

But then Jay ran headlong into the prophecy of the suffering Messiah in Isaiah 53. It boggled his mind. *I have to be misreading the text,* Jay thought. He grabbed the Jewish text, but the description of the suffering Messiah seemed just as clear. How did he resolve this new crisis of belief?

Jay did what any aspiring lawyer might do. He examined the evidence. Taking out a sheet of paper and drawing a line down the middle, he listed ways Jesus fit the description of the Messiah on the right side and ways He did not on the left. "I kept looking for a traditional Jewish explanation that would satisfy but found none. The only plausible explanation seemed to be Jesus."

"I'd always thought my cultural Judaism was sufficient, but in the course of studying about the Messiah who would die as a sin-bearer, I realized that I needed a Messiah to do that for me."

A few days later Jay went to hear a Jews for Jesus singing group named the Liberated Wailing Wall. He felt enormous relief when he realized that other Jews believed in Christ as the Messiah. At the conclusion of the service, the group invited people to give their lives to Christ. Jay did just that, and everything changed.

Now that God had this young law student's fervent heart, He began to prepare Jay's mind for the challenges that were ahead. Jay would need a lot of trial experience and the ability to take firm stands for unpopular causes. God had just the ticket—the Internal Revenue Service. "I began my career at law as a prosecutor for the IRS. In one sense it's a miserable job; prosecuting people for fraud and tax evasion never won anybody a popularity contest. What made it worthwhile was that I was trying

as many as 12 cases per week. That kind of experience can really launch a person into a terrific career."

When the IRS requested that Jay relocate, he left government work and entered private practice. Jay's law firm flourished, as did a real-estate development company that Jay started on the side. But the thing that motivated Jay most was the work he was doing as a board member for Jews for Jesus, helping the organization that first introduced him to Christ.

When the opportunity came to work for them as general counsel, Jay immediately left his lucrative private practice. Before long he was defending the rights of Jews to share the gospel in airports, arguing before the highest court in the land at the age of 30. He won the case with a rare unanimous ruling from the nine justices.

Today Jay Sekulow heads one of the top public-interest law firms in the country, the American Center for Law and Justice. He heads a large staff of lawyers who take on hundreds of cases a year. Jay himself has argued at the Supreme Court nine times, always defending the religious freedoms guaranteed by our Constitution.

In a 1990 case involving the constitutionality of Bible and prayer clubs on public-school campuses, Jay cleared the way for generations of public-school students to share the gospel with their classmates. Three years later another case guaranteed the rights of churches and religious groups to use school facilities after hours.

Talk to Jay for five minutes or listen to his daily radio talk show, and you'll be amazed at the passion and energy he brings to his work. He loves it. The law fascinates him, and the tension energizes him. And in the midst of all the fevered activity, Jay never loses sight of the fact that God, not the court, is ultimately in control. That thought always calms him in the storm.

God looked out at the future on June 10, 1956, and knew He would one day need a good constitutional lawyer. So He created Jay Sekulow and began to prepare him for his calling.[1]

Take a moment to thank God for attorneys who work to protect our religious liberties. Ask the Lord to raise up other Christian lawyers and judges who will seek justice and will rule according to God's purposes for humanity.

Wherever you are today and in whatever circumstances you find yourself, God is calling you by name to a special plan and an incredible adventure. Want to join Him? Read on.

DAY 1

Principle I: God's Unique Plan

TODAY'S WORD ON WORK

"God ... set me apart from birth and called me by his grace."
Galatians 1:15

RESPONDING PRAYER

Lord, You called Paul the apostle by Your grace. And You called and prepared Jay Sekulow. I pray that You will reveal to me Your purposes for my service to Your kingdom. I want to participate in Your plan for my world. Amen.

> **Read and think about "Today's Word on Work" in the margin and respond to the Lord in prayer.**

Last week we introduced you to eight principles for a life that counts.

1 **Fill in the blanks below to review the eight principles for a life that counts. If you need help, see page 15.**

1. God prepared a unique _____ and _____ for your life even _____ you were born.

2. God calls you to a life-changing _____ with Him through _____ _____.

3. God calls you to partner with Him in a _____ that is _____ than you are.

4. God calls you to be on _____ with Him right where you are—starting _____.

5. God reveals His mission through His _____, His _____, wise _____, and His work in _____ around you.

6. God repeatedly brings you to a crossroads of _____ as He _____ you for His mission.

7. God _____ and _____ for your mission one _____ at a time.

8. When you _____ God's call, you experience His _____ and _____ your world.

Today let's focus on the first principle to discover how it fits into your search for your life purpose.

2 **Read principle 1 several times, giving special attention to the words that are bold and underlined.**

God prepared a unique **plan** and **calling** for your life even **before** you were born.

3 **Now personalize the principle by rewriting it below. Change *your* to *my* and *you were* to *I was.***

_____

_____

4 **Complete your response to principle 1. Refer to page 19 if you need to.**

Seek to _____, _____,

and _____ in God's plan.

God created you with a purpose in mind. And the Master Designer knew just what it would take for you to accomplish that purpose in complete reliance on Him.

Think about the many ways God expresses this principle in Scripture. He said to Jeremiah:

"Before I formed you in the womb I knew you,
   before you were born I set you apart;
I appointed you as a prophet to the nations" (Jeremiah 1:5).

5 **When did God set apart Jeremiah to be a prophet?**

_____

God is all-knowing. He knows the past, present, and future. He creates with the end in mind, not just the beginning. God explained that He knew Jeremiah before He created him in his mother's womb. God had a unique plan and calling for Jeremiah before he was born.

"That's just Jeremiah," we say. "Maybe God made Jeremiah perfectly suited to his task. But look at me; I'm no Jeremiah!" But God knows what He's doing. And lest we think that this was a special concept that applied only to Old Testament prophets, God revealed a similar thought to the Apostle Paul: "God … set me apart from birth and called me by his grace" (Galatians 1:15).

6 **Read Galatians 1:15-17 in the margin. Why did God set apart Paul from birth, call him, and reveal His Son [Jesus] in him? "So that [he] might**

_____."

"When God, who set me apart from birth and called me by his grace, was pleased to reveal his Son in me so that I might preach him among the Gentiles, I did not consult any man, nor did I go up to Jerusalem to see those who were apostles before I was, but I went immediately into Arabia and later returned to Damascus."
Galatians 1:15-17

God set apart Paul from birth to preach the gospel of Jesus Christ to the Gentiles (non-Jews). Paul did not learn about this calling until after he met Jesus on the road to Damascus. Jesus said to him: " 'Go into Damascus. There you will be told all that you have been assigned to do' " (Acts 22:10).

In Damascus God sent Ananias to Paul with this message: " ' "The God of our fathers has chosen you to know his will and to see the Righteous One and to hear words from his mouth. You will be his witness to all men of what you have seen and heard" ' " (Acts 22:14-15). Jesus explained to Paul that He was sending Paul to the Gentiles " ' "to open their eyes and turn them from darkness to light, and from the power of Satan to God, so that they may receive forgiveness of sins and a place among those who are sanctified by faith in me" ' " (Acts 26:18).

God had a unique plan and calling for Paul's life. God prepared that plan before Paul was born. When the time was right, Jesus revealed the plan to Paul, and God enabled and used Paul to change his world.

In his letter to the church in Ephesus, Paul made it plain that this concept applies to every believer.

7 **As you read Ephesians 2:10 below, underline the reason God created you and when He prepared these assignments for you.**

We are God's workmanship, created in Christ Jesus to do good works, which God prepared in advance for us to do (Ephesians 2:10).

God created you for good works. He made those plans for you in advance. The word translated *workmanship* is the Greek word that means *masterpiece*. This awesome God, the One who created the majesty of the universe, says that we are His masterpiece, a work of art, specially created for a world-changing purpose.

God did not create masterpieces just to put us on display. He created us to enjoy a relationship with Him and to make a difference for Him. He created us to do good works that accomplish His purposes in His world. Our response is to seek to recognize, understand, and participate in that plan.

8 **Review today's summary ideas and respond to God in prayer. Thank Him for making you as a masterpiece with a special plan for your life.**
- God prepared a unique plan and calling for your life even before you were born.
- Your response is to seek to recognize, understand, and participate in that plan.
- God created you with a purpose in mind.
- God creates with the end in mind, not just the beginning.
- God created you for good works.

> God created you for good works.

DAY 2

God's Plan for John the Baptist

Read and think about "Today's Word on Work" in the margin and respond to the Lord in prayer.

TODAY'S WORD ON WORK

" 'Produce fruit in keeping with repentance. ... Every tree that does not produce good fruit will be cut down and thrown into the fire.' "
Luke 3:8-9

About eight hundred years before Jesus came to earth, the prophet Isaiah brought comforting words to God's people:

> A voice of one calling:
> "In the desert prepare
>   the way for the Lord;
> make straight in the wilderness
>   a highway for our God.
> Every valley shall be raised up,
>   every mountain and hill made low;
> the rough ground shall become level,
>   the rugged places a plain.
> And the glory of the Lord will be revealed,
>   and all mankind together will see it.
> For the mouth of the Lord has spoken" (Isaiah 40:3-5).

RESPONDING PRAYER

Lord, You've created me for good works—to produce good fruit. Please accomplish Your will and purposes in and through my life so that people might see Jesus in me. Amen.

Many years later God sent a message through the prophet Malachi that a prophet like Elijah would come to "turn the hearts of the fathers to their children, and the hearts of the children to their fathers" "before that great and dreadful day of the Lord comes" (Malachi 4:6,5). When Jesus was about to come and fulfill God's redemptive work for the world, the way needed to be prepared for Him. So God planned to send John the Baptist to prepare the way for the coming of the Lord. First God sent an angel to a priest named Zechariah.

1 **Read the angel's message and answer the questions that follow.**
The angel said to him: "Do not be afraid, Zechariah; your prayer has been heard. Your wife Elizabeth will bear you a son, and you are to give him the name John. He will be a joy and delight to you, and many will rejoice because of his birth, for he will be great in the sight of the

Lord. He is never to take wine or other fermented drink, and he will be filled with the Holy Spirit even from birth. Many of the people of Israel will he bring back to the Lord their God. And he will go on before the Lord, in the spirit and power of Elijah, to turn the hearts of the fathers to their children and the disobedient to the wisdom of the righteous—to make ready a people prepared for the Lord" (Luke 1:13-17).

a. What was Zechariah to name the son who was promised?

_____

b. When would the boy be filled with the Holy Spirit?

_____

c. How would many of the people of Israel respond?

_____

d. What would John's assignment be? To make ready ...

_____

> John would bring many people in Israel back to the Lord.

Zechariah was to name his son John. John would be filled with the Holy Spirit from the time of his birth, and he would bring many people in Israel back to the Lord. John the Baptist's assignment from before birth was to "make ready a people prepared for the Lord" (verse 17).

When John began his ministry in Israel, he preached "a baptism of repentance for the forgiveness of sins" (Luke 3:3) to prepare the way for the Lord Jesus.

2 **Read some of the events in John's ministry. Underline the instructions he gave about what people should do.**

"What should we do then?" the crowd asked.

John answered, "The man with two tunics should share with him who has none, and the one who has food should do the same."

Tax collectors also came to be baptized. "Teacher," they asked, "what should we do?"

"Don't collect any more than you are required to," he told them.

Then some soldiers asked him, "And what should we do?"

He replied, "Don't extort money and don't accuse people falsely—be content with your pay."

The people were waiting expectantly and were all wondering in their hearts if John might possibly be the Christ. John answered them all, "I baptize you with water. But one more powerful than I will come, the thongs of whose sandals I am not worthy to untie. He will baptize you with the Holy Spirit and with fire. ..." And with many other words John exhorted the people and preached the good news to them (Luke 3:10-18).

John's message was very practical. He called people—
- to share clothes and food with those who had none;
- to collect no more taxes from people than required;
- not to extort money;
- to be content with their pay.

John's ministry prepared the way for the ministry of Jesus Christ. When Jesus came and was baptized by John, John said, " 'Look, the Lamb of God, who takes away the sin of the world!' " (John 1:29). Later to his own followers John said of Jesus, " 'He must increase, but I must decrease' " (John 3:30, NKJV).

3 Review in the margin the first principle for a life that counts and your response. How does John's life illustrate this principle?

_____

_____

_____

Before John was born, God planned an assignment for his life. John received the assignment God gave him, and he fulfilled his mission. Jesus gave this evaluation of John's life and work: " 'I tell you the truth: Among those born of women there has not risen anyone greater than John the Baptist' " (Matthew 11:11). What an affirmation of a life lived according to God's unique plan!

4 Suppose someone in the future reviewed your life. Which of the following characteristics of John's ministry would you like to be said of you? Check all that apply and write your first name in the blank for each one you check.

❏ a. _____ pointed people to Jesus Christ, the Lamb of God, who takes away the sin of the world.

❏ b. _____'s recognition decreased as Jesus' fame and recognition increased.

❏ c. _____ received his or her God-given assignment and fulfilled the mission God gave.

5 Review today's summary ideas and respond to God in prayer. Pray that you too will know and fulfill your mission in a way that lifts up Jesus and that prepares people's lives to receive Him.

- John said of Jesus: " 'He must increase, but I must decrease' " (John 3:30, NKJV).
- Before John was born, God planned an assignment for his life. John received the assignment God gave him, and he fulfilled his mission.

PRINCIPLE 1
God prepared a unique plan and calling for your life even before you were born.

YOUR RESPONSE
Seek to recognize, understand, and participate in God's plan.

DAY 3

Sacred or Secular Calling?

TODAY'S WORD ON WORK

" 'My prayer is not that you take them out of the world but that you protect them from the evil one.' "

John 17:15

RESPONDING PRAYER

Lord Jesus, thank You for praying for me. I want to be Your servant in the world. Please protect me from the evil influences around me so that Your light can shine through me into the darkness. Amen.

> **Read and think about "Today's Word on Work" in the margin and respond to the Lord in prayer.**

1 **Review the personalized expression of principle 1 by filling in the blanks below.**

God prepared a unique _____ and _____ for my life even _____ I was born.

God is at work in the world all around you. He has a divine purpose He wants to accomplish. He has a unique plan and calling for your life that are part of His larger plan to restore the people of the world to right relationships with Him. Before you were born, God looked into the future and planned an amazing mission that He wants you to complete.

2 **In your opinion which of the following careers are acceptable callings from God? Check all that apply.**

- ❏ Pastor
- ❏ Missionary
- ❏ Evangelist
- ❏ Seminary professor
- ❏ Minister on church staff
- ❏ Chaplain
- ❏ Christian concert artist
- ❏ Teacher in Christian school
- ❏ Newspaper reporter
- ❏ Judge
- ❏ Assembly-line worker
- ❏ Janitor
- ❏ Accountant
- ❏ Lawyer
- ❏ Insurance salesperson
- ❏ Politician

Did you check only items in the left column, or did you check all of the careers? Most of us grew up thinking that God's call on a person is defined by where they work and the religious nature of their work. In that view only jobs in the left column would qualify because they relate to sacred (associated with church, religion, or God) topics and activities in sacred places. Some would even exclude the teacher, professor, and concert artist because they are probably not ordained (set apart for God's work in a special service).

All too often members of our churches who feel called to secular professions (like those in the right column) are treated like second-class citizens in the church. It's almost as if we have taken this first principle—that God prepared a unique plan and calling for our lives even before we were born—and added a stipulation: if you're truly spiritual, that unique plan and calling will be to the mission field or to a ministry in a church. How many times have we heard a pastor or a missionary leader plead with us to leave behind our secular pursuits and put them on the altar for Christ? How many times have we witnessed a commissioning service for those going to the mission field or an ordination service for those surrendering to full-time Christian ministry?

Now consider this: how many times have we been in a commissioning service for people determined to make a difference for Christ in some of the most challenging yet influential professions in America? How many lawyers, politicians, entertainers, educators, journalists, and businessmen or business-women consider themselves commissioned into the service of Christ in their fields of work? Rarely do we celebrate believers' decisions to join God in His work right where they are! That needs to change. That's why we've written *Made to Count Life Planner* for you.

Sacred or secular calling has more to do with whom the call came from than to what area of service a person is called. The important question is whether God is present in the person and is working through the person. If the call came from God and He is present in and actively working through the person, the calling is sacred no matter what the profession or location of the service. If the call began with a person's own thoughts or ambitions and if God is not present in and working through the person, then the calling is secular no matter what the profession or location of the work.

3 **In each of the following pairs, check the factor that most clearly makes a job or career sacred.**
a. ❑ The work takes place in a church building.
   ❑ God is present in the person and is working through the person.
b. ❑ God is the One who called the person and gave the unique assignment to be done.
   ❑ The job involves religious activity or requires ordination.

This activity could give rise to a debate over technicalities. A job or a career, however, is more clearly sacred when God is present in the person, when He is working through the person, and when He called the person and gave the unique assignment. God makes a job or a career truly sacred, not the place or the activity.

Many refer to Hebrews 11 as the faith hall of fame. Looking back over history, the author listed men and women whom God commended for their faith (see 2 Chronicles 16:9). The lives of these men and women counted because of their faith and faithfulness to the Lord. The list is remarkable for those who made it and those who didn't. For instance, only one

"The eyes of the Lord range throughout the earth to strengthen those whose hearts are fully committed to him."
2 Chronicles 16:9

> As they obediently joined what God was doing around them, God made their lives count for eternity.

prophet/priest, Samuel, made the list by name. This is not a list of famous clergy. It is primarily a list of ordinary people who responded in faith to God's call on their lives. As they obediently joined what God was doing around them, God made their lives count for eternity. They are on the list because of their faith, not their positions.

4 As you read this roll call of faith, underline the word in each description that identifies the career(s) of the person of faith. We've underlined the first one for you.

- Abel was a <u>herdsman</u> (kept flocks) and "a righteous man" (Hebrews 11:4) who brought acceptable offerings to God.
- Noah was a righteous man God called into the business of building an ark (a boat). He obeyed God's call to build the ark even though he and the world had never seen rain up to that time.
- Abraham was a nomadic herdsman who followed God's call to a far-off land, "even though he did not know where he was going" (Hebrews 11:8).
- Isaac and Jacob followed in their father and grandfather Abraham's career as nomadic herdsmen and claimed God's promise of a land for their descendants.
- Joseph became a powerful political ruler in Egypt.
- Moses was a shepherd when God called him to lead the nation of Israel out of Egypt and to the promised land.
- God's people were commended for their faith as they followed the military general Joshua and conquered the walled city of Jericho.
- Rahab had been a prostitute when she reached a major crossroads in life. She chose to side with the God of Israel and to give protection to two spies, and her family was spared because of her faith.
- Gideon was a farmer who responded to God's call and became a military leader.
- David was a shepherd turned war hero, who later became king.
- Samuel was the one prophet/priest who made the list by name.

5 Based on this list, which of the following statements is true? Write a *T* beside the true one.

____ a. The biblical people most commended for their faith were primarily chosen from among the religious leaders, or clergy.

____ b. The biblical people most commended for their faith were primarily chosen from among common, ordinary people who were willing to obey God.

The people most frequently commended for their faith in Hebrews 11 were laymen and women (*b*), not clergy. These were ordinary folks who were called by an extraordinary God to turn their world upside down. They were distinguished not by their abilities but by their faith.

6 **How would you classify yourself, based on your present career or job position? Check one.**
   ❑ a. Religious leader, clergy, full-time religious missionary
   ❑ b. Layperson, secular worker
   ❑ c. Other: _____

If you checked *b*, you qualify as someone God could call to walk with Him by faith. The good news for those who checked *a* is that God can and will use you too! God can even use those whose past reputations are blemished, like Rahab. Together with many others, these men and women were included in Hebrews 11 to inspire us and cheer us on. The writer of Hebrews said, "Since we are surrounded by such a great cloud of witnesses, let us throw off everything that hinders and the sin that so easily entangles, and let us run with perseverance the race marked out for us" (Hebrews 12:1). *Made to Count Life Planner* was written to help you prepare for and run that race!

7 **Read about one believer's calling in "Called to Be a News Correspondent" on this page.**

CALLED TO BE A NEWS CORRESPONDENT

Peggy accepted Christ during her college years and became active in a campus ministry to focus her life. She wanted to be a fully committed Christian. "I thought a committed Christian went into full-time vocational work. I was a little confused. So I became very involved in a campus ministry, but every time I wanted to get involved in campus politics or the Journalism Department, it took me away from some of my ministry activities. I was chided by ministry leaders for spending too much time in activities that took me away from the ministry. But I kept asking, 'Shouldn't we be active in the world outside the church?' I felt ashamed if I couldn't make it to ministry activities because I was too busy with other campus events. I got the message very clearly that I should go into full-time ministry if I was really a dedicated Christian."

But Peggy also loved the idea of touching her world and being involved in campus leadership outside her Christian circles. Moving from major to major, she finally landed in a journalism class and found that it fired her passion, maximized her strengths, and gave her a sense that God had planned something special for her in that arena. "I sensed this is what I was created to do. It was a fit for me!"

Peggy had to choose between following this plan that God had been preparing for her or staying in the full-time ministry box constructed by others. If Peggy Wehmeyer had stayed in that box, she probably would not have become the first religion correspondent on "ABC World News Tonight," reporting to Peter Jennings.[2]

Knowing exactly what would be needed, God created you, His masterpiece, just as perfectly suited to your own calling as Peggy Wehmeyer is suited to being a religion correspondent for "ABC World News Tonight," Jay Sekulow is suited to being a constitutional lawyer, and Rick Husband was suited to being an astronaut. Now God calls you by name and invites you to be part of the greatest adventure you'll ever experience.

⑧ Review today's summary ideas and respond to God in prayer.

- God is at work in the world all around you.
- Before you were born, God looked into the future and planned an amazing mission that He wants you to complete.
- Rarely do we celebrate believers' decisions to join God in His work right where they are! That needs to change.
- Sacred or secular calling has more to do with whom the call came from than to what area of service a person is called. The important question is whether God is present in the person and is working through the person.
- God calls you by name and invites you to be part of the greatest adventure you'll ever experience.

DAY 4

God's Plan for Joseph

TODAY'S WORD ON WORK

"Trust in the Lord with all your heart
and lean not on your own understanding;
in all your ways acknowledge him,
and he will make your paths straight."
Proverbs 3:5-6

RESPONDING PRAYER

That's a hard thing for me to do, Lord. I've been taught to depend on myself and my understanding. But at Your command I trust in You. I trust You to make my paths straight. Amen.

> **Read and think about "Today's Word on Work" in the margin and respond to the Lord in prayer.**

If you are like many people, you are inspired when you hear success stories about people who have worked their way from an entry-level position to the top of a corporation. You may envy someone who didn't go to college but has built a multimillion-dollar company. Business people buy books and go to seminars to learn the secrets of success. When people tell their success stories about work, they seem to focus primarily on important habits, personality traits, skills, ideas that motivate, and so forth.

1. **Below is a list of commonly stated keys for success in the workplace. Check those you have heard used to describe the way someone achieved success in a profession.**

❏ Wisdom   ❏ Being proactive   ❏ Results-oriented
❏ Courage   ❏ Good luck   ❏ Effective planner
❏ Empathy   ❏ Ingenuity   ❏ Priorities in order
❏ Loyalty   ❏ Initiative   ❏ Personal integrity
❏ Creativity   ❏ Discipline   ❏ Negotiation skills
❏ Decisiveness   ❏ Intentionality   ❏ Ability to motivate
❏ Flexibility   ❏ Trustworthiness   ❏ Focus on excellence
❏ Aggressiveness   ❏ Common sense   ❏ Clear mission statement
❏ Assertiveness   ❏ Perseverance   ❏ Persuasive communicator
❏ Brilliance   ❏ Clear life goals   ❏ Knowledge of the right people
❏ Energy   ❏ Vision   ❏ Good time manager

These are the kinds of traits that the world looks to for success. One most important trait is missing from the previous list. Let's look at the story of Joseph to identify that missing trait.

God revealed to Joseph that he would one day rule over his own family members. When his jealous brothers sold Joseph into slavery, the slave traders took him to Egypt and sold him to an Egyptian leader named Potiphar. Joseph literally began working on his career path from the bottom of a pit.

> Joseph literally began working on his career path from the bottom of a pit.

2. **Read the following Scripture and look for the key to Joseph's success when he became a slave in Egypt. Underline the reason for his success each time it is described.**

The Lord was with Joseph and he prospered, and he lived in the house of his Egyptian master. When his master saw that the Lord was with him and that the Lord gave him success in everything he did, Joseph found favor in his eyes and became his attendant. Potiphar put him in charge of his household, and he entrusted to his care everything he owned. From the time he put him in charge of his household and of all that he owned, the Lord blessed the household of the Egyptian because of Joseph. The blessing of the Lord was on everything Potiphar had, both in the house and in the field. So he left in Joseph's care everything he had (Genesis 39:2-6).

3. **What was the key to Joseph's success in everything he did?**

_____

4 **What effect did Joseph's relationship with the Lord have on his boss's home and business? Check one.**
   ❏ a. Potiphar's home and business suffered loss because of Joseph's commitment to the Lord.
   ❏ b. Potiphar's home and business were greatly blessed because of Joseph's relationship with the Lord.

> The Lord was with Joseph, and He caused everything Joseph did to prosper.

Joseph's key to success was not any of the traits we would find in today's secular business books. The Lord was with Joseph, and He caused everything Joseph did to prosper. Joseph probably had several of the character traits in the previous list of the world's keys to success. But the primary reason for Joseph's success was that God was with him. God caused this pagan slave owner's home and business to prosper. Potiphar was blessed because of Joseph's walk with God.

5 **Could God cause your company or employer to prosper for a similar reason?**   ❏ Yes   ❏ No

Joseph went from being sold as property to being a privileged manager in his master's family business. Then Joseph hit bottom again when he refused to sleep with the boss's wife. He was thrown into prison when the rejected wife falsely accused him of rape. From a human perspective Joseph's integrity didn't count for much. Had God let him down? No. God used every turn of events for kingdom purposes. Even though Joseph was in prison for 13 years, he didn't stay on the bottom.

6 **Read the following Scripture and underline the next key to Joseph's success.**

> While Joseph was there in the prison, the Lord was with him; he showed him kindness and granted him favor in the eyes of the prison warden. So the warden put Joseph in charge of all those held in the prison, and he was made responsible for all that was done there. The warden paid no attention to anything under Joseph's care, because the Lord was with Joseph and gave him success in whatever he did (Genesis 39:20-23).

Joseph's favor with the warden and success in prison was due to God's involvement in his life. God blessed Joseph and gave him success in everything he did. Because God blessed Joseph's work, the prison was a much better place.

   Joseph's final rise to the top came when he correctly interpreted some dreams, first for two prisoners and then for Pharaoh himself. Even in the greatest promotion of his career, Joseph still realized that God was his source of success. To the two prisoners Joseph said, " 'Do not interpretations belong to God?' " (Genesis 40:8). Joseph interpreted their dreams, and both dreams came true just as he said they would.

When Pharaoh had a dream, no one could interpret it for him. Then one of these former prisoners remembered Joseph and recommended his skill to Pharaoh, who sent for Joseph and said: " 'I had a dream, and no one can interpret it. But I have heard it said of you that when you hear a dream you can interpret it' " (Genesis 41:15).

God enabled Joseph to interpret Pharaoh's dream. Joseph was careful to attribute his ability to God and not to claim the power for himself. Read Pharaoh's response in the margin.

Did you notice that even pagan Pharaoh recognized the reason for Joseph's skill, wisdom, and discernment? He realized that God was with Joseph and was the source of Joseph's success. Consequently, Pharaoh elevated Joseph to second in command. Because God revealed that a famine was coming, Joseph began storing grain. When the famine came, Joseph became one of history's greatest grain futures traders. God had a unique plan for Joseph's life. He used Joseph to spare the lives of many, including His chosen people Israel.

No one would deny that Joseph was successful. But before our study is over, you will understand that success in God's kingdom may be defined very differently than it is by the world's standards. The important lesson for now is that a life that counts for eternity depends on a right relationship with God.

> " 'Can we find anyone like this man, one in whom is the spirit of God?'
>
> "Then Pharaoh said to Joseph, 'Since God has made all this known to you, there is no one so discerning and wise as you. You shall be in charge of my palace, and all my people are to submit to your orders. Only with respect to the throne will I be greater than you.'
>
> "So Pharaoh said to Joseph, 'I hereby put you in charge of the whole land of Egypt.' "
> Genesis 41:38-41

7 Review in the margin the first principle for a life that counts and your response. How do you see this principle at work in Joseph's life?

_____

_____

Joseph's brothers sold him as a slave, but God used that event to get Joseph to Egypt. God used Joseph's prison experience to connect him with Pharaoh's butler. God then worked through the butler to get Joseph an audience with Pharaoh. God accomplished His purposes in spite of others' actions and opposition. Here is how Joseph summed it up to his brothers: " 'God sent me ahead of you to preserve for you a remnant on earth and to save your lives by a great deliverance. So then, it was not you who sent me here, but God' " (Genesis 45:7-8). " 'You intended to harm me, but God intended it for good to accomplish what is now being done, the saving of many lives' " (Genesis 50:20).

God had a plan, and Joseph was a part of that plan. God made Joseph's life count in a way that saved a nation from starvation. Joseph accepted God's sovereignty over His life and was faithful even in difficult circumstances. He later understood that God is able to accomplish His purposes even when people seem to oppose His work.

> **PRINCIPLE 1**
> God prepared a unique plan and calling for your life even before you were born.
>
> **YOUR RESPONSE**
> Seek to recognize, understand, and participate in God's plan.

Being a Christ-follower is not easy. You will encounter situations that call you to respond differently than most people in the world would respond. When Christ has shaped your value system, priorities, and motives, you may find yourself at odds with the world's agenda where you work. Remember that God is the One who can accomplish His work where you are. He makes your life count: "In all things God works for the good of those who love him, who have been called according to his purpose" (Romans 8:28).

8 **Review today's summary ideas and respond to God in prayer.**
- The primary reason for Joseph's success was that God was with him.
- God blessed Joseph and gave him success in everything he did.
- Joseph was careful to attribute his ability to God and not to claim the power for himself.
- Success in God's kingdom may be defined very differently than it is by the world's standards.
- God had a plan, and Joseph was a part of that plan.

DAY 5

Faithfulness Without Success

TODAY'S WORD ON WORK
"Now it is required that those who have been given a trust must prove faithful."
I Corinthians 4:2

RESPONDING PRAYER
Lord, I realize that I've been entrusted with much—Your Spirit, gifts, time, health, resources, opportunity—more than I can name. Enable me to be a faithful servant. Amen.

Read and think about "Today's Word on Work" in the margin and respond to the Lord in prayer.

God calls us to be a part of His kingdom work. He can enable us to accomplish what He calls us to do, and success is a wonderful fruit of God's activity in us. Not every assignment from God, however, is guaranteed success in the world's eyes. Sometimes God's plan is just for faithfulness. At the conclusion of the first list of the faith hall of fame in Hebrews 11 we read the success side: "[Others] through faith conquered kingdoms, administered justice, and gained what was promised; who shut the mouths of lions, quenched the fury of the flames, and escaped the edge of the sword; whose weakness was turned to strength; and who became powerful in battle and routed foreign armies. Women received back their dead, raised to life again" (Hebrews 11:33-35).

We don't want to mislead you into thinking that what humanity considers success is always the outcome of obedience to God's calling.

1 **Read in the margin about other faithful hall of famers in Hebrews 11. Underline what they were commended for.**

We wouldn't judge this group as successful. In fact, we would probably nominate these souls not for a hall of fame but for something with a less pleasant title. Although these saints were not successful from a human standpoint, "these were all commended for their faith" (Hebrews 11:39).

2 **Review the personalized expression of principle 1 by filling in the blanks below.**

God prepared a unique _____ and _____ for my life even _____ I was born.

Sometimes God's call and unique plan for your life are for an assignment that requires faithfulness but does not guarantee success. We need to be ready to accept God's assignment even when He lets us know that the outcome will be negative when viewed from a human perspective.

Earlier this week we examined the ministry of John the Baptist. He was faithful in preparing the way for the Lord Jesus to come. Some of John's disciples even followed Jesus when John pointed them to the Lamb of God. But do you know how John concluded his ministry? Here's his story.

3 **Read about the conclusion of John's ministry and answer the questions that follow.**

Herod had arrested John and bound him and put him in prison because of Herodias, his brother Philip's wife, for John had been saying to him: "It is not lawful for you to have her. ..."

On Herod's birthday the daughter of Herodias danced for them and pleased Herod so much that he promised with an oath to give her whatever she asked. Prompted by her mother, she said, "Give me here on a platter the head of John the Baptist." The king was distressed, but because of his oaths and his dinner guests, he ordered that her request be granted and had John beheaded in the prison. His head was brought in on a platter and given to the girl, who carried it to her mother. John's disciples came and took his body and buried it. Then they went and told Jesus (Matthew 14:3-12).

"Others were tortured and refused to be released, so that they might gain a better resurrection. Some faced jeers and flogging, while still others were chained and put in prison. They were stoned; they were sawed in two; they were put to death by the sword. They went about in sheepskins and goatskins, destitute, persecuted and mistreated—the world was not worthy of them. They wandered in deserts and mountains, and in caves and holes in the ground. These were all commended for their faith." Hebrews 11:35-39

a. When John spoke out against the king's immorality, where did he end his ministry? _____

b. How did John the Baptist die? _____

c. How would you evaluate the success of John's final ministry?
   ❑ He was a failure. He died in disgrace.
   ❑ He was a martyr. I'd give him hero status.
   ❑ He was so successful that others would want to follow him.

God made John's life count!

John ended his career in prison and was cruelly beheaded at an evil woman's request. Many would see his end as failure. Yet this is the man about whom Jesus said, " 'I tell you the truth: Among those born of women there has not risen anyone greater than John the Baptist' " (Matthew 11:11). John was faithful, and God commended him. God made John's life count!

Isaiah was one of the great Old Testament prophets. Through him God gave us vivid descriptions of the coming Suffering Servant, Jesus Christ. Isaiah was in the temple when he received his calling from God. After a time of worship, confession, and cleansing, God asked: " 'Whom shall I send? And who will go for us?' " (Isaiah 6:8).

In response Isaiah volunteered: " 'Here am I. Send me!' " (Isaiah 6:8). At times God may call us to follow before He gives us the details. After Isaiah had volunteered for this unknown assignment, God explained that he was to preach, but the people would not listen or respond. Isaiah asked, " 'For how long, O Lord?' " (Isaiah 6:11), and God responded:

"Until the cities lie ruined
   and without inhabitant,
until the houses are left deserted
   and the fields ruined and ravaged,
until the Lord has sent everyone far away
   and the land is utterly forsaken" (Isaiah 6:11-12).

④ **If God called you to such an assignment, how do you think you would respond? Check an answer or write your own.**
   ❑ a. I would be faithful to preach regardless of the response.
   ❑ b. I would ask the Lord for a different and more successful assignment.
   ❑ c. I would withdraw my offer to volunteer.
   ❑ d. Other: _____

⑤ **How did Isaiah fulfill the first principle for a life that counts? It is printed in the margin on page 45.**

_____

Isaiah was a faithful servant. When we look at his ministry from God's perspective, he was completely successful because he faithfully fulfilled his mission. Thousands of years later, we still read his message and know his name. Be prepared to accept the assignments God gives. Sometimes faithfulness and not human success is what God desires.

Lest we forget the most successful ministry ever, remember what God called Jesus to do. From a human perspective His ministry would not have been seen as much of a success. He served in public ministry for only three years. His remnant of followers was small in numbers. The religious leaders of His day rejected His message and publicly accused Him of being a devil. He was executed as a criminal.

6 **How did Jesus fulfill the first principle for a life that counts?**

_____

_____

_____

_____

Jesus obeyed unto death. He completely finished the mission God the Father had given Him. And this was the Father's assessment of His life: " 'This is my Son, whom I love; with him I am well pleased' " (Matthew 3:17).

7 **Examine in the margin your response to principle 1. How willing are you to accept God's plan even though it may lead to hardship?**
   ❑ I'm ready to find and participate in God's plan, no matter what.
   ❑ I'm not sure.
   ❑ Suffering? That's not for me.

8 **Review today's summary ideas and respond to God in prayer. Also talk to Him about your response to the previous activity.**
   • Not every assignment from God is guaranteed success in the world's eyes.
   • John was faithful, and God commended him.
   • Isaiah was completely successful because he faithfully fulfilled his mission.
   • Be prepared to accept the assignments God gives. Sometimes faithfulness and not human success is what God desires.
   • Jesus completely finished the mission God the Father had given Him.

---

[1]Quotations by Jay Sekulow are based on his testimony provided on the Jews for Jesus Web site, *www.jewsforjesus.org/stories/sekulow.html.* Information about his current cases and the results of previous Supreme Court cases can be found at the Web site for the American Center for Law and Justice, *www.aclj.org/about/aboutj.asp.*
[2]Authors' interview, 17 March 2003.

> Be prepared to accept the assignments God gives. Sometimes faithfulness and not human success is what God desires.

> **PRINCIPLE 1**
> God prepared a unique plan and calling for your life even before you were born.
>
> **YOUR RESPONSE**
> Seek to recognize, understand, and participate in God's plan.

WEEK 3

Called to a Relationship

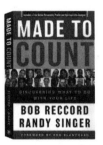

THIS WEEK'S SUPPLEMENTARY READING
Chapters 5–6, *Made to Count*

John Newton had seen the worst of the British slave trade. He had known men who tried to impregnate as many slave girls as possible on voyages to the New World. He had seen men so cynical that their whole mission on the slave ships was to find a Christian, ridicule him, and try to talk him out of his faith. He had seen men whip the skin off the back of a young deckhand for a minor infraction. And he was reminded of the worst of those offenders every morning when he looked in the mirror. John Newton, a former slave trader, knew a thing or two about the slave trade.

But John Newton had also experienced God's amazing grace. He heard the call to ministry and served as a pastor for more than 25 years. He also wrote hymns like "Amazing Grace." His burning passion was to find a way to abolish the evil that he had once propagated.

His outspoken views won converts—like a 27-year-old member of Parliament who in 1785 requested a secret meeting with Reverend Newton. To avoid anyone's finding out, they met at the parsonage rather than the church. The strain showed on the face of young William Wilberforce. He told Reverend Newton that he had heard him preach when he was just a boy, but he "was afraid to surrender to Christ for fear of what others might say."

"And now?" Newton asked.

"Now I have come to a crisis of my soul," answered the grim-faced member of Parliament. "I am afraid of turning my back on Christ. But I also fear losing face and prestige. If my constituents were to hear that I embraced … religion, my career would be over." Wilberforce paused and shifted in his seat, then gave Newton a determined half-smile. "But maybe that would not be so bad. You have always inspired me, Reverend Newton. When I used to go to Olney and hear your sermons, I felt like jumping up and asking you to help me be a preacher like you.

"When I returned to London, that enthusiasm cooled, and I even-

tually got into politics. Still, as I read the Bible and Christian books, I am convinced that I must act on what I have read. I've come to see you about this before I go out of my mind."

For the next few hours Reverend John Newton explained the way of the cross and total surrender to Christ. Wilberforce wept and gave his life to Christ. Now he was ready to follow Newton into the ministry and face the consequences.

But Newton wisely counseled against it: "If God can use an ex-slave trader for His work, imagine what He can do through a gifted member of Parliament. There's nothing in the Bible that says you cannot be both a Christian and a statesman. True, these two are seldom found in one person, but it happens."

Wilberforce accepted this advice and remained where he was to serve God. He went public with his newfound faith, enduring ridicule and then winning grudging respect from his contemporaries. He turned his energy toward abolishing the slave trade, a blight on the soul of the British Empire.

In 1788, after a stirring 3½-hour oratory on the subject, Wilberforce made his first motion to abolish the slave trade. His impassioned speech had such an impact on the other members of Parliament that the local papers predicted sure passage of the bill. The prediction, however, was premature. Wilberforce lost the first of many votes on this critical issue.

Every year for the next 17 years, Wilberforce would make a motion to abolish the British slave trade. But Wilberforce never forgot the words of Newton, and the conviction that he was called to fight for Christian principles in Parliament never left him.

In 1806 Wilberforce finally heard the sweet sound he had longed for. After votes were counted on his motion to abolish the slave trade, the ranking member of Parliament said very simply, "The ayes have it!" Wilberforce had won.

But Wilberforce wasn't satisfied. Never flinching from his call, he continued to work tirelessly against the institution of slavery. Just four days before his death in 1833, Parliament passed a vote to abolish slavery in all the British territories. Wilberforce the Christian had remained Wilberforce the member of Parliament. And God had used him mightily.[1]

Pause to pray that God will clarify your calling to serve Him. Pray that He will continue to call Christian men and women to be salt and light for Christ in the world of government.

DAY 1

Principle 2: A Life-Changing Relationship

TODAY'S WORD ON WORK

"Jesus replied, 'If anyone loves me, he will obey my teaching. My Father will love him, and we will come to him and make our home with him.' "

John 14:23

RESPONDING PRAYER

Jesus, what a promise this is! I long to have such a love for You that You and the Heavenly Father will come to live in a relationship with me. Let it be, Lord. Amen.

> **Read and think about "Today's Word on Work" in the margin and respond to the Lord in prayer.**

> **Principle 2:** God calls you to a life-changing relationship with Him through Jesus Christ.
>
> **Your response:** Enter the relationship and submit to God's transforming work in your life.

1 **Read principle 2 several times, giving special attention to the words that are bold and underlined.**

God calls you to a life-changing **relationship** with Him through **Jesus Christ**.

2 **Now personalize the principle by rewriting it. Change *you* to *me*.**

_____

_____

3 **Fill in the blanks below with the missing words and review all eight principles for a life that counts.**

1. God prepared a unique _____ and _____ for your life even _____ you were born.

2. God calls you to a life-changing _____ with Him through _____ _____.

3. God calls you to partner with Him in a **mission** that is **bigger** than you are.

4. God calls you to be on **mission** with Him right where you are—starting **now**.

5. God reveals His mission through His **Word**, His **Spirit**, wise **counsel**, and His work in **circumstances** around you.

6. God repeatedly brings you to a crossroads of **choice** as He **forges** you for His mission.

7. God **guides** and **provides** for your mission one **step** at a time.

8. When you **answer** God's call, you experience His **pleasure** and **change** your world.

God prepared a unique plan and calling for your life even before you were born. He had a plan and purpose for John Newton and William Wilberforce. Both entered a personal and life-changing relationship with Jesus Christ. When God's love, life, and justice flowed through their lives in power, they saw the abolition of slavery throughout the British Empire.

God doesn't call you just to get you to do something for Him. His calling is actually twofold. First, God's call is to a life-changing relationship with Him. Then He calls you to a life-fulfilling mission alongside Him. The God of all creation, who is powerful, mighty, just, holy, and altogether awesome, is also a loving God. His first purpose for your life is a love relationship with Him.

> First, God's call is to a life-changing relationship with Him. Then He calls you to a life-fulfilling mission alongside Him.

4 What are two things God calls you to?
a. A life-changing _____
b. A life-fulfilling _____

When Saul (later Paul) met Jesus Christ on the road to Damascus, he believed. Placing His trust in Christ as the true Messiah, he was filled with God's Spirit. His life was radically changed, and the Jews saw and heard the difference. Not only did God call Paul to a relationship, but He also called Paul to a life-fulfilling mission—a mission to preach the gospel of Jesus Christ to the Gentile world.

God is love, and He has loved us with an everlasting love. With that unfailing love He draws us to Himself. His love compelled Him to bridge the huge gap that existed between Him and us because of our sinful nature. We are all separated from God because of a sinful, self-focused nature. We have a natural tendency to want to chart our own course and do things our own way instead of seeking what God desires. We want what we want when we want it and the way we want it. We have all sinned.

The Bible compares us to sheep that have gone astray wandering away from the Shepherd. The reality is that all of us have a heart condition. If we are not in a personal and intimate relationship with God the Creator,

" 'God so loved the world that he gave his one and only Son, that whoever believes in him shall not perish but have eternal life.' "
John 3:16

"God demonstrates his own love for us in this: While we were still sinners, Christ died for us."
Romans 5:8

"God made him who had no sin to be sin for us, so that in him we might become the righteousness of God."
2 Corinthians 5:21

" 'Salvation is found in no one else, for there is no other name under heaven given to men by which we must be saved.' "
Acts 4:12

we have a terminal spiritual disease. Yet from His great love, God sent the prescription and solution for our ruptured relationship with Him.

5 **Read the four Scriptures in the margin and underline in each one what God does for us through His Son Jesus Christ.**

Jesus Christ gave His life so that we would not perish but have eternal life. He became sin for us and died for us so that we would be saved and become the righteousness of God.

If we want a life filled with adventure, significance, and impact, we must first make sure that we are in a personal, intimate relationship with the Creator of all life. For God's first call is for us to enter a personal relationship with Him by faith in the person and work of Jesus Christ.

Such a relationship is a pure gift from God. It's God who takes the initiative to draw people to Himself and offer them the gift of eternal life. Each individual will respond—some receiving the free gift and some rejecting it. Each will make a personal choice—a willful and eternal choice.

However, to be authentic, a decision for Christ is more than simply intellectually believing some facts about Christ. When Scripture says, " 'Believe in the Lord Jesus, and you will be saved' " (Acts 16:31), it does not mean merely acknowledging that some facts about Christ are true. The word *believe* is taken from a Greek word that refers to faith. But because *faith* is not a verb in English, it has been translated *believe*. The point is that we must place the full weight of our trust for a personal relationship with God in what Jesus Christ has accomplished in His death, burial, and resurrection alone. It cannot be Christ plus anything. It must be Christ alone!

6 **Mark the following statements *T* for *true* and *F* for *false*.**
___ a. I am the one who takes the initiative in a relationship with God. I choose to ask Him for the relationship, and He responds to me.
___ b. If I intellectually believe the facts about Jesus' life and death, I have all the relationship required for salvation.
___ c. To believe in Christ, I must place the full weight of my trust in what Jesus did for me through His death and resurrection.

Only the third statement is true. God is the One who takes the initiative. He pursues the love relationship with us first. We respond to Him. This love relationship is more than just intellectual belief in historical facts. To believe in Jesus, we put the full weight of our trust in what He did for us on the cross. He won the victory for us through His resurrection.

7 **Have you entered a personal relationship with God through faith in Jesus Christ and His sacrifice for you?** ❑ Yes ❑ No

If so, briefly describe when and how you entered that relationship. If not, describe your feelings about entering such a relationship with God through Jesus Christ.

_____

_____

8 **Review today's summary ideas and respond to God in prayer about your relationship with Him by faith in Jesus.**
- God's call is to a life-changing relationship with Him.
- Then He calls you to a life-fulfilling mission alongside Him.
- We are all separated from God because of a sinful, self-focused nature.
- If we want a life filled with adventure, significance, and impact, we must first make sure that we are in a personal, intimate relationship with the Creator of all life.
- It's God who takes the initiative to draw people to Himself.
- To believe in Jesus, we put the full weight of our trust in what He did for us on the cross.

DAY 2

Zacchaeus Was Called to a Life-Changing Relationship

Read and think about "Today's Word on Work" in the margin and respond to the Lord in prayer.

TODAY'S WORD ON WORK

"If anyone is in Christ, he is a new creation; the old has gone, the new has come!" 2 Corinthians 5:17

1 **Read the account of Jesus and Zacchaeus and notice the difference Jesus made in Zacchaeus and his work life. Underline what Zacchaeus decided to do differently after his encounter with Jesus.**

Jesus entered Jericho and was passing through. A man was there by the name of Zacchaeus; he was a chief tax collector and was wealthy. He wanted to see who Jesus was, but being a short man he could not, because of the crowd. So he ran ahead and climbed a sycamore-fig tree to see him, since Jesus was coming that way.

RESPONDING PRAYER

I'm so glad that You paid the price so that I could be made new. Help me live in that newness of life for You. Amen.

When Jesus reached the spot, he looked up and said to him, "Zacchaeus, come down immediately. I must stay at your house today." So he came down at once and welcomed him gladly.

All the people saw this and began to mutter, "He has gone to be the guest of a 'sinner.' "

But Zacchaeus stood up and said to the Lord, "Look, Lord! Here and now I give half of my possessions to the poor, and if I have cheated anybody out of anything, I will pay back four times the amount."

Jesus said to him, "Today salvation has come to this house" (Luke 19:1-9).

In Jesus' day tax collectors were notorious for taking advantage of people through excessive taxation. By supporting the oppressive Roman government and overtaxing the people, tax collectors were considered sinners. But when Zacchaeus met Jesus, everything changed.

When Zacchaeus turned to Jesus Christ in faith and made Him Lord, he made two decisions about the use of his resources. First, he pledged to give half to the poor. Jesus did not require this, Zacchaeus volunteered it. He changed from someone with a calloused heart to someone with a tender heart for the needy. Second, Zacchaeus agreed to pay back four times anything he had overcharged. Making restitution for past sin indicated a change in his heart. When Jesus saw that Zacchaeus's mind, heart, and actions had changed, He knew that salvation had come to this household.

② **In the margin are some Scriptures describing the natural human nature that is bent toward sin. Below are Scriptures describing the traits of a person who has been born again by the Spirit of God. As you read both sets of Scriptures, see which side best describes you. Talk to the Lord about your findings.**

THE NEW CREATION

The fruit of the Spirit is love, joy, peace, patience, kindness, goodness, faithfulness, gentleness and self-control. Against such things there is no law. Those who belong to Christ Jesus have crucified the sinful nature with its passions and desires (Galatians 5:22-24).

Those who live in accordance with the Spirit have their minds set on what the Spirit desires. ...The mind controlled by the Spirit is life and peace. ... You, however, are controlled not by the sinful nature but by the Spirit, if the Spirit of God lives in you. ... But if Christ is in you, your body is dead because of sin, yet your spirit is alive because of righteousness (Romans 8:5-10).

THE OLD, SINFUL NATURE

"The acts of the sinful nature are obvious: sexual immorality, impurity and debauchery; idolatry and witchcraft; hatred, discord, jealousy, fits of rage, selfish ambition, dissensions, factions and envy; drunkenness, orgies, and the like. I warn you, as I did before, that those who live like this will not inherit the kingdom of God."
Galatians 5:19-21

"Those who live according to the sinful nature have their minds set on what that nature desires. ... The mind of sinful man is death. ... The sinful mind is hostile to God. It does not submit to God's law, nor can it do so. Those controlled by the sinful nature cannot please God. ... And if anyone does not have the Spirit of Christ, he does not belong to Christ."
Romans 8:5-9

3 **If God evaluated your life based on the previous verses about the old nature and the new creation, what would He conclude? Pray now and ask Him. Then check your response.**

❏ a. I am in Christ because I have a new nature. My old, sinful nature is past. Christ and His nature now live in me.

❏ b. Nothing much has changed since I decided to become a Christian and joined the church. My old, sinful nature is still very strong. I may not be in Christ as I thought.

❏ c. I've always had this old, sinful nature, and I realize that I am a sinner. I have never repented of my sin and turned to Christ to be born again.

❏ d. Other: _____

Principles and good work habits can be important in a workplace. A vision, personal goals, and hard work may also help you get ahead. In fact, you may be able to achieve great success in the world's eyes by working this way. But if God Himself is not present in you and is not actively involved in your life and work, you will not accomplish anything that is of lasting value to God. The key to success in God's kingdom is a right relationship with God—the King. Apart from Him you can do nothing of kingdom value: " 'I am the vine; you are the branches. If a man remains in me and I in him, he will bear much fruit; apart from me you can do nothing' " (John 15:5).

> The key to success in God's kingdom is a right relationship with God—the King.

4 **Try to write from memory the second principle for a life that counts. Also write your response. Look back at page 48 if you need to.**

Principle 2: _____

_____

My response: _____

_____

Before God calls us to make a difference, He calls us to Himself— to a personal love relationship.

5 **Review today's summary ideas and respond to God in prayer as you consider your personal relationship with Him.**

• When Zacchaeus met Jesus, everything changed.

• When Jesus saw that Zacchaeus's mind, heart, and actions had changed, He knew that salvation had come to this household.

• The key to success in God's kingdom is a right relationship with God.

• Apart from Him you can do nothing of kingdom value.

DAY 3

Relationship, Not Religion

TODAY'S WORD ON WORK

" 'You diligently study the Scriptures because you think that by them you possess eternal life. These are the Scriptures that testify about me, yet you refuse to come to me to have life.' "
John 5:39-40

RESPONDING PRAYER

Lord, I see that I can be very religious and miss the relationship with You. I don't want to go there. Draw me near to Yourself. Let me know and experience a deep, personal relationship with You. Amen.

> **Read and think about "Today's Word on Work" in the margin and respond to the Lord in prayer.**

1. **Based on your reading of John 5:39-40, label each definition below as religion or relationship.**

   _____ a. Living in communion with Jesus in such a way that I experience His presence, know His guidance, and experience His power at work in and through me

   _____ b. Being faithful to do the activities expected of a Christ-follower from duty and obligation, often primarily for others to see

A huge difference exists between religion (*b*) and relationship (*a*). God doesn't call us to more religion. He calls us to an intimate relationship. Religion is activity; relationship is intimacy. While religion focuses on words and works, relationship is a walk.

Churches are filled with good people who live nice lives but fail to have a personal relationship with the One who designed them. Their lives are pleasant, and they're not rocking any boats. But God intended more. From the beginning of creation, God desired a personal, intimate relationship with His highest creation—us! When we go through the motions without any of the meaning, all we have is empty religious ritual. Jesus made it plain that He would never be satisfied with that kind of insipid existence, nor would we. He declared, " 'I came that [you] may have and enjoy life, and have it in abundance (to the full, till it overflows)' " (John 10:10, AMP).

2. **Answer the following questions.**
   a. Have you felt the power of God in your life?   ❑ Yes   ❑ No
   b. When was the last time you had something happen that could be explained only by the awesome work of the Holy Spirit?

   _____

   c. When was the last time the words of Scripture jumped off the pages at you, and you felt that you were reading a personal love letter from God?

   _____

d. When was the last time you found yourself in such deep, intimate prayer that time flew by and you were surprised at the length of time you had spent in prayer?_____

e. When was the last time you worshiped with your whole being, almost feeling transported to God's presence?

_____

If it's been a while or if the answer is never, then you really need to camp out on this principle before going any further.

3 **Write your personalized form of principle 2, which you first wrote on page 48.**

_____

_____

God calls us to a life-changing relationship with Him through Jesus Christ. And this new relationship changes everything.

4 **Which of the following most nearly describes your experience of Jesus Christ at the present time? Check one.**
- ❏ a. I'm going through the motions of being a Christ-follower. I'm doing the right things, but I don't sense a nearness to Christ.
- ❏ b. I experience Christ's nearness and guidance. Although I sometimes stray, my relationship with Him is real and deeply personal.
- ❏ c. I can't say that I have religion or relationship. Working through this study is the closest I've come to either.

Religion (*a*) can appear good on the outside, but inside it is filled with emptiness and deadness. Life and vitality don't keep company with religious activity for the activity's sake. Turning from your sin, personally inviting Jesus Christ into your life, and making a commitment to live as a Christ-follower are the beginning of a relationship with God. The Bible tells us, " 'There is salvation in and through *no one else*, for there is no other name under heaven given among men by and in which we must be saved' " (Acts 4:12, AMP, italics added).

To find God's call and plan for your life, be sure you've entered a personal relationship with the One who created you for a purpose. Who could know the purpose for your life better than the One who designed you? It sounds simple, doesn't it? Yet so many people miss it. Jesus Himself knew that would be the case. Stop and read His words in the margin from two different Bible versions.

It almost sounds as if Jesus was frequenting the same bookstores we do and was getting bombarded by the same self-help nonsense. Those surefire

" 'Enter through the narrow gate; for wide is the gate and spacious and broad is the way that leads away to destruction, and many are those who are entering through it. But the gate is narrow (contracted by pressure) and the way is straitened and compressed that leads away to life, and *few are those who find it'.* "
Matthew 7:13-14, AMP, italics added

" 'Don't look for shortcuts to God. The market is flooded with surefire, easygoing formulas for a successful life that can be practiced in your spare time. Don't fall for that stuff, even though crowds of people do. The way to life—to God!—is vigorous and requires total attention.' "
Matthew 7:13-14, MSG

formulas might make you a little better at doing the things you can already do, but they won't help you do what you can't do alone. They won't radically change your life. They won't bring you into a personal relationship with the Heavenly Father, who wants to help you go where you can't go alone.

When we invite Christ in, He does some serious housecleaning. Old desires, hangouts, and philosophies that focus on us are carried out to the trash. New desires, hangouts, and philosophies that focus on Him are brought in. We become, in Paul's words, an entirely new creation. The old has gone. The new has come!

5 **If you realize that you don't have a relationship with Jesus Christ, now is a good time to start.**
- Agree with God about your sin and your failure to measure up to His standards.
- Ask Him to forgive you, to release you from the weight and guilt of your past.
- Place your trust in what Jesus Christ did for you by paying your penalty for sin on the cross.
- Invite Him to come into your life and become your Lord. Pledge to follow Him.
- If you sense that you need more help, talk to a friend who is a follower of Jesus Christ or to a pastor you know.

This fresh start with Christ has two inevitable impacts on the mission for our life. First, we will dare to do things we could never do alone. And second, we won't do anything or go anywhere unless we know that God has called us to it and will go with us through it.

Are you willing to go anywhere God calls you and do anything He asks you to do? Or do you want to leave some room to rely on those self-help formulas to help you run your own race and depend on your own abilities and resources to make life count?

6 **Read "From Religion to Relationship" on page 57 and see if you identify with any of Andy's experiences of religion rather than relationship. If you identify with him, don't wait 60 years. Enter the relationship now!**

Relationships take time to build and maintain. A few minutes here and there or prayer on the run will not be sufficient for your walk with the Lord. Intimacy requires unhurried time. Add a regular assignment to your life in Christ. Take time this week to begin taking unhurried time with your Heavenly Father.

7 **Read the suggestions in the margin for unhurried time with your Heavenly Father. Plan to take that time soon.**

UNHURRIED TIME WITH YOUR HEAVENLY FATHER

1. Get away from the interruptions of your daily routine. Find a quiet place at home or an outdoor space where you can enjoy an unhurried time with your Heavenly Father.
2. Don't worry about an agenda. Let His Spirit guide your conversations.
3. Learn to enjoy being in His presence. Receive His love.

FROM RELIGION TO RELATIONSHIP

Born in Ireland, Andy was one of 13 children. He grew up attending church every time the doors were open. "It seemed like we went every night of the week plus three times on Sunday. We walked about a mile and a half, so I figured I'd walked about 4,000 miles for Jesus by the time I was 17, and I was getting sick and tired of it."

Andy made a commitment to Christ at age 11, but by age 17 he'd had enough of the disciplines of home, the regimen of church, and the expectations of family. So he joined the navy and turned his back on his faith for 10 years. "But God never left me. He was so faithful, and my mother prayed so much. There wasn't a night of my life in those 10 years that I didn't know something was wrong and missing inside me."

Andy left the service, got married, and launched a career of all-out service at Johnson Wax and later at Xerox. He focused on doing a job, doing it well, and giving everything he had. After 18 years he had given so much that he was fried emotionally and physically.

Deciding that he needed a career change, Andy jumped at the opportunity to become the COO of a home-decorating empire. He attacked this new job as he had the others—full bore, holding nothing back. "After another 18 years of exhausting devotion, I was totally burned out, very depressed, and very unhappy. I was struggling in every relationship possible."

Although time was at a premium, Andy had made time for church. He served as a deacon, taught Bible study, and participated in church visitation. "I would have won an Academy Award outwardly. But inside I'd lost my joy, my peace, and I was filled with ego. I wanted to let the church know how great I was working for Jesus. And frankly, I did a great job at that, but I became an empty shell. I was doing a lot of things for Jesus, but I could never really get any peace that I was in His will."

Struggling with whether to go to the mission field, the ministry, or someplace else where he could make a radical difference for Christ, Andy found himself on a mission trip with a friend, Dr. David Wyrtzen. Andy told him: "I wish God would call me into ministry. I've been waiting all my years for Him to call me."

After a long pause, David turned to Andy and asked: "Do you think that God would put you through all He has in the business world just for you to get into something brand-new and go to the mission field at age 60? Why don't you become a minister in the workplace?"

"Not long after that I was lying in bed and came to a crisis. I told God: 'I'm not going back into sales. I'm just not going to go there. Lord, I just can't do it.'"

And in the quiet stillness of his bedroom, Andy heard God saying, "Andrew, I've been waiting 40 years for you to tell Me you can't do something. Now let Me do it for you."

At this moment, as a 60-year-old man, Andy discovered God's will and call for his life. He went back into direct sales, but this time things were different. Andy decided to abide in Christ, leaving the results to his Lord, and to depend on Him as a safeguard from his own frantic work habits and self-reliance.

Andy Horner launched Premier Designs, Inc., a jewelry business that takes fashion jewelry to neighborhood home shows. "We're a corporation built on biblical principles," Andy explains. "We started this company so that moms could stay at home with their children and yet have a job and an income that pays the bills."

Andy's company is built on the servant model. Although every distributor is in jewelry sales, she understands that she is sent to practice the love of Christ, loving people as they are and serving people every chance she gets. God has blessed Andy as he focused on the ministry first and left the results to God.

Now more than 16,000 independent distributors visit more than 100,000 homes, sharing Christ as they show their wares. Andy realizes that his job is to abide peacefully in Christ rather than dwell on the bottom line of his business. "I was 60 years old, I think, before God could trust me. There was just too much of me and not enough of Him in my life. I realized my strength had become my weakness. I admitted I couldn't do it, but He could, and He simply responded with the words I'll never forget: 'Then let Me do it!' And God has."[2]

DAY 4
Abiding in Christ

TODAY'S WORD ON WORK

" 'I am the vine, you are the branches. He who abides in Me, and I in him, bears much fruit; for without Me you can do nothing.' "
John 15:5, NKJV

RESPONDING PRAYER

Lord Jesus, I want that kind of abiding relationship with You so that Your life will flow through me and bring forth much fruit. Show me how to have that kind of relationship with You. Amen.

" 'I am the true vine, and my Father is the gardener. He cuts off every branch in me that bears no fruit, while every branch that does bear fruit he prunes so that it will be even more fruitful. You are already clean because of the word I have spoken to you. Remain in me, and I will remain in you. No branch can bear fruit by itself; it must remain in the vine. Neither can you bear fruit unless you remain in me.

'I am the vine; you are the branches. If a man remains in me and I in him, he will bear much fruit; apart from me you can do nothing.' "
John 15:1-5

> **Read and think about "Today's Word on Work" in the margin and respond to the Lord in prayer.**

Human-centered philosophies and self-help gurus are me-focused. The power is within me. If I can dream it, I can achieve it. I must believe in myself, have faith in my abilities! In contrast, Christ-followers are called to die to self and to abide in Christ. The focus is not on me but on Him.

That's why the second principle for a life that counts is so important.

1 **Write the second principle for a life that counts, as well as your response.**

Principle 2: _____

_____

My response: _____

_____

The second principle states that God calls you to a life-changing relationship with Him through Jesus Christ. Only when we abide in (remain in intimate relationship with) Christ do we realize the full potential of our calling and avoid the me-centered philosophy that robs us of our destiny—the mission God has for us. The power lies not within us but within our relationship with Christ.

2 **Where does the power come from for you to fulfill your mission, your destiny? Check one.**
❑ a. From inside me, from my strengths and abilities
❑ b. From the Spirit of Christ, who lives in and through me

3 **Read Jesus' words in the margin and answer these questions.**
a. Who is the Vine? _____
b. Who is the branch? _____
c. Who is the Gardener? _____
d. How much can the branch do by itself? _____

e. What does the Gardener do with a branch that doesn't bear fruit?

_____

f. What does the Gardener do to a branch to cause it to bear more fruit?

_____

g. What is the job of the branch in relationship to the Vine?

_____

The power to fulfill your mission and destiny in God's unique plan comes not from you but from the Spirit of Christ, who lives in and through you. In the parable of the Vine, Jesus described the relationship we need with Him. He is the Vine. You are a branch. God the Father is the Vinedresser. By itself the branch can do nothing. When the branch bears no fruit, the Father disposes of it. But when a branch bears fruit, the Vinedresser prunes it to make it even more fruitful. The job of the branch is not to bear fruit; that is the job of the Vine working through the branch. The job of the branch is to remain (abide) in a close, personal relationship with the Vine.

Every Christ-follower needs to grasp an important corollary to this distinction between the self-help philosophies and the biblical view of calling. Self-help philosophies tell you to focus almost exclusively on your strengths— unlock their full potential, and you will change your world. The Bible takes a different view.

④ **Read 2 Corinthians 12:9-10 in the margin and fill in the blanks.**
Paul said that when he was weak, he was _____.
Paul said that God's _____ was made perfect in Paul's weakness.

> "He said to me, 'My grace is sufficient for you, for my power is made perfect in weakness.' Therefore I will boast all the more gladly about my weaknesses, so that Christ's power may rest on me. That is why, for Christ's sake, I delight in weaknesses, in insults, in hardships, in persecutions, in difficulties. For when I am weak, then I am strong."
> 2 Corinthians 12:9-10

Although this concept seems counterintuitive, it is absolutely key to realizing the full potential of your calling. God shares His glory with no one. When He works through our weaknesses in the most improbable ways, no one can question who should get the credit. If we focus exclusively on our strengths, we may miss a major part of what God wants to do through our lives.

⑤ **Why does God choose to work through your weaknesses?**

_____

Of course, we don't turn a blind eye to our God-given strengths and try to operate exclusively in our areas of weakness. We should evaluate both our strengths and weaknesses with a focus on God, not on ourselves. Through the prism of His sufficiency we see our strengths as gifts and talents that God hard-wired into us. Recognizing what we do best and giving our Creator the glory for it are important parts of our calling. But an equally important part is honestly acknowledging our weaknesses. We must manage the weaknesses that might lead us into sin, while leaving room for God to work in spite of—no, because of—the weaknesses in our lives.

Abiding in Christ means that we allow Him both to maximize our strengths and to work powerfully through our weaknesses. When He does, heads will shake in disbelief at what God alone has accomplished.

6 **Which is the most appropriate conclusion to draw when God works through your weaknesses?**
   ❏ a. Because of my weaknesses I worked harder and longer than ever. Look what I've done!
   ❏ b. Apart from Christ working in me, I can do nothing. God is the One who has worked in and through me. Look at what He has done! I praise Him!

7 **Which is the most appropriate conclusion to draw when God works through your strengths?**
   ❏ a. Because of my strengths I was able to do this job well.
   ❏ b. Apart from Christ working in me, I can do nothing of kingdom value. God is the One who has worked in and through me. Look at what He has done! I praise Him!

Did you check *b* in each case? When you deal with things of the kingdom and eternity, you can do nothing of lasting value in the area of your strengths *or* weaknesses. Christ in you is the One doing His work. Either way, He is the only One who gets the glory. He is the only One worthy of praise.

How do you abide in Christ so that you can have a fruitful life? We've got some suggestions for you. Keep in mind, however, that this is a relationship, not just religious activity.

8 **Read the suggestions in the margin for abiding in Christ. Then spend time with the Lord in prayer and in His Word. Watch for another opportunity to spend unhurried time with your Heavenly Father.**

SUGGESTIONS FOR ABIDING IN CHRIST

I. Spend time reading God's Word and listening for ways to adjust your life to God and His ways.

2. Spend time in two-way prayer seeking God's will and desires for what you ask. Bring yourself into agreement with Him rather than trying to get Him to agree with you.

3. Regularly examine your life alongside the standards in Scripture. Turn from sin and walk in newness of life.

4. Spend time with God's people to help one another, encourage one another, seek God's counsel together, and enjoy His presence.

DAY 5

Prayer as a Relationship

Read and think about "Today's Word on Work" in the margin and respond to the Lord in prayer.

Many people see prayer as a religious activity. Therefore, they plan special times for prayer, have a special place they go to pray, or participate in an interecessory-prayer ministry. These actions are appropriate as long as we recognize that prayer is more than just an activity to complete.

1 Review principle 2 for a life that counts by filling in the blanks below.
God calls you to a life-changing _____ with Him
through _____ _____.

What is your response?
Enter the _____ and _____ to God's
transforming _____ in your life.

Principle 2, which has been this week's focus, teaches you that God calls you to a life-changing relationship through Jesus Christ. When you enter that relationship, you submit to God's transforming work in your life. Prayer is a relationship with God, and it is a very important way you submit to God's work in your life. When you genuinely pray, you interact with the God of the universe, who invites you to come into the throne room of heaven with your requests. Throughout the day God is present with you and available to interact with you in prayer. Having special time to focus on prayer is a good practice. Having a special place and time to pray and participating in a prayer ministry are also wonderful disciplines for a Christ-follower. But if you see prayer as just an item on your to-do list, you are missing the experience of prayer as a vital relationship with the Lord.

2 Which of the following most nearly describes the way you think about prayer? Check a response or write your own.
  ❑ a. I see prayer as a constant relationship. I realize that I can talk with God at any time and that when He speaks, I'm listening. My day is saturated with an attitude of prayer because God is always with me.

TODAY'S WORD ON WORK

" 'Again, I tell you that if two of you on earth agree about anything you ask for, it will be done for you by my Father in heaven. For where two or three come together in my name, there am I with them.' "
Matthew 18:19-20

RESPONDING PRAYER

Lord, that is a very big promise. I want to know that kind of power in prayer, and I want to know that extra measure of Your presence. Teach me how to pray in agreement with others. Amen.

❑ b. I tend to think of prayer as something I need to do at certain times and in special places. Because it's my duty as a Christ-follower, I discipline myself to devote time to prayer.

❑ c. Quite honestly, I don't think about prayer very much. It is seldom a part of my day or my life.

Disciplining yourself to have regular times and places for prayer is a good practice. But if you think of prayer more as a religious activity or duty, let God bring you into the experience of prayer as a personal relationship with Him.

③ **If you think of prayer as just a religious activity, stop and ask the Lord to draw you to Himself and to help you experience prayer as an intimate relationship with your Heavenly Father.**

Let's look at three purposes God has in calling you to a prayer relationship with Him.

One purpose God has for a prayer relationship is to mold and shape you to be like Him. Prayer is your time to talk with your Heavenly Father. It's a time to worship Him in praise and with thanksgiving. When you begin to see Him for who He really is, you will also see yourself as you really are in comparison. That will prompt you to confess your sin and turn to Him. God uses such prayer to mold and shape you to be more like His Son, Jesus Christ. He shows you worldly behaviors and attitudes to put off and godly behaviors and attitudes to put on.

PURPOSE 1
To mold and shape you to be like God

④ **What is one purpose for a prayer relationship?**
God uses it to _____.

⑤ **If you can think of a time when God used a time of prayer to change you, correct you, mold you, or shape you more nearly into the image of Christ, briefly describe that occasion.**

_____
_____

PURPOSE 2
For you to participate with God in the work He wants to do

A second purpose of a prayer relationship is for you to participate with God in the work He wants to do. In one sense prayer is a mystery; why would God wait to act until He has someone pray? As our Heavenly Father and Master, God takes great pleasure in allowing us to participate with Him in His work. When we do, we experience life at its best. We get to be coworkers with the God of the universe in His kingdom pursuits. God invites our prayer for His kingdom work. Then when He accomplishes what we've prayed for, we experience the spiritual adrenaline rush of knowing that we're part of something bigger than we are.

6 **What is the second purpose for a prayer relationship?**

For me to _____ with God in the work He wants to do

7 **If you can think of a time when God prompted you to ask for something that He later did in answer to your prayer, briefly describe it.**

_____

_____

A third purpose of a prayer relationship is for God to reveal to you what He is planning to do so that you can adjust your life to Him and join His work. Jesus described this kind of relationship with His Father while He was involved in His earthly ministry: "Jesus said to them, 'My Father is always at his work to this very day, and I, too, am working.' … 'I tell you the truth, the Son can do nothing by himself; he can do only what he sees his Father doing, because whatever the Father does the Son also does. For the Father loves the Son and shows him all he does' " (John 5:17-20).

In a prayer relationship with His Father, Jesus received the directions He needed to know what He was to do and say. After an evening of healing people and casting out demons, Jesus went out early the next morning to pray for His Father's will (see Luke 4:42-43). The masses wanted to spend time with Jesus that day, but because He had been up early praying, He knew that His Father wanted Him to go preach the good news of the kingdom to other towns. God often reveals His directions and gives His assignments to you in times of prayer. Prayer is a relationship in which God reveals His plans to His servants.

8 **What is a third purpose of a prayer relationship?**

God uses it to _____

so that I can adjust my life to Him and join His work.

9 **If you can think of a time when God revealed a specific assignment He had for you during a time of prayer, briefly describe that occasion.**

_____

_____

10 **Review the three purposes of a prayer relationship and respond to God in prayer. Ask Him to teach you how to experience the fullest dimensions of what He intends a prayer relationship to be.**

> **PURPOSE 3**
> To reveal to you what God is planning to do so that you can adjust your life to Him and join His work

"At daybreak Jesus went out to a solitary place. The people were looking for him and when they came to where he was, they tried to keep him from leaving them. But he said, 'I must preach the good news of the kingdom of God to the other towns also, because that is why I was sent.' "
Luke 4:42-43

---

[1]Joe Musser, *The Infidel* (Nashville: Broadman and Holman, 2002), 349–50. Precisely what was said in this first meeting is a product of Mr. Musser's informed imagination based on known historical facts.
[2]Authors' interview, 13 May 2003.

WEEK 4
Called to a Mission

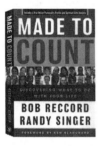

THIS WEEK'S SUPPLEMENTARY READING

Chapter 7, *Made to Count*

Pat was seven when his younger brother Larry died. While Pat's father turned to God and the church for comfort, his mother turned to alcohol to deal with the pain. Soon his parents divorced, and his father moved from their home in Philadelphia to south Florida. Two years later Pat's mother took her sons and moved to Florida to reconcile with her husband. But after three months the boys came home from school one day to find that their mother had returned to Philadelphia and left them with their father.

Pat excelled in sports, but while playing baseball in college, he realized he wouldn't become a professional player. During his senior year he married his best friend and sweetheart, but the weight of the world seemed to press in on him: "I had to figure out what I was going to do for a living after I got out of college. I had to deal with a newlywed with no money in a strange city. … I was living the life of the prodigal son. At 21 years old, I was broken because for the first time in my life, my priority was not baseball; it was everything other than baseball. My self-esteem, as a result, was collapsing. I wound up in the hospital six or seven times thinking I was having a heart attack, but it was just stress."

Lonely, broken, and feeling strained in his marriage, Pat walked into a church and met Christ. "I completely and totally surrendered myself," he said. "I felt a sense of relief that He accepted the burdens that were on my back and was willing to accept all of my shortfalls. I sensed that as the prodigal son I was returning, and He was willing to accept me just the way I was."

Pat's health returned, and he finished college. Even though he would have preferred a sports career, his wife's resistance led him to choose a career in business. Pat recalls: "I honored her and wound up in business. As I look back now, I believe that God had a plan for both of us and that my wife was going to discourage me from sports because God wanted me in the financial marketplace."

Today Pat Flood's marketplace is HomeBanc, headquartered in Atlanta, Georgia. With 1,200 employees and $170 million in annual revenue, HomeBanc is one of *Fortune Magazine*'s top one hundred places to work. From a small start-up bank in 1985 to this

major corporation, God has guided Pat on the mission. "I tell people that if you look back at the successes of HomeBanc, you'll find God's hand. If you look at the failures, you'll find the times when I forgot that it was actually His and not mine."

Pat believes that part of God's call is for him and HomeBanc to be examples of the difference God can make when He and His principles are honored in the workplace. Pat seeks the Lord's guidance when he faces conflicts in the workplace, and he guides his company to follow Christ's example of servanthood to others with honor and integrity. Pat reflected: "As I continued to sense the Holy Spirit helping me in what were significant workplace confrontations, I continued to feel His encouragement. It always turned out way better than I could have possibly contemplated it. I continued to get messages from people in the marketplace and from people who were around me that this was something they thought I was called to do."

Pat realizes that the greatest assets in his company are the people who work there. Their health and well-being are vital concerns. There-

fore, Pat asked a prominent pastor in Atlanta to accept the responsibility of shepherding the employees and guiding the corporate culture by Judeo-Christian values. Today Ike Rieghard serves as the chief people officer for HomeBanc.

One morning as Pat was at work praying and reviewing the Ten Commandments, his attention was drawn to "Honor your father and mother." God began to speak to him about a plan to rescue his mother from alcoholism and to forgive her. He called his two brothers, who also work for HomeBanc, and shared the plan. They offered her and her new husband a home in south Florida on the condition that they would get help and give up drinking. That was six years ago, and Pat's mother hasn't had a drink since moving to Florida. She is regular in church and is devoted to prayer. In this way and in other ways Pat sees his calling as an opportunity to build a legacy that honors Christ.[1]

Pray and ask the Lord to reveal the mission He has for you. Ask Him to reveal how your work can build a legacy that honors Him and contributes to His kingdom work.

DAY 1

Principle 3: Called to a Mission

TODAY'S WORD ON WORK

"All this is from God, who reconciled us to himself through Christ and gave us the ministry of reconciliation: that God was reconciling the world to himself in Christ, not counting men's sins against them. And he has committed to us the message of reconciliation. We are therefore Christ's ambassadors, as though God were making his appeal through us. We implore you on Christ's behalf: Be reconciled to God."
2 Corinthians 5:18-20

RESPONDING PRAYER

Thank You, Lord, for doing through Christ what was necessary for me to be right with You. Now that You've committed this message and ministry to me, teach me when and how to be an ambassador for Christ. Amen.

> **Read and think about "Today's Word on Work" in the margin and respond to the Lord in prayer.**

This week we will focus on principle 3 for a life that counts.

Principle 3:	God calls you to partner with Him in a mission that is bigger than you are.
Your response:	Receive God's assignments and begin obeying by faith.

1 **Read principle 3 several times, giving special attention to the words that are bold and underlined.**

God calls you to partner with Him in a **mission** that is **bigger** than you are.

2 **Now personalize the principle by rewriting it. Change *you* to *me* and *you are* to *I am*.**

_____

_____

3 **Fill in the blanks below with the missing words and review all eight principles for a life that counts.**
1. God prepared a unique _____ and _____ for your life even _____ you were born.
2. God calls you to a life-changing _____ with Him through _____ _____.
3. God calls you to partner with Him in a _____ that is _____ than you are.
4. God calls you to be on **mission** with Him right where you are—starting **now**.
5. God reveals His mission through His **Word**, His **Spirit**, wise **counsel**, and His work in **circumstances** around you.

6. God repeatedly brings you to a crossroads of **choice** as He **forges** you for His mission.

7. God **guides** and **provides** for your mission one **step** at a time.

8. When you **answer** God's call, you experience His **pleasure** and **change** your world.

Principles 2 and 3 teach us a twofold call of God. Last week we learned through principle 2 that God calls us to a life-changing relationship with Him. Principle 3 teaches us that God calls us to a life-fulfilling mission alongside Him, a mission that is bigger than we are.

④ **What are the two parts of God's twofold call? Fill in the blanks.**
  1. A life-changing _____ with Him.
  2. A life-fulfilling _____ alongside Him.

Too often we speak of doing things for God, as if we come up with the idea, create the plan, and execute the strategy. But when we carefully read the Bible, we learn that God says He will do the planning, guiding, and directing. God does not leave us to guess His mission for us. He guarantees His guidance for all who have entered a personal relationship with Him (read the first three Scriptures in the margin). And therein lies a big difference! God is not nearly as concerned about what we are going to do for Him as He is about whether we are willing to be work alongside Him and be obedient in what He is already doing.

Our mission is a partnership in which God controls the planning process while we make ourselves available to execute *His* plan. Contrary to what we have heard, we are not called to live for Christ. We are called to live in Christ. The Christian life is not only one of imitation but also one of habitation: "God has chosen to make known among the Gentiles the glorious riches of this mystery, which is Christ in you, the hope of glory" (Colossians 1:27).

Throughout Scripture and throughout history God always blessed people in order for them to bless others. People were saved in order to be sent. They were changed in order to become change agents in the lives of others (see 1 Peter 2:9). God still works in people's lives that way today.

⑤ **Mark each statement *T* for *true* or *F* for *false*.**
  ___ a. God calls me to make up plans for what I will do for Him, and then I carry out the plans.
  ___ b. God makes plans and asks me to allow Him to work through me to accomplish them.
  ___ c. God has blessed me in order for me to bless others.

"I will guide you along the best pathway
    for your life.
I will advise you and watch over you."
Psalm 32:8, NLT

"Whether you turn to the right or to the left,
your ears will hear a voice behind you,
saying, 'This is the way; walk in it.' "
Isaiah 30:21

"Trust in the LORD with all your heart
    and lean not on your own
    understanding;
in all your ways acknowledge him,
    and he will make your paths straight."
Proverbs 3:5-6

"You are a chosen people, a royal priesthood, a holy nation, a people belonging to God, that you may declare the praises of him who called you out of darkness into his wonderful light."
I Peter 2:9

You probably indicated that *b* and *c* are true. Salvation is a gift, but it brings with it a responsibility. Findley Edge said it well: "The call to salvation and the call to ministry are one and the same call."[2] Edge went on to explain: "Salvation is a gift, wholly a gift, but this gift is given only on the basis of the quality of response which God Himself sets. The One who called us to this mission and the fulfilling of it, who gifted us, who appointed some to equip us, and who empowers us and gives us His presence through the Holy Spirit expects us to fulfill this mission when we say to Him, 'I give You my life.' Authentic faith is a faith that fulfills that to which God has called us."[3]

Step by step the God who designed us for a unique destiny, then called us into a life-changing relationship with Himself, also guides us into a life-changing mission alongside Him.

When Jesus met Saul on the road to Damascus, He not only called him to salvation, but He also called Saul to a mission: " 'Now get up and stand on your feet. I have appeared to you to appoint you as a servant and as a witness of what you have seen of me and what I will show you. I will rescue you from your own people and from the Gentiles. I am sending you to them to open their eyes and turn them from darkness to light, and from the power of Satan to God, so that they may receive forgiveness of sins and a place among those who are sanctified by faith in me' " (Acts 26:16-18).

6 **What was the mission Jesus called Saul to accomplish?**

_____

_____

> When God called you to a personal relationship through Jesus Christ, He had a mission in mind for you as well.

God called Saul to a relationship with Him, but He also called Saul to carry the message of salvation to the Gentiles so that they could come to saving faith in Jesus Christ. When God called you to a personal relationship through Jesus Christ, He had a mission in mind for you as well.

7 **Review today's summary ideas and respond to God in prayer.**
- God calls us to a life-fulfilling mission alongside Him, a mission that is bigger than we are.
- God says He will do the planning, guiding, and directing.
- The Christian life is not only one of imitation but also one of habitation.
- God always blessed people in order for them to bless others.
- "The call to salvation and the call to ministry are one and the same call."

DAY 2

Titus Was Called to a Mission

Read and think about "Today's Word on Work" in the margin and respond to the Lord in prayer.

Paul sent a letter to a coworker in the ministry named Titus. Evidently, Paul and Titus had started some churches on the island of Crete. Paul left Titus there with a mission to "straighten out what was left unfinished and appoint elders in every town" (Titus 1:5).

1 **How do you think Titus's assignment illustrates principle 3 for a life that counts? Review the principle on page 66 if you need to.**

_____

_____

Titus's mission was a tough assignment. Already some people were teaching false doctrine for personal financial gain. The greater problem was that the people of Crete had a terrible reputation in the world. An ancient poet had said, " 'Cretans are always liars, evil brutes, lazy gluttons' " (Titus 1:12). Paul said this was true about the people of Crete.

2 **Read Titus 1:15-16 in the margin. Underline descriptions of the corrupt.**

3 **How can a person publicly deny knowing God even though he or she claims to know Him?**

_____

Those who do not believe in Christ are corrupted in mind and conscience, impure, detestable, disobedient, and unfit for doing anything good. A person who lives like that denies God by his or her actions.

4 **If someone in your workplace claims to be a Christian but lives like the rest of the world, how do unbelievers respond? Check all that apply.**
❏ a. They ridicule the church and Christ: "If that is what being a Christian means, I don't want to have any part of it."
❏ b. They use this hypocrite as an excuse to reject Christ: "Why should I be a Christian? Look at _____. He's a Christian, and I live a better life than he does."

TODAY'S WORD ON WORK

"Teach slaves to be subject to their masters in everything, to try to please them, not to talk back to them, and not to steal from them, but to show that they can be fully trusted, so that in every way they will make the teaching about God our Savior attractive."
Titus 2:9-10

RESPONDING PRAYER

Lord, I'd like to set that kind of example in my work—an example that makes You attractive to others. Teach and enable me to live like that. Amen.

"To the pure, all things are pure, but to those who are corrupted and do not believe, nothing is pure. In fact, both their minds and consciences are corrupted. They claim to know God, but by their actions they deny him. They are detestable, disobedient and unfit for doing anything good."
Titus 1:15-16

❑ c. They reject Christ and the church as irrelevant: "Christians are no different from anybody else. If they want to waste their time with that religious stuff, it's OK with me."

❑ d. Other: _____

Christians' hypocrisy and bad examples can be the greatest hindrances to the spread of Christ's kingdom. Christians in the workplace must be different as they allow Christ to live through them. Paul gave a couple of reasons: "Our people must learn to devote themselves to doing what is good, in order that they may provide for daily necessities and not live unproductive lives" (Titus 3:14) and "… so that in every way they will make the teaching about God our Savior attractive" (Titus 2:10).

5 **Why should Christ-followers devote themselves to doing what is good? Complete these phrases.**

To provide for _____

and not live _____

to make the teaching about God _____

The Christians of Crete needed to change their conduct to reflect Christ's character in them. They needed to devote themselves to doing what is good to provide for daily necessities and to be productive. They needed to live in such a way that the message about Christ as their Savior would be attractive. Do you realize that God can use the way you live and work to attract others to Christ? God wants to put you on public display to show what a difference Christ makes in a life.

Paul wanted Titus to teach the Christians in Crete to honor Christ by their actions. But first he challenged Titus to practice what he was to teach: "In everything set them an example by doing what is good. In your teaching show integrity, seriousness and soundness of speech that cannot be condemned, so that those who oppose you may be ashamed because they have nothing bad to say about us" (Titus 2:7-8).

Let's look at what Titus was to teach the Christians of Crete.

6 **In the following Scriptures we've identified the people Titus was to teach with bold and italic type. Underline words that describe the behavior desired. We have underlined a couple as examples.**

You must teach what is in accord with sound doctrine. Teach the ***older men*** to be <u>temperate</u>, worthy of respect, self-controlled, and sound in faith, in love and in endurance.

Likewise, teach the ***older women*** to be reverent in the way they live, not to be slanderers or addicted to much wine, but to teach what

> God wants to put you on public display to show what a difference Christ makes in a life.

is good. Then they can train the younger women to love their husbands and children, to be self-controlled and pure, to be busy at home, to be kind, and to be subject to their husbands, so that no one will malign the word of God.

Similarly, encourage the *young men* to be self-controlled (Titus 2:1-6).

Teach *slaves* to be subject to their masters in everything, to try to please them, not to talk back to them, and not to steal from them, but to show that they can be fully trusted, so that in every way they will make the teaching about God our Savior attractive.

For the grace of God that brings salvation has appeared to *all men*. It teaches us to say "No" to ungodliness and worldly passions, and to live self-controlled, upright and godly lives in this present age, while we wait for the blessed hope—the glorious appearing of our great God and Savior, Jesus Christ, who gave himself for us to redeem us from all wickedness and to purify for himself a people that are his very own, eager to do what is good (Titus 2:9-14).

Remind the *people* to be subject to rulers and authorities, to be obedient, to be ready to do whatever is good, to slander no one, to be peaceable and considerate, and to show true humility toward all men (Titus 3:1).

I want you to stress these things, so that *those who have trusted in God* may be careful to devote themselves to doing what is good. These things are excellent and profitable for everyone (Titus 3:8).

Paul's instructions called for these groups to be obedient, good, peaceable, doctrinally sound, considerate, humble, self-controlled, upright, godly, trust-worthy, temperate, respected, loving, persistent, sober, pure, kind, and subject to authority. If Christians worked like this in the workplace, people would eventually notice the difference. Christians should be honest and trustworthy. They should be hard workers and productive. They should be kind and considerate to others and maintain right relationships with them in public and in private. They should show proper respect for lines of authority. As Pharaoh said of Joseph, people in the workplace should say, " 'Can we find anyone like this man, one in whom is the spirit of God?' " (Genesis 41:38).

> Christians should be honest and trustworthy.

7 **If God evaluated the impact of your life and witness in your workplace or on the people in your world up to now, what would He find? Check one or write your own response.**

❑ a. The quality of my work, my attitudes, my integrity, the way I treat others, and my witness about Christ's work in my life make the "teaching about God our Savior attractive" (Titus 2:10).

❑ b. People probably do not know I'm a follower of Christ.

❑ c. I'm afraid that my life and testimony currently have (or would have) a negative influence on the people in my workplace.

❑ d. My life and witness are so neutral that people probably would not care to know what I think about Christ.

❑ e. Other: _____

_____

_____

8 **Do you want your workplace to change and function the way God intends?** ❑ **Yes** ❑ **No**

9 **If you answered yes, are you willing to be an example to other Christ-followers and to the world so that no one will have anything bad to say about you, other Christians, or the church of Jesus Christ? Review in the margin principle 3 for a life that counts, along with your response, and write your commitment to the Lord.**

_____

_____

_____

_____

_____

_____

PRINCIPLE 3

God calls you to partner with Him in a mission that is bigger than you are.

YOUR RESPONSE

Receive God's assignments and begin obeying by faith.

Christ wants to restore obedience to Him in your workplace, regardless of whether it is a religious organization that has drifted from His will or a secular corporation, whether it has 5 employees or 50,000. He needs a place to start. We pray that you and others in your small group will be the starting point for Christ's redemptive work in the world around you—in your workplace or through the platform of your position or profession.

10 **Review today's summary ideas and respond to God by praying that He will work in you through His Holy Spirit to reflect Christlike qualities to those in your workplace or profession.**

• Christians in the workplace must be different as they allow Christ to live through them.

• They needed to live in such a way that the message about Christ as their Savior would be attractive.

• Christ wants to restore obedience to Him in your workplace.

DAY 3

Preparing for Your Mission

Read and think about "Today's Word on Work" in the margin and respond to the Lord in prayer.

This week we are focusing on principle 3 for a life that counts.

1. **Fill in the blanks to recall principle 3 and your response to the principle.**

   Principle 3: God calls you to partner with Him in a _____ that is _____ than you are.

   Your response: Receive God's _____ and begin obeying by _____.

Just as an astronaut trains for a mission in space or military personnel train for a mission in a combat zone, God will prepare you for the mission He has in store for you. The bigger and the more significant the mission, the larger the character required to carry out the assignment. Here are some ways God prepares you for your mission.

1. God wants to develop your intimacy with Him in prayer so that you hear and know His voice as He guides you. If God has not given you a clear assignment yet, keep working on developing your relationship with Him. God spent 40 years with Moses in the desert before He gave Moses the assignment to lead the nation of Israel out of Egypt.

2. God wants to set you apart from sin. God uses clean vessels (lives): "We know that our old self was crucified with him so that the body of sin might be done away with, that we should no longer be slaves to sin" (Romans 6:6). "You have been set free from sin and have become slaves to righteousness" (Romans 6:18).

3. Like a potter with clay, God molds and shapes your life, your personality, your wisdom, and your abilities to match the assignment He has uniquely planned for your life. Give Him the time He knows is required to complete the preparation.

4. God develops your relationships with people to prepare you to work with them in the body of Christ or as God's representative to them.

TODAY'S WORD ON WORK

"Dear friends, I urge you, as aliens and strangers in the world, to abstain from sinful desires, which war against your soul. Live such good lives among the pagans that, though they accuse you of doing wrong, they may see your good deeds and glorify God on the day he visits us."
I Peter 2:11-12

RESPONDING PRAYER

Lord, I want to bring You glory. I thank You that I can choose to abstain from sinful desires that war inside me. Show me how to live my life in a such way that my testimony will bring You glory. Amen.

2 **Pause to pray. Give God permission to mold and shape your life to be exactly what He knows will be needed for your mission assignment(s). Pray about these areas:**
   a. Your relationship with Him in prayer
   b. Your holiness, righteousness, and freedom from sin
   c. Your character, wisdom, and gifts to match a mission assignment
   d. Your relationships with people inside the body of Christ and with people in the world around you

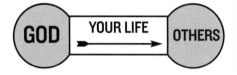

When you think about preparing for your mission in these areas, picture your life as a pipe.[4] It is a channel through which Jesus—the Living Water—flows. On one end of your pipe you must be connected to God by a saving relationship with Him through Jesus Christ, your Savior. On the other end of your pipe you are connected to other people through relationships. God's desire and mission are to work through your life in such a way that others will come to saving faith in His Son—that they will be reconciled to God. We could illustrate your life with the drawing in the margin.

Some people have a problem with their pipe. Because it is clogged up, the Living Water cannot flow through it as intended. Sin can clog up your pipeline by shutting off your access to the Holy Spirit's power and filling presence. God's holiness and righteousness cannot be revealed (flow) through a dirty life. To be ready for your mission assignment, you need a clean life.

Love of pleasure and love of the world or the things of the world can clog up your pipe. The Scriptures say, "Do not love the world or anything in the world. If anyone loves the world, the love of the Father is not in him" (1 John 2:15). God's first and greatest command to us is this: " 'Love the Lord your God with all your heart and with all your soul and with all your mind' " (Matthew 22:37). God's love cannot flow through a life that is filled with the love of other people, activities, or things in place of a wholehearted love for God. Love of self can also keep the Living Water from flowing.

3 **Is your pipe clogged by sin, self, or the love of something that takes the place of your love for God? Then you need to get your pipe cleaned out. Clean out your pipe by—**
   • confessing and repenting of your sin;
   • daily denying yourself in order to follow Christ;
   • putting away idols of the heart and returning to your first love for God.

Another problem can exist with the flow of Living Water through your pipe. If you have a broken relationship with a person, you have a cap on the end of your pipe that stops the flow. The person may not be willing to listen to you or receive the Living Water from your life. Broken relationships in the body of Christ have an effect on your relationship with God as well. Two kinds of broken relationships may be present in your relationships with others.

In one case you may have sinned against the other person or group. Jesus gave this command to you: " 'If you are offering your gift at the altar and there remember that your brother has something against you, leave your gift there in front of the altar. First go and be reconciled to your brother; then come and offer your gift' " (Matthew 5:23-24).

Even your worship is not acceptable to God if you have a broken relationship that has not been reconciled. Reconciling that relationship by seeking forgiveness and, if necessary, making restitution removes the cap from your pipe so that the Living Water can flow once again.

4 **Pray and ask the Lord to reveal to you anyone within or outside the body of Christ whom you have sinned against. If names come to mind, write their initials below and take the actions necessary to reconcile your relationships.**

_____

The other kind of broken relationship is one in which you have been offended (or sinned against) by the other person. If you are withholding forgiveness, your pipe will be capped. If that is the case, Jesus has two things to say to you: " 'If you forgive men when they sin against you, your heavenly Father will also forgive you. But if you do not forgive men their sins, your Father will not forgive your sins' " (Matthew 6:14-15). " 'When you stand praying, if you hold anything against anyone, forgive him, so that your Father in heaven may forgive you your sins' " (Mark 11:25).

When you have been sinned against, forgive. This will uncap your pipe so that God's grace and love can flow through your life. Forgiveness is a command, not an option. The wonderful thing about this command is that the Holy Spirit of Christ in you can enable you to forgive in obedience to the command. When you forgive though the other person does not deserve it, you reveal God's grace and forgiveness. So forgive and uncap your pipe. You are most Christlike when you forgive.

> **You are most Christlike when you forgive.**

5 **Pray and ask the Lord to reveal to you anyone within or outside the body of Christ whom you need to forgive. If names come to mind, write their initials below and forgive them. You will need the help of Christ to forgive. Ask Him for that help and forgive as He has commanded.**

_____

When your pipe is clean and clear of all clogs, the Living Water can flow through you. When relationships with others are right and clear, they become opportunities for you to reveal Christ and His grace, mercy, and love.

⑥ **Which kind of pipe best describes your life? Circle one:**
Clogged   Capped   Clean and clear

⑦ **Review today's summary ideas and respond to God in prayer. Take the actions needed to prepare for the mission assignment God has for you.**
- The bigger and the more significant the mission, the larger the character required to carry out the assignment.
- Sin can clog up your pipeline by shutting off your access to the Holy Spirit's power and filling presence.
- God's love cannot flow through a life that is filled with the love of other people, activities, or things in place of a wholehearted love for God.
- Forgiveness is a command, not an option.
- You are most Christlike when you forgive.

DAY 4

Guidelines for Mission Assignments

TODAY'S WORD ON WORK

"I urge you, brothers, in view of God's mercy, to offer your bodies as living sacrifices, holy and pleasing to God—this is your spiritual act of worship. Do not conform any longer to the pattern of this world, but be transformed by the renewing of your mind. Then you will be able to test and approve what God's will is—his good, pleasing and perfect will."
Romans 12:1-2

RESPONDING PRAYER

Lord, I give You my life, body, mind, and heart. I want to be conformed to Your Son Jesus and His ways. Renew my mind so that I can learn Your perfect will. Amen.

> **Read and think about "Today's Word on Work" in the margin and respond to the Lord in prayer.**

Today we want to help you begin thinking about the mission assignments God may have for you. The 10 guidelines you will study today may challenge previous assumptions or teachings about God's will. So as you study, it will help to keep in mind the following facts about God.
- God is sovereign. He alone has the right to direct your life. Do not put Him in a box that limits what He might want to do.
- This mission assignment is about God's work. He cares about its accomplishment more than you do. If your mind and heart are set to receive His assignment and obey it whatever the cost, God will not let you miss the assignment. You can talk to Him about these matters as you seek understanding from Him.

- God is infinite. His ways and thoughts are far above our ways and thoughts. We cannot define all the ways God may work or anticipate all that God may want to say or do.
- Knowing what God has already willed for people and the world as revealed in Scripture is an important foundation for knowing how you fit into that plan. Allow God's Word to grow in importance for you.

① As you read the following 10 guidelines, underline important ideas. When a specific thought or application comes to mind, write notes for yourself in the margin. If you have questions, write them in the margin to discuss with your small group.

NOTES

1. God takes the initiative to reveal the assignment(s). You do not choose your own assignment. Assignments are not discovered; they are revealed.

2. Assignments may change over the years, so don't lock yourself into one assignment and ignore others by saying, "That's not my gift." If God calls you to a new assignment, He will grant you spiritual gifts for the new assignment as He did with Moses. A spiritual gift is the manifestation of the Holy Spirit working through you to accomplish a God-given assignment. Because the gift normally follows the giving of the assignment, you will usually not see the gift until you are obeying the assignment.

3. Not every need or opportunity is an assignment from God. Therefore, you need to pray about your role. God entrusts you as the manager of the gifts and resources He has given you. Trust Him to guide you through prayer, His Word, and interaction with other believers to discern the assignments He has for you. Then don't hesitate to say, "I don't sense that this is an assignment God is calling me to at this time" when that is the case. But also understand that changing circumstances may indicate God's timing for you to assume this assignment. Keep your relationship with God very intimate and up-to-date so that you will recognize and hear His voice.

4. When you do not sense God's leadership for an assignment, focus on developing your love relationship with Him in prayer and in His Word. Allow Him to develop your character for the upcoming assignment. At the same time, don't neglect any assignments God may have already made clear in Scripture. Some assignments are simply acts of obedience to the clear teaching in Scripture that you already know.

5. Realize that some assignments will come to an end. You will usually recognize the end of one assignment when God calls you to the next one. Gracefully end an assignment, but don't hesitate to move on in obedience to the Lord's leadership.

NOTES

_____
_____
_____
_____
_____
_____
_____
_____
_____
_____
_____
_____
_____
_____
_____
_____
_____
_____
_____

PRINCIPLE 3

God calls you to partner with Him in a mission that is bigger than you are.

YOUR RESPONSE

Receive God's assignments and begin obeying by faith.

---

6. Stay focused on the assignment(s) God has given you. Sometimes the enemy will tempt you to be distracted into doing good things that are not God's assignments for you.

7. Be very careful about trying to delegate an assignment. God may use you to connect a need with a source to meet that need. However, if God wants to give you an assignment, don't try to delegate it to someone else.

8. When you are confronted with a major new assignment, review your spiritual markers—times in your life when you clearly knew that God spoke, guided, or worked in and through you for His kingdom purposes. Often new assignments will consistently flow in the directions God has been working in your life through the years. New assignments may call for new spiritual gifts, but they often flow consistently with the pattern of God's prior activity in your life.

9. Make prayer a primary work strategy. You will not clearly discern God's directions for your assignments without a focused, intimate prayer life. Pray with others about your assignments from time to time. Keep in mind that prayer is not just a religious activity; it is a relationship with a Person.

10. Realize that sometimes your assignment is not just for you but for the body of Christ of which you are a part. Whenever possible, allow your work to be connected to the body of Christ. Christ loved the church and gave Himself for it. The church is Christ's incarnation in our day. Be careful not to bypass the church—your own congregation or one you may join for a particular assignment.[5]

② Review principle 3 and your response in the margin. Then review your notes, questions, and underlining in today's lesson. Talk to the Lord about what He is saying or doing in your life that might help you understand His mission for you.

DAY 5

Types of Mission Assignments

Read and think about "Today's Word on Work" in the margin and respond to the Lord in prayer.

Your mission in Christ's kingdom is not about where you work or whether your work is classified by the world as secular or sacred. It does not depend on whether you work around Christian people or unbelievers. It is all about a very special relationship you have through Jesus Christ with your Heavenly Father. In that relationship God will reveal what He is doing where you are. You are then invited to join Him in His work. Here's the way Jesus described His approach to knowing and doing His Father's will: " 'My Father is always at his work to this very day, and I, too, am working. ... I tell you the truth, the Son can do nothing by himself; he can do only what he sees his Father doing, because whatever the Father does the Son also does. For the Father loves the Son and shows him all he does" (John 5:17-20).

Henry Blackaby sums up Jesus' approach this way: "Watch to see where God is at work and join Him!"[6] Sometimes people wait for God to give them a big and exciting assignment, and they get frustrated when that assignment doesn't come. God may be waiting to see how you obey Him in assignments He has already commanded.

1 **Pray as you read this list of things God has commanded or modeled in Scripture. Ask God if He has an assignment like one of these in mind for you now. If a person or a situation comes to mind as you read and pray, that may be God's assignment. Talk to Him about those that come to mind. Jot down notes in the margin. If God uses one of these admonitions to catch your attention, read the accompanying Scripture for more information.**

- Speak up for those who cannot defend themselves (see Proverbs 31:8-9).
- Act justly, love mercy, and walk humbly with God (see Micah 6:8).
- Shine spiritual light for those in spiritual darkness (see Matthew 5:14-16).
- Love your enemies (see Matthew 5:43-48).
- Give to the needy (see Matthew 6:1-4).
- Give a cup of cold water in Christ's name (see Matthew 10:42).
- Meet needs of others as a servant and slave (see Matthew 20:25-28).

TODAY'S WORD ON WORK

"It was he who gave some to be apostles, some to be prophets, some to be evangelists, and some to be pastors and teachers, to prepare God's people for works of service, so that the body of Christ may be built up."
Ephesians 4:11-12

RESPONDING PRAYER

Lord, thank You for giving the body of Christ gifted leaders to help us. Use them to equip me to do my part in building up the body. Amen.

NOTES

_____

_____

_____

_____

_____

_____

_____

_____

_____

_____

_____

_____

_____

_____

NOTES

_____
_____
_____
_____
_____
_____
_____
_____
_____
_____
_____
_____
_____
_____
_____
_____
_____
_____
_____
_____
_____
_____
_____
_____

- Minister to Christ by meeting the needs of others (see Matthew 25:34-40):
  - Give food to the hungry.
  - Give water to the thirsty.
  - Invite the stranger in.
  - Give clothes to the naked.
  - Care for the sick.
  - Visit the prisoner.
- Make disciples, teaching them to obey everything Christ commands (see Matthew 28:19-20).
- Preach the good news to all creation (see Mark 16:15).
- Love one another and show the world that you are His disciple (see John 13:34-35).
- Show Christian unity among believers so that the world will know that Jesus is God's Son (see John 17:20-23).
- Be a faithful manager of resources entrusted to you (see 1 Corinthians 4:2).
- Plead with others to be reconciled to Christ (see 2 Corinthians 5:20).
- Be rich in doing good, generous, and willing to share (see 1 Timothy 6:17-19).
- Set an example by doing good, showing integrity, and using sound speech (see Titus 2:6-8).
- Live in peace with all people and be holy (see Hebrews 12:14).
- Look after orphans and widows in their distress (see James 1:27).
- Demonstrate love toward your neighbor (see James 2:8).
- Turn a sinner from the error of his way (see James 5:19-20).
- Live godly lives among pagans so that they will glorify God (see 1 Peter 2:11-12).
- Submit yourself to every authority and show respect (see 1 Peter 2:13-17).
- Be prepared to give a reason for the hope that is in you (see 1 Peter 3:15).

In week 1 we listed some arenas in which God may give you a mission assignment. He will have assignments for you in more than one of these areas, but His primary mission for you may focus on one of these areas. God did not use a human cookie cutter to make you. His assignment to you may be very different than the one for your spouse or a fellow Christ-follower. Don't allow others' expectations to dictate an emphasis that is contrary to what God reveals for you. But at the same time, listen to others just in case God needs to speak to you through their wise counsel.

Look at some places God may have a mission assignment for you.

1. _The structures of culture and society._ The norms and mores of our culture and society are shaped by laws, media, education, and many other forces. God may have a mission for you in government, higher education, media, or law that can affect our culture and society.

2. _Your daily workplace._ God's primary mission field for your life may be your workplace. It may be a place where people need the Lord, and you are His witness to them. God may want to work through your job to minister to needy people in your area or around the world. He may use

you to seek justice, stand for righteousness, insist on honesty and integrity, or set a model for others to follow. He may work through you to accomplish a breakthrough that will benefit all of humanity.

3. *The platform of your profession or career.* God may work through you to benefit others in or through your profession or career. He may want to influence a union, a guild, an association, or other people you connect with through your profession. This area may also be a field in which you can share the gospel of Christ.

4. *The needy people of society or the world.* God may call you to a mission that is a volunteer assignment or that relates to your paid work. People, communities, tribes, cities, and even nations or continents may be the object of your mission. When people are needy, God cares. You may get involved in short- or long-term projects to meet needs. At God's direction you may lead your company to launch a project that touches a nation or a people group. Meeting a humanitarian need may open doors for the gospel to flow into new territory.

5. *Your home and extended family.* God's primary mission assignment may be for you to rear a child or encourage and support a spouse whom God plans to use in a significant way. In the verses in the margin, Paul stated that some plant, some water, and God causes the growth. All have a part to play, but God alone gets the glory. Being a full-time mom or a supportive husband or wife may be the big assignment God has for you. You may not know His ultimate purpose now, but in the future you will understand the significance of your obedience.

6. *Your other circles of influence or relationships.* God may call and give you gifts to work through relationships to touch people significantly for His kingdom. Your hospitality, mercy, friendship, and demonstrations of love may create opportunities to influence people for Christ. Your mission may be to lead them to faith in Christ; to disciple, minister to, and encourage other Christ-followers so that they can be strong and whole; or to do carry out both of these roles.

7. *The organizational life of the church.* Many people have been taught that this arena is the only option for serving the Lord. The fact is that God calls to the other arenas we have named, but He also gives assignments within the organized church. Notice what Paul taught about mission assignments: "It was he who gave some to be apostles, some to be prophets, some to be evangelists, and some to be pastors and teachers, to prepare God's people for works of service, so that the body of Christ may be built up" (Ephesians 4:11-12). God calls some people to be apostles, prophets, evangelists, and pastors/teachers. Their job is to equip other members of the body of Christ to carry out their mission assignments (ministries)—to build up the body to be all God intends it to be so that it can penetrate the world with the light of Christ.

"I planted the seed, Apollos watered it, but God made it grow. So neither he who plants nor he who waters is anything, but only God, who makes things grow. The man who plants and the man who waters have one purpose, and each will be rewarded according to his own labor."
I Corinthians 3:6-8

SEVEN ARENAS FOR MISSION ASSIGNMENTS

I. The structures of culture and society

2. Your daily workplace

3. The platform of your profession or career

4. The needy people of society or the world

5. Your home and extended family

6. Your other circles of influence or relationships

7. The organizational life of the church

② **Look back over the seven arenas for mission assignments. Do you sense that God is already guiding you to a mission in one or more of these arenas? If so, record what you sense that He may be saying about your mission.**

_____

_____

_____

_____

_____

God's mission assignments will vary in length, depending on what He has in mind. Some mission assignments will last only minutes in response to an immediate need. Others may involve a special project that will end after a limited time. Still others may be short-term assignments that extend over a season of life—years or decades. And some missions may last a lifetime.

③ **How long does a mission assignment last? Match each type of mission with its time frame.**

___ 1. A special project   a. A lifetime

___ 2. One primary assignment   b. A season in life

___ 3. An immediate need   c. A limited time

___ 4. A short-term assignment   d. A very brief time

You were correct if you answered 1. _c,_ 2. _a,_ 3. _d,_ 4. _b._ God may or may not reveal to you the timetable on the front end. Let Him be God. He controls those details, and He does it well!

God is in control of His universe. He is your Master, and you are His servant. He does not have to act at your request or on your timetable. Be very careful not to put God on your timetable. When you set a time limit or demand an answer by a certain time, you are overstepping your boundary as God's servant. If you are not hearing from God, keep working on your relationship. Make sure you are walking rightly with the Lord and then enjoy being in His presence. As you seek His will, He will let you know when He is ready for you to take action.

④ **Which of the following responses is more indicative of a servant? Check one.**

❏ a. I tell God what I've decided to do and when and how I expect Him to come through for me as I do this work for Him.

❏ b. I patiently wait for God to reveal His mission assignments, ready to obey the very moment He makes clear His will to me. In the meantime I keep doing everything else He has already made clear to me.

Learn to let God be God. He is in charge. He is the One who takes the initiative. He has the plan for your mission, and He knows the right time for your involvement.

5 **Write principle 3 for a life that counts and your response.**

Principle 3: _____

_____

My response: _____

_____

6 **Review your notes and spend time in prayer seeking God's direction for your mission assignments. Remember to be patient!**

---

[1]Authors' interview, 18 July 2003.

[2]Findley Edge, *The Doctrine of the Laity* (Nashville: Convention Press, 1985), 44.

[3]Ibid., 37.

[4]Adapted from Claude V. King, *Final Command Action Manual* (Murfreesboro, TN: Final Command Resources, 2001), 51–53. Used by permission.

[5]Adapted from Claude V. King, *With Grateful Hearts* (Murfreesboro, TN: Final Command Resources, 2003), 43–45. Used by permission. The workbook *Experiencing God: Knowing and Doing the Will of God* by Henry Blackaby and Claude V. King (Nashville: LifeWay Press, 1990) will help you more fully understand how to know and do God's will.

[6]Henry Blackaby and Claude V. King, *Experiencing God: Knowing and Doing the Will of God* (Nashville: LifeWay Press, 1990), 15.

WEEK 5
Called Now

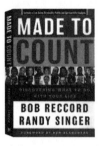

THIS WEEK'S
SUPPLEMENTARY READING

Chapters 8–9, *Made to Count*

Mark was one of the good kids. "I attended a small church in Chesapeake, Virginia, every Sunday," Mark recalls. "I was working on my points. I figured if I obeyed my parents, worked hard, and racked up enough good points, then one day I would go to heaven."

Mark's theology seemed comfortable enough until his Sunday school teacher entered class claiming to be a changed man. "Gary Bradley just walked in, plopped Bibles on the table for every student in the class, and said, 'This week I became a Christian.' "

This came as quite a shock to an impressionable high-school senior who assumed that everyone in his church was already a Christian. But Mark had a lot of respect for his Sunday school teacher, so he agreed to join a Bible study on the Gospel of John. One night "the proverbial light bulb went on," Mark recalls. That night he knelt by his bed and asked Christ into his heart. No blinding light. No angelic trumpets. Not even hot tears streaming down his cheeks. Just a quiet resolve to follow Christ wherever He might take him.

Mark attended William and Mary, majoring in religion and preparing for missions work. "I was serious about following Christ. To me, being 100 percent sold out meant full-time Christian ministry." That commitment took him to the mission field in the Philippines, working with The Navigators in campus ministry. While there Mark felt God's stirring again. This time it was not toward the international mission field but away from it.

The more God turned Mark's thoughts toward his homeland, the more Mark realized how fragile America's liberties and freedoms are. "I had this deep sense that we can't rely on the commitment of our forefathers alone, that every generation has to make a fresh and new commitment to the democratic and religious principles of the founders. And I started to think I could make a difference."

"Called from the mission field into politics?" we asked Mark. "You've got to be kidding. What did others think about that?"

"The advice I got was well-intentioned, but most people urged me to stay in full-time ministry rather than consider the public square as a mission field to which I was now being called," admits Mark. "I think it's because the

church has used the idea of calling as referring to geography, occupation, or people. But I discovered that God's calling is really to Himself. I am called to fellowship with Jesus. In that context God will place me wherever He wants me to be, and that pursuit will become holy."

Holiness and politics. It was this brash, idealistic notion that Mark brought back to America. He went to law school and worked for a few years in private practice. Then he moved into the political arena as a state senator and later became the attorney general of Virginia.

During those years Mark forged a strange coalition for a Republican: schoolteachers, religious conservatives, and minority voters. "I spent a lot of time in the African-American community," Mark explains, "working hard on issues of racial reconciliation." He also developed a mentorship program for at-risk kids throughout the commonwealth and started a Bible study for Virginia legislators.

"I constantly remind myself," Mark told us, "that Christ came to redeem and reign over every square inch of His creation," including politics.

In 2001 Mark accepted the Republican nomination for governor of Virginia. Mark lost a tough election in a supercharged political climate. Early the next morning Mark got right back to basics, reminding himself that God had a plan for his life and that it was still a good plan. "I got up the next morning, had my quiet time, and wrote at the top of my journal, *Things I Believe Today.* Then I prayed, 'Lord, I eagerly anticipate and wait for Your direction of where You want me to go and what You want me to do.' "

Two days later Chuck Colson called. "We've been praying for four years for the next Prison Fellowship president, and God has led us to you. Would you consider praying about this with us?"

Now as the president of Prison Fellowship, Mark Earley can hardly contain his enthusiasm and wonder at this part of God's plan. "Prison Fellowship," he says, "was an opportunity for me to be involved in all of the things I've ever had a passion about since I became a Christian: evangelism, disciple making, missions, public policy, the criminal-justice system, and caring for those on the margins of life."[1]

Thank God for Christ-followers like Mark, who have been called to bring Christ's holy presence to cultural and political environments. Are you ready to pray Mark's prayer: "Lord, I eagerly anticipate and wait for Your direction of where You want me to go and what You want me to do"?

DAY 1

Principle 4: Called Now

TODAY'S WORD ON WORK

"Whatever you do, work at it with all your heart, as working for the Lord, not for men."
Colossians 3:23

RESPONDING PRAYER

Lord, I love You, and I want to serve You with all my heart. Open my mind to understand that all my work can be done as working for You and not for people. Amen.

Read and think about "Today's Word on Work" in the margin and respond to the Lord in prayer.

This week we will examine the next principle for a life that counts.

> **Principle 4:** God calls you to be on mission with Him right where you are—starting now.
>
> **Your response:** Receive God's assignments and begin obeying by faith.

1 **Read principle 4 several times, giving special attention to the words that are bold and underlined.**

God calls you to be on **mission** with Him right where you are—starting **now**.

2 **Now personalize the principle by rewriting it. Change *you* to *me* and *you are* to *I am.***

_____

_____

3 **Fill in the blanks below with the missing words and review all eight principles for a life that counts.**

1. God prepared a unique _____ and _____ for your life even _____ you were born.
2. God calls you to a life-changing _____ with Him through _____ _____.
3. God calls you to partner with Him in a _____ that is _____ than you are.
4. God calls you to be on _____ with Him right where you are—starting _____.

5. God reveals His mission through His **Word**, His **Spirit**, wise **counsel**, and His work in **circumstances** around you.

6. God repeatedly brings you to a crossroads of **choice** as He **forges** you for His mission.

7. God **guides** and **provides** for your mission one **step** at a time.

8. When you **answer** God's call, you experience His **pleasure** and **change** your world.

When a person repents of sin and places his or her full faith in Jesus Christ, God places His Holy Spirit in the person. With the presence of God's Spirit inside, even young and new Christ-followers can immediately begin obeying Him. Although God may guide you to prepare for a future ministry and although His larger mission assignments may lie in the future, you can begin serving Him on mission right now, right where you are.

Jesus and His disciples encountered a demon-possessed man by the Sea of Galilee one day. He was in such bondage that he was naked, wild, and homeless. Jesus cast out the demons, and the man was radically transformed. The man was ready to join Jesus and His disciples, but Jesus had a different mission for him.

4 **Read and underline the mission Jesus gave the man.**

"Go home to your family and tell them how much the Lord has done for you, and how he has had mercy on you." So the man went away and began to tell in the Decapolis how much Jesus had done for him. And all the people were amazed (Mark 5:19-20).

One way Jesus works through people to make a significant difference is to use the recent testimony of a life transformed by God's power. The sooner this testimony begins, the better. This man wanted to travel with Jesus to other mission fields, but his testimony would have been far less effective among people who did not know his past. Instead Jesus sent him home, where his testimony of transformation would amaze those who heard him.

When Paul was converted, he followed a similar pattern. He immediately began to preach Christ (see Acts 9:20-22). Although Paul did not begin his missionary journeys to plant churches among the Gentiles until later, he began witnessing right away about the Christ who had become his Messiah and Savior. His testimony astonished the people who heard him.

When you begin to think about the mission God has for you, you probably want to know the what and the where of your work. *Here* and *now* are the first responses God usually gives. However, His unique plan for you may involve a change in your career path. Following are three types of career assignments He may give.

"At once he began to preach in the synagogues that Jesus is the Son of God. All those who heard him were astonished and asked, 'Isn't he the man who raised havoc in Jerusalem among those who call on this name? And hasn't he come here to take them as prisoners to the chief priests?' Yet Saul grew more and more powerful and baffled the Jews living in Damascus by proving that Jesus is the Christ."
Acts 9:20-22

> "As Jesus walked beside the Sea of Galilee, he saw Simon and his brother Andrew casting a net into the lake, for they were fishermen. 'Come, follow me,' Jesus said, 'and I will make you fishers of men.' At once they left their nets and followed him.
>
> "When he had gone a little farther, he saw James son of Zebedee and his brother John in a boat, preparing their nets. Without delay he called them, and they left their father Zebedee in the boat with the hired men and followed him."
>
> Mark 1:16-20

1. *New career.* Mission assignments will vary from person to person. God knows how He wants to use each one. Sometimes Christ may call you to a new career as He did Peter, Andrew, James, and John (see Mark 1:16-20). They left their fishing businesses and moved into full-time work that was eventually church-related. God may call you to change careers and become a missionary, a pastor, a church-staff member, an evangelist, or another church-related worker. He may move you to a different type of career that is not considered church-related or sacred. That's what God did with Mark Earley, whose story began this week's study.

5 **What is one type of career assignment to which God may call you?**

_____

2. *New focus for your present career.* Although God may call you to a new career, more often He wants to change people and leave them in their workplaces to reveal the difference Christ can make. This is what He did with Zacchaeus, who did not quit being a tax collector after he was born again. He became a very different kind of tax collector. Jesus healed or cast demons out of many people. When they wanted to follow Him, He instructed them to go home and tell the great things God had done for them. They didn't have to change jobs to be on mission with God. Christ wants to leave most of the people who study this course in their present jobs and workplaces—but as different persons with a kingdom focus.

6 **What is a second type of career assignment God may give you?**

_____

3. *New location for your present career.* God may leave you where you are to do kingdom work in your current workplace. But sometimes God may give you an assignment that changes the location of your work but not the basic type of work. In Scripture Aquila and Priscilla were tentmakers. They worked as tentmakers in Rome until the Jews were run out of town. Paul met them and worked as a tentmaker with them in Corinth. They were still tentmakers, but they were permitted to join Paul in his missionary work. Later they moved their business to Ephesus. God called Aquila and Priscilla to pursue the same career but in a different location.

7 **What is a third type of career assignment God may give you?**

_____

8 **How would you describe your present career or job?**

_____

9 **Review today's summary ideas and respond to God. Ask Him to guide your career path according to His divine plan.**

- You can begin serving God on mission right now, right where you are.
- One way Jesus works through people to make a significant difference is to use the recent testimony of a life transformed by God's power.
- *Here* and *now* are the first responses God usually gives.

DAY 2

Aquila and Priscilla on Mission Now

Read and think about "Today's Word on Work" in the margin and respond to the Lord in prayer.

In week 1 when we first looked at the way Paul turned his world upside down, we met a couple of tentmakers—Aquila and Priscilla. They were a ministry team themselves, the kind of people who served the Lord wherever they found themselves. They are an example of principle 4 at work.

1 **Write principle 4, to which you were introduced yesterday. Look back at page 86 if you need to.**

_____

_____

Aquila and Priscilla illustrated this principle by serving on mission with God right where they were in the now of each day.

2 **Read the accounts of Aquila and Priscilla in the Scriptures that follow and answer the questions.**

Paul left Athens and went to Corinth. There he met a Jew named Aquila, a native of Pontus, who had recently come from Italy with his wife Priscilla, because Claudius had ordered all the Jews to leave Rome.

TODAY'S WORD ON WORK

"Every day they continued to meet together in the temple courts. They broke bread in their homes and ate together with glad and sincere hearts, praising God and enjoying the favor of all the people. And the Lord added to their number daily those who were being saved."
Acts 2:46-47

RESPONDING PRAYER

Lord, when I read about the early followers of Christ, I envy them. Their joy, their love for one another, and their fruitfulness are things I would like to experience. Show me how I can experience the fullness of what You created Your church to be. Amen.

Paul went to see them, and because he was a tentmaker as they were, he stayed and worked with them. Every Sabbath he reasoned in the synagogue, trying to persuade Jews and Greeks (Acts 18:1-4).

a. Where did Paul first meet Aquila and Priscilla? _____

b. Where had they lived before moving to Corinth? _____

c. What was the career they held in common with Paul?

_____

Meanwhile a Jew named Apollos, a native of Alexandria, came to Ephesus. He was a learned man, with a thorough knowledge of the Scriptures. He had been instructed in the way of the Lord, and he spoke with great fervor and taught about Jesus accurately, though he knew only the baptism of John. He began to speak boldly in the synagogue. When Priscilla and Aquila heard him, they invited him to their home and explained to him the way of God more adequately.

When Apollos wanted to go to Achaia, the brothers encouraged him and wrote to the disciples there to welcome him. On arriving, he was a great help to those who by grace had believed. For he vigorously refuted the Jews in public debate, proving from the Scriptures that Jesus was the Christ (Acts 18:24-28).

d. Where were Aquila and Priscilla when they met Apollos? _____

e. When they realized that this gifted speaker didn't know the full story about Jesus and baptism following salvation, what did they do?

_____

_____

"If we have sown spiritual seed among you, is it too much if we reap a material harvest from you? If others have this right of support from you, shouldn't we have it all the more?

"But we did not use this right. On the contrary, we put up with anything rather than hinder the gospel of Christ. ...

"What then is my reward? Just this: that in preaching the gospel I may offer it free of charge, and so not make use of my rights in preaching it."
1 Corinthians 9:11-18

Paul first met this ministry couple in Corinth. They came there as religious refugees when the Jews were expelled from Rome. Aquila and Priscilla were tentmakers by trade. Since Paul was also a tentmaker, they worked together six days a week. Then on the Sabbath Paul went to the synagogue to reason with the Jews. Paul made tents to earn a living so that he could preach and plant churches free of charge (see 1 Corinthians 9:11-18). Can you imagine what a privilege Aquila and Priscilla had to sit and talk with Paul six days a week? They received special training at the feet of this great apostle.

When Paul went from Corinth to Ephesus, Aquila and Priscilla went with him. After Paul had left Ephesus, a gifted preacher named Apollos came to town. When Aquila and Priscilla heard him, they realized that his message was powerful but incomplete. Rather than embarrass him in public, they privately invited him to their home, where they mentored him. God had equipped them through Paul to serve as spiritual shepherds for this gifted young preacher.

Aquila and Priscilla were mature in their faith to the degree that this lay couple could mentor a gifted preacher like Apollos. As we look at Paul's letters, we find another interesting fact about this couple. From Ephesus Paul wrote a letter back to Corinth saying: "The churches in the province of Asia send you greetings. Aquila and Priscilla greet you warmly in the Lord, and so does the church that meets at their house" (1 Corinthians 16:19).

③ Earlier Aquila and Priscilla mentored a preacher in their home. Now what was going on in their house?

_____

Because early churches didn't have church buildings, believers met in homes or other places. One church in Ephesus met in the home of Aquila and Priscilla. This couple obviously had a gift for hospitality, so they used their home as a ministry tool. First it was a place to mentor a young preacher. Then it became the location for a church to meet. Homes provide a great place for a small group of Christ-followers to explore the Scriptures and encourage one another in their faith. Spending time around the church planter Paul had its effect on this gifted lay couple.

In Corinth Aquila and Priscilla served the Lord right where they were as they encouraged Paul in his efforts. When they moved to Ephesus, they continued to serve right where they were. They were on call when God wanted to use them to teach Apollos. They continued to be on mission with God by nurturing a fledgling congregation in their home.

When Paul wrote to the church in Rome, we find that Aquila and Priscilla had moved back to town.

④ Read in the margin Paul's greeting in Romans 16:3-5 and underline what was taking place in Aquila and Priscilla's home in Rome.

Aquila and Priscilla served the Lord wherever they went. As they had done in Ephesus, they hosted a church in their home in Rome. Although we don't know the details, they had also risked their lives for Paul. Both he and the Gentile churches were grateful to Aquila and Priscilla.

Have you ever thought about hosting a church in your home like Aquila and Priscilla? In many places today churches are blessed to have buildings in which to worship and study the Bible. However, too often the modern church revolves around a building. A church is people, not a building.

If we are going to effectively reach our world, we will need many more churches in places where people are. Full-time, seminary-trained pastors are

"Greet Priscilla and Aquila, my fellow workers in Christ Jesus. They risked their lives for me. Not only I but all the churches of the Gentiles are grateful to them. Greet also the church that meets at their house." Romans 16:3-5

not plentiful enough to start churches in every place they are needed. In many cases the number of Christ-followers is not large enough to fund a full-time pastor even if one were available. Some churches have realized that they need to release the laity to begin minichurches (small or miniature churches).

These minichurches can be started in homes or highrise apartment buildings. They can be started in trailer parks, on college campuses, in community centers, in hotel banquet rooms, in movie theaters, and even in corporate offices or at a storefront business. They can be started in villages and towns where no evangelical church exists. They can be started with ethnic groups who need a church that studies and worships in the heart language of the people.

If we delay until we have full-time seminary-trained pastors and money to pay them, we will never have enough churches to reach the masses of people in our world. We need more church planters like Aquila and Priscilla!

> We need more church planters like Aquila and Priscilla!

5 **Read "Tentmakers Start New Churches." Could God be calling you to help start a new church in your home, apartment building, community center, or another location? Would you pray in the following ways?**

- Pray that your church will see the need for new churches and begin praying for, training, and sending out those God calls to start new churches. (Churches have different ways to start churches. Discuss this process and pray with your pastor.)
- Pray that every town, apartment community, and people group will have access to a church.
- Pray that God will call and equip people to start new churches in ways and numbers that rival the growth of the New Testament church that turned the world upside down through Christ.
- Ask God if He wants you to participate in starting a new church.

TENTMAKERS START NEW CHURCHES

Jean Baptiste Thomas, a Haitian immigrant, moved to New York City in the 1960s and went to work for a bank in Manhattan. A group of immigrants began meeting in his home for Bible study and worship. Thomas studied theology on the side while serving as a pastor to the church that met in his home.

Thomas taught his people, "When you get saved, you get a job." As members began to sense the direction God was leading them to be on mission, the church would provide training to help them effectively serve the Lord. Now the church runs more than one thousand in their French and English services. But they still have no full-time paid staff. Pastor Thomas has been serving free for 40 years now.

Pastor Thomas also taught his people, "If you have a job, you can start a church." As God calls members to start churches in other communities, the church affirms God's leadership, provides training, and sends them out with their blessing. To date the church has begun more than 40 other congregations, some of which are now megachurches. The church this congregation started in Connecticut has already begun seven or more churches, using the same pattern of church planting.[2]

DAY 3

Ways God Can Work Through You

Read and think about "Today's Word on Work" in the margin and respond to the Lord in prayer.

1 **Review principle 4 for a life that counts by filling in the blanks below.**

God calls you to be on _____ with Him right where you are—starting _____.

God's mission for you is for the here and now. He may have a stage of preparation He wants you to experience for a future mission assignment, but you don't have to wait to get involved in God's mission. You can and should "make the most of every opportunity" (Colossians 4:5).

Sometimes the reason Christ-followers do not have a more significant impact on the world around us is that we don't understand the ways God works. God may be setting the stage for us to partner with Him in a mission, and we miss it because we don't recognize God's work around us.

2 **Read the following list of ways God can work through you as you live your life at home, work, and play. Underline ways that seem to be especially meaningful. If you read one and realize that you missed an opportunity to be used by God or recognize that God used you that way, underline it and write a brief note in the margin about the experience. If you have questions, write them in the margin also.**

1. *God works in answer to your prayers to reveal Himself to those with or for whom you pray.* Watch for opportunities to pray with and for people so that they will experience God when He answers the prayer.
2. *God works to reveal Christlikeness in purity, holiness, honesty, integrity, humility, and obedience.* People need to see Christ in flesh. We are the body of Christ for our generation. Allow God to refine you and live in you in such a way that Christ shines through.

TODAY'S WORD ON WORK

"Be wise in the way you act toward outsiders; make the most of every opportunity. Let your conversation be always full of grace, seasoned with salt, so that you may know how to answer everyone."
Colossians 4:5-6

RESPONDING PRAYER

Master, when I have been surrounded by outsiders, too often I have been timid about my faith. Please give me wisdom, grace, and answers for the needy world around me. Let me be the salt of the earth that flavors and preserves vitality of life. Amen.

NOTES

_____
_____
_____
_____
_____
_____

NOTES

_____

_____

_____

_____

_____

_____

_____

_____

_____

_____

_____

_____

_____

_____

_____

_____

_____

_____

_____

_____

_____

_____

_____

_____

_____

3. ***God works to demonstrate His love by meeting the needs of others.*** When you hear of someone in your circles of influence who has a need, ask the Lord whether you or your group should meet that need in the name of Jesus. Let God's love flow through you.

4. ***God works by revealing His mercy through your forgiveness of others who have offended you.*** The world expects you to get mad, fight back, or get even. It doesn't expect forgiveness. You are never more like Jesus than when you forgive an offense. Show His mercy by forgiving.

5. ***God works by reconciling people to God through Christ.*** People who are not right with God are missing the abundant life their Creator has to give them. God has given you a ministry and message of reconciliation. Help people get right with God.

6. ***God works as you lead the way to repentance for wrongs.*** Pride and arrogance are common human traits that offend God. When you publicly repent of wrongs done in public and when you lead a group to repent of corporate sins, the world sees something it does not often see. Your humility and repentance may spark repentance in others.

7. ***God works as you function as a peacemaker to resolve conflict.*** Broken relationships can rob people of joy and can drain energy. When the Prince of Peace works through you to reconcile, people can experience Him and can be drawn to Him.

8. ***God works as you demonstrate your love for your enemies by doing good, meeting needs, and returning good for evil.*** They don't expect love from you. Jesus gave some hard commands that run counter to human nature and reason. When you love your enemies, Christ can work through you to draw them to His love.

9. ***God works as you endure persecution with courage and grace.*** When Paul and Silas sang praises in prison after being beaten, they got the attention of a jailer, who came to faith with his whole household (see Acts 16:22-34). Facing persecution like Christ reveals Him to those who are watching.

10. ***God works as you demonstrate your faith by your deeds.*** What you say with your lips doesn't mean much if your life doesn't reflect the same faith. " 'Let your light shine before men, that they may see your good deeds and praise your Father in heaven' " (Matthew 5:16).

11. ***God works by revealing answers to critical problems that seem humanly impossible to solve.*** When God gave wisdom to Joseph for the needs of a pending crisis in Egypt, Pharaoh realized that God was with Joseph (see Genesis 41:37-38). Don't hesitate to take seemingly impossible problems to the Lord for counsel. If God gave you an answer, you would have the opportunity to give glory to Him.

12. ***God works as your attitudes and behavior make the gospel of Christ appealing to those who observe your life.*** Live your life in such a way

that people will want what they see in you. The true gospel really is good news for those who are living in spiritual darkness and deadness.

13. *God works by giving you divine wisdom for critical decisions.* When you ask and God gives wisdom, it will have a divine quality that gives glory to Him.

14. *God works as you reveal peace, calmness, or courage in a crisis.* Coming to America in a boat with Moravian Christians, John Wesley saw their peace and calmness in the face of a life-threatening storm, and he realized that they had something he didn't. Back in London in a Moravian chapel, Wesley came to genuine faith in Christ, and God unleashed a mighty spiritual awakening in England and in the United States.[3] Allow God to give you a peace that passes human understanding.

15. *God works as you grieve with hope in the face of significant loss.* Facing death is a natural part of life. Those who have no hope for a future with Christ grieve as those without hope. When you have hope of eternity with Christ, it should show in the way you grieve. People will be watching.

16. *God works as you reveal selflessness in a selfish world.* When the world seeks materialism and is self-serving, people see the contrast in someone who gives and serves in a selfless way. Jesus said that greatness comes by way of service (see Matthew 20:25-28).

Every problem, crisis, challenge, obstacle, sinful act, or broken relationship can afford you the opportunity to reveal Christ in the way you respond. As you allow the life and mind of Christ to be revealed in your daily walk, others will have the opportunity to see Him and come to know Him.

3 **Review the items you underlined, the notes you took, or the thoughts you had about ways God can work through you to make an impact on others. Ask God to reveal ways He wants to work through you here and now to make a difference in the lives of others. If He reveals something, write it below.**

_____

_____

_____

_____

_____

_____

_____

_____

NOTES

_____

_____

_____

_____

_____

_____

_____

_____

_____

_____

_____

_____

_____

DAY 4

My Faith at Work Assessment

TODAY'S WORD ON WORK

"Do your best to present yourself to God as one approved, a workman who does not need to be ashamed and who correctly handles the word of truth."
2 Timothy 2:15

RESPONDING PRAYER

Lord, I want to be a workman who is approved by You. I don't want to be ashamed. Please encourage and guide me to be such a workman. Amen.

Read and think about "Today's Word on Work" in the margin and respond to the Lord in prayer.

As God guides you into the middle of His plan and activity, the primary thrust of His work may focus on one area more than another. That focus may change from time to time. His primary mission assignment for you at the present time may be in any one of the following arenas.

- Your home with your immediate family and/or with relatives
- Your church or the larger body of Christ in your city, denomination, nation, or world
- Your community, your neighborhood, or the public sector
- Your workplace or profession
- A distant mission field in your nation or somewhere else in the world (short- or long-term)

1 **Fill in the blanks to complete the fourth principle for a life that counts.**

God calls you to be on _____ with Him right where you are—starting _____.

Your workplace is a setting in which you can implement principle 4 by going on mission now. Let's focus on your workplace to identify ways God might be at work there.

At the back of your *Life Planner* we have provided a special Made to Count Tool Kit. There you will find some tools that will help you apply what you are learning to your process of discovering the mission God has planned for you. Throughout the remainder of your study, a tool-kit logo in the margin designates an assignment to use one of these special tools.

2 **Turn to "My Faith at Work Assessment," beginning on page 190 in the Made to Count Tool Kit. Follow the instructions and complete this assessment of your workplace. You will have an opportunity to share some of your findings with your small group. Place a check in this box when you have completed the assessment:** ❏

3 Review in the margin principle 4 for a life that counts and your response. Initial here if you are willing to accept God's assignment to be on mission right where you are, right now: _____

4 Read "Delivering Faith over Lunch" on this page. Then review "My Faith at Work Assessment" on pages 190–93 in the Made to Count Tool Kit. What ideas have come to mind about a way you might live your faith in a more intentional way in your workplace? Respond below. If nothing has come to mind, spend time talking to the Lord about the way He wants you to be on mission here and now.

_____

_____

_____

_____

_____

_____

_____

_____

_____

_____

_____

_____

_____

PRINCIPLE 4
God calls you to be on mission with Him right where you are—starting now.

YOUR RESPONSE
Receive God's assignments and begin obeying by faith.

DELIVERING FAITH OVER LUNCH

Jonathan Stoudenmire is a construction manager for strip-mall developments throughout the Southeast. He discovered early that a busy construction site could be a tough place to share the gospel. But he also learned that construction workers let down their guard when they gather around the table to eat. So Jonathan and his wife devised a plan. Once a month she would deliver a large lunch to the construction site. On that day lunch would be a feast, and it would be free for everyone.

As Jonathan relaxed with the men over lunch, he worked hard to gain their respect by treating them the way he wanted to be treated. His affirmation was quick, his smile ready, his encouragement strong, and his support total. Jonathan would look for a chance to be vulnerable and let down his guard. And the men didn't miss that temperament. After all, it wasn't what they expected on construction sites—especially from the boss.

The result? Inevitably, Jonathan would get an opportunity to share his faith over lunch. No three-point sermons and tons of memorized Scripture. Just a humble and authentic explanation of how much Christ had changed his life. Often some of the men would respond to his vulnerability with an openness of their own. Many men came to know Jesus Christ as Savior because one man and his wife creatively and intentionally found a nonthreatening way to share the most important aspect of their lives.[4]

DAY 5

Prepared to Do Any Good Work

TODAY'S WORD ON WORK

"In a large house there are articles not only of gold and silver, but also of wood and clay; some are for noble purposes and some for ignoble. If a man cleanses himself from the latter, he will be an instrument for noble purposes, made holy, useful to the Master and prepared to do any good work."
2 Timothy 2:20-21

RESPONDING PRAYER

Yes, Lord! I want to be holy; useful to You, my Master; and prepared for any good work You may desire from me. Help me cleanse myself to be used by You for noble purposes. Let my life count! Amen.

Read and think about "Today's Word on Work" in the margin and respond to the Lord in prayer.

1 Review the first three principles for a life that counts. Then fill in the blanks to complete the fourth principle.

1. God prepared a unique plan and calling for your life even before you were born.

2. God calls you to a life-changing relationship with Him through Jesus Christ.

3. God calls you to partner with Him in a mission that is bigger than you are.

4. God calls you to be on _____ with Him right where you are—starting _____.

As you continue to seek the Lord's directions about His mission and your role in it, you should also prepare your life to be one that God can use in significant ways. He chooses to use clean vessels for His noble purposes. As you read in Today's Word on Work, "a man cleanses himself" (2 Timothy 2:21). We want to help you do that.

2 Turn to "My Personal Prayer Guide" on pages 194–95 in the Made to Count Tool Kit. Follow the instructions to—
a. pray for cleansing;
b. pray for your calling and your workplace.
Place a check in this box when you have finished: ❑

3 Read "Ministering Through Prayer" on page 99, the story of someone who joined God's mission through prayer.

MINISTERING THROUGH PRAYER

During a political campaign the owner of a newspaper interviewed Vernadette Broyles. According to Vernadette, normally the owner wouldn't have given her the time of day, but because of the political race, the woman's focus was attentive and unwavering. Throughout the interview something deep in Vernadette's heart told her that the woman was experiencing something very difficult.

Vernadette could not shake the uneasiness she had felt with the newspaper owner. Before leaving the area, she went back to the newspaper office and found the owner, who was just about to leave. And then the door opened. "I don't want to scare you or sound rude, but I just really feel in my heart that God wants me to say something to you and that maybe you're going through some very difficult times. If you'd like, I'd be happy to pray for you."

Stunned, the woman stared at Vernadette. Then tears began cascading down her cheeks. "Oh, Vernadette, if you only knew!" And then the difficulty came pouring out. Off to the side and away from the crowds, Vernadette was able to step into the woman's life and give her comfort and counsel from the One who could handle any trouble. She was able to take the woman into His presence in prayer.[5]

4 **Fill in the blanks to complete your response to principle 4.**

Receive God's _____ and begin obeying
by _____.

5 **Praying for others is one way you can accept God's assignment to be on mission and to obey in faith. Close in prayer by asking the Lord to touch others through you. Memorize the question "How may I pray for you?" and watch for ways to minister to others through prayer.**

---

[1]Authors' interview, 1 July 2003.

2Authors' interview.

3John Greenfield, *Power from on High: The Story of the Great Moravian Revival of 1727* (Bethlehem, PA: Interprovincial Board of Communication, 1989), 31-40.

[4]Authors' interview, 17 May 2003.

[5]Authors' interview, 4 April 2003.

WEEK 6

Called to a Great Commission

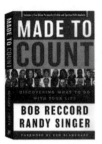

THIS WEEK'S SUPPLEMENTARY READING

Chapter 10, *Made to Count*

Graham grew up in a very strict Christian church. "I thank God today for that Christian heritage that grounded me in the Word. At a very young age, however, I felt that we were great at being Christians in a very introverted way, but we made no impact on the outside world. And I had a hunger for all those people out there." One Sunday night at age 14 Graham brought a tramp to church so that he could hear the gospel. This night changed Graham forever.

"When I got home, my mother told me never again to do what I'd done that night, that I'd somehow brought disgrace on the family. I knew with every fiber of my being that she was wrong. That day I made a secret commitment that no matter what my mother thought, I would find a way to make a difference for lonely and beaten-down people."

Today Graham Lacey is an international businessman and entrepreneur and a friend to England's royal family, politicians, and religious leaders throughout the world. While living in New York City, Graham was involved in a Bible-study group that shared a common desire to make an impact on New York. "We felt that if we made a difference in New York, it could in turn touch the world."

The group planned to have a Thanksgiving lunch, and Graham suggested that they invite the loneliest couple in New York City. When asked who that might be, he quickly named an ambassador and his wife from a Muslim country. This country had come under great criticism and pressure due to its actions on the international scene, and tensions with the United States were great. Graham wrote an invitation, but weeks went by with no response. The group continued to pray for the couple.

Thanksgiving Day arrived, and just as the group sat down to eat, the intercom in the apartment sounded. It was the ambassador, his wife, and their security detachment.

"We sat around the table, and I asked a group member to pray. During the prayer the ambassador

started to cry. At the end of the prayer I asked the ambassador if anything had been said that offended him. He said: 'No, but as I listened to your friend praying, I was so moved that you would invite us into your home. If the people in New York knew who we were, they'd spit in our faces; yet you invited us to share your Thanksgiving meal. You showed us friendship.' "

That Thanksgiving luncheon led to an extraordinary relationship between Graham and the ambassador. "I got to know him and his wife as well as his family. I took him to a Baptist church to hear the gospel. I met with him one-on-one and talked to him about Christ. I prayed with him on numerous occasions in his office."

Graham was invited to the ambassador's homeland. While there Graham met with the Islamic leadership and, at their request, shared his faith in Christ. He also spent time with the country's leader. "I started by giving him an Arabic copy of the New Testament and Psalms and then shared my faith and talked to him about Christ. It was a very energetic conversation. At the end of our time, I asked him if I might pray with him. I got down on one knee and prayed for

him, his wife, and his family. I prayed that the Holy Spirit would break out in revival power in his country. When I finished praying, the leader embraced me, kissed me three times, and then once again spoke in Arabic to his colleague. The translator said that the distinguished leader would like me to pray again. When I asked why, he told me that no one had ever prayed for him before, and this leader wanted their television cameras to film me praying for him." While the cameras rolled, Graham again prayed for revival to fall on the nation.

Since that time this country's government-sponsored television station opens and closes with excerpts from that prayer for revival. "I believe that God is limited in what He can do only by the limitations we place on Him through our lack of faith in His promises. If we'll just dare to believe Him and challenge Him, God will open the windows of heaven and pour out blessings so great that our storehouses won't be able to contain them. We just have to dare to believe and find that the almighty God of Abraham is the same yesterday, today, and forever."[1]

Ask God to give you love and compassion like His for the people in your circles of influence who need to know Christ.

DAY 1
Jesus' Final Command

TODAY'S WORD ON WORK

"Then said Jesus to them again, Peace be unto you: as my Father hath sent me, even so send I you."
John 20:21, KJV

RESPONDING PRAYER

Lord Jesus, You came to seek and save the lost. Now that You're in heaven, you've entrusted that assignment to Your people. I want to obey Your assignment for me. Please help me carry out Your command. Amen.

PRINCIPLE 3
God calls you to partner with Him in a mission that is bigger than you are.

PRINCIPLE 4
God calls you to be on mission with Him right where you are—starting now.

Read and think about "Today's Word on Work" in the margin and respond to the Lord in prayer.

Events that significantly alter history or culture become etched into our minds. They are vivid. We remember. For instance …

1 **On September 11, 2001, our world changed when terrorists attacked the World Trade Center and the Pentagon. Where were you, and how did you hear about the attacks?**

During His last 40 days on earth, Jesus gave His disciples one final command. He repeated it in different ways in different settings because the future of His kingdom would depend on His disciples' obedience to this command. That Scripture is known as the Great Commission: " 'All authority in heaven and on earth has been given to me. Therefore go and make disciples of all nations, baptizing them in the name of the Father and of the Son and of the Holy Spirit, and teaching them to obey everything I have commanded you. And surely I am with you always, to the very end of the age' " (Matthew 28:18-20).

As you are going, make disciples (followers) who obey everything Jesus has commanded. That's a God-sized mission! This mission assignment was not just for the first band of disciples. It is the church's standing order for fulfilling its purpose in the world. When we studied principles 3 and 4, we learned that God has called us to partner with Him in a mission that is bigger than we are, and that mission starts now where we are. The Great Commission is the summary statement of God's calling on all of us.

2 **Based on your understanding of this mission assignment, have you and your church faithfully obeyed the command? Check your response.**
❑ Yes ❑ No ❑ We've been only partially obedient.

Every church and every Christ-follower has a role to play in going to all nations and making disciples. An important part of discovering God's purpose for your life is understanding and accepting Jesus' final command to take the good news to all the world. For this reason we will focus this week on carrying out God's mission by embracing our responsibility to accept and participate in Jesus' Great Commission.

When Jesus was ready to ascend into heaven, He knew the event would be etched into the memories of His disciples. He carefully crafted His last words to summarize the assignment He was depending on the disciples to carry out. He didn't want us to forget this one. We must remember and obey Jesus' timeless words, printed in the margin.

Then Jesus disappeared into the clouds, and angels appeared to comfort the watching disciples. The event and the words were etched into their memories. Realizing this was a significant message, the disciples waited in Jerusalem as instructed, and the Holy Spirit came on them 10 days later. When Peter walked into the streets and preached a message, three thousand people from all over the known world came to faith in Christ (see Acts 1:41).

From that day the early church assumed its responsibility to obey Christ's final command by going on mission to the four areas Jesus named. We can think of these mission fields as ever-increasing concentric circles.

> " 'You will receive power when the Holy Spirit comes on you; and you will be my witnesses in Jerusalem, and in all Judea and Samaria, and to the ends of the earth.' "
> Acts l:8

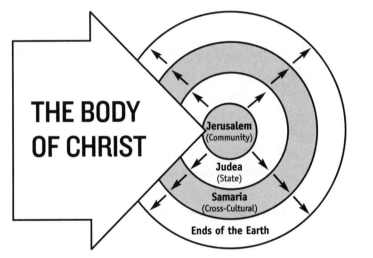

③ **Read again Acts 1:8 in the margin and underline the four areas where Jesus said His followers would be His witnesses.**

Now the assignment is ours. We have His Holy Spirit. We are His witnesses. We must—
- start in Jerusalem (at home, in your city);
- continue into Judea (extended family, surrounding communities, county, state, or province);
- proceed to Samaria (crossing racial, ethnic, and religious barriers);
- continue to the ends of the earth.

Although these mission fields have a logical progression, God never intended for us to limit ourselves to one area at a time. We don't have to finish reaching one circle before moving to the next. God may even call us to an outer circle first. The focus is this: as we go, we are to be His witnesses.

> As you begin praying for the people in your circles of influence, God can begin to use you to make disciples as you go about your daily life.

If you think about the billions of people in the world, this mission assignment may be so overwhelming that you don't know where to start. Let's start by identifying your world. In what part of this huge world has God placed you? Who are the people in your circles of influence? As you begin praying for the people in your circles of influence, God can begin to use you to make disciples as you go about your daily life.

4 Turn to "My Circles of Influence," beginning on page 196 in the Made to Count Tool Kit. Follow the instructions to begin making lists of the people in your circles of influence who do not yet believe in Christ. Today spend a few minutes working on each circle of influence. As time permits in days to come, continue to prepare thorough lists.

The people you listed are some of the people who are part of your world. God may use you to point them to Jesus Christ. In the remainder of this week's study, we will provide you with practical help to begin cultivating a relationship, praying, and eventually introducing these people to the Savior.

5 Of all the people you just added to "My Circles of Influence," which one person would you most like to come to faith in Jesus Christ?

_____

6 Pray and ask God to work through you to draw this person to Jesus Christ. Tomorrow we'll guide you to pray for the people you listed in your circles of influence. But if you want to get a jump on praying more specifically, turn to "Praying for Those Yet to Believe" on page 201 in the Made to Count Tool Kit and review some ways to pray.

7 Review today's summary ideas. Tell the Lord of your desire to obey His final command—His Great Commission. Ask Him to empower you to be His witness to your world.
- The future of His kingdom would depend on His disciples' obedience to this command.
- " 'Go and make disciples of all nations' " (Matthew 28:19).
- This mission assignment was not just for the first band of disciples. It is the church's standing order for fulfilling its purpose in the world.
- " 'You will be my witnesses in Jerusalem, and in all Judea and Samaria, and to the ends of the earth' " (Acts 1:8).

DAY 2

Called to Be Fishers of Men

Read and think about "Today's Word on Work" in the margin and respond to the Lord in prayer.

As Jesus walked beside the Sea of Galilee, he saw Simon [Peter] and his brother Andrew casting a net into the lake, for they were fishermen. "Come, follow me," Jesus said, "and *I will make you fishers of men.*" At once they left their nets and followed him.

When he had gone a little farther, he saw James son of Zebedee and his brother John in a boat, preparing their nets. Without delay he called them, and they left their father Zebedee in the boat with the hired men and followed him (Mark 1:16-20, italics added).

When Jesus was ready to select 12 disciples who would be with Him and become leaders in His kingdom, He didn't go to the top religious leaders. He went to the Sea of Galilee and called ordinary men, issuing this invitation: " 'Come, follow me, and I will make you fishers of men' " (Mark 1:17).

Just as Peter and Andrew used a net to catch fish, we can cast spiritual nets to fish for men and women. When one person is transformed by Christ, we immediately need to walk with this new Christ-follower to introduce his family, friends, relatives, and coworkers to Christ.

1 Read about Peter's fruitfulness as a spiritual fisherman in Acts 10:24,44. Underline the words that describe the harvest.

The following day [Peter] arrived in Caesarea. Cornelius was expecting them and had called together his relatives and close friends. While Peter was still speaking these words, the Holy Spirit came on all who heard the message (Acts 10:24,44).

When Peter preached to Cornelius, his whole household, including relatives and close friends, experienced salvation. Peter used a net to fish for men and women. But how did Peter know where to go fishing?

God had already been working with the Gentile Cornelius, a God-fearing man and a man of prayer. About three in the afternoon, a Jewish time for prayer, an angel appeared, telling Cornelius to send for Peter (see Acts 10:1-8).

TODAY'S WORD ON WORK

" 'The harvest is plentiful, but the workers are few. Ask the Lord of the harvest, therefore, to send out workers into his harvest field.' "
Luke 10:2

RESPONDING PRAYER

Lord, our world needs You. Apart from You, conflict and sin make life miserable. I know the world around me needs a spiritual harvest. Please call many workers into the spiritual harvest. Show me my place in the harvest too. Amen.

> Depend on the Lord to focus your attention on those with whom He is presently working to bring to faith in Christ.

The next day, while Peter was praying, he fell into a trance, and God began to reveal a new attitude Peter needed to develop toward Gentiles. As the men with Cornelius's invitation approached, God instructed Peter, " 'Do not hesitate to go with them, for I have sent them' " (Acts 10:20).

God had a plan for Cornelius and Peter to accomplish a major break-through in the spread of the gospel to the Gentile world. As they prayed, God spoke to both men independently. Cornelius gathered the people in his circles of influence to hear Peter, and history was made that day.

Yesterday you started listing people in your circles of influence. As your list grows, depend on the Lord to focus your attention on those with whom He is presently working to bring to faith in Christ. One way to identify people on whom God wants you to focus attention is to watch for His activity in the lives of those on your lists.

2. Review your lists of people in "My Circles of Influence," pages 196–99 in the Made to Count Tool Kit. Then follow the instructions for using "God's Activity Watch List" on page 200 and notice whether God begins to focus your attention on one or more people who have not yet believed. After you have completed this activity, check this box: ❏

3. Write the name of one person on whom you sense that God wants you to focus attention. If you don't have that sense of focus, leave the line below blank and keep watching for God's activity.

_____

Specific prayer is the next step in identifying where to go fishing for those who need Christ. As we saw with Peter and Cornelius, God often speaks in times of prayer.

4. Turn to page 201 in the Made to Count Tool Kit and follow the instructions to complete "Praying for Those Yet to Believe." Begin praying for the people in your circles of influence, especially those on whom God is leading you to focus attention.

DAY 3
Cultivating Relationships

Read and think about "Today's Word on Work" in the margin and respond to the Lord in prayer.

TODAY'S WORD ON WORK
"I have become all things to all men so that by all possible means I might save some. I do all this for the sake of the gospel, that I may share in its blessings."
I Corinthians 9:22-23

To be on mission with God to the people around you, you may need to cultivate new or closer relationships through which God can work.

1 **Read 1 Corinthians 9:19-23 in the margin and look for ways Paul built redemptive relationships. Underline the people he sought to reach.**

2 **Paul was free in Christ. Why did he make himself a slave to everyone?**

_____

_____

_____

_____

RESPONDING PRAYER
Heavenly Father, I know that You desire that people come to faith in Your Son Jesus. I want to do my part. Show me the people and the way I am to cultivate relationships through which Your life and love can flow. Amen.

3 **What was Paul's primary strategy for building redemptive relationships? Check one.**

❑ a. He caught people in times of weakness and manipulated them into making decisions for Christ.

❑ b. He argued with people to convince them to become Christians.

❑ c. He set up a church and waited until people came to him seeking help. Then he led them to Christ.

❑ d. He identified himself with others so that he could understand life from their perspective. Then he shared the gospel in terms they could understand. He became a servant to help them enter the kingdom.

"Though I am free and belong to no man, I make myself a slave to everyone, to win as many as possible. To the Jews I became like a Jew, to win the Jews. To those under the law I became like one under the law (though I myself am not under the law), so as to win those under the law. To those not having the law I became like one not having the law (though I am not free from God's law but am under Christ's law), so as to win those not having the law. To the weak I became weak, to win the weak. I have become all things to all men so that by all possible means I might save some. I do all this for the sake of the gospel, that I may share in its blessings."
I Corinthians 9:I9-23

Paul became a servant and a slave to others in order to win them to faith in Christ. He didn't manipulate them, argue with them, or wait until they sought his help. Paul identified himself with other people and shared the gospel in terms they could understand *(d)*.

"When I came to you, brothers, I did not come with eloquence or superior wisdom as I proclaimed to you the testimony about God. For I resolved to know nothing while I was with you except Jesus Christ and him crucified. I came to you in weakness and fear, and with much trembling. My message and my preaching were not with wise and persuasive words, but with a demonstration of the Spirit's power, so that your faith might not rest on men's wisdom, but on God's power."
I Corinthians 2:I-5

4 Read 1 Corinthians 2:1-5 in the margin. What was Paul's primary tool for helping the Corinthians come to faith in Christ? Check one.
❑ a. Paul allowed Christ to live through him in such a way that people saw a demonstration of the Spirit's power. The focus of his message was on the sacrificial death of Jesus Christ.
❑ b. Paul used his speaking skills, human wisdom, and persuasive words to intellectually convince people to turn to Christ. His message focused on practical lessons for ways they could enjoy life.

5 Which of the following was more true about Paul's public image?
❑ a. Paul appeared proud, confident, and superior.
❑ b. Paul appeared humble, weak, fearful, and trembling.

6 In which of the following do you believe Paul placed his confidence?
❑ a. He was confident in himself and his human abilities.
❑ b. He was confident in Christ and His Spirit's power to change lives.

Paul's primary tool was to preach Christ and to allow God to demonstrate the Spirit's power to change lives (*a*). He was not proud. He did not assume a superior position. Paul was humble, recognizing that he could do nothing without Christ (*b*). His confidence rested in Christ alone (*b*).

7 If you have intentionally built a relationship with another person or group to create a channel through which God's love and life can flow, briefly describe what you did and what the outcome has been to date.

_____

_____

As God gives you a special concern for a person yet to believe, you may realize that your relationship with that person is shallow. You may need to spend time cultivating the relationship before you will be in the ideal position to reveal God and introduce Jesus Christ. This relationship becomes a channel through which Christ's love can flow to the person. As we've seen, Paul cultivated relationships in order to reach people for Christ.

God may call you to carry out a project to reach a particular group of people, not just one individual. One couple had a wayward son who played in a rock band at a nightclub. Rather than fight with their son to change his behavior, they decided to influence his peers for Christ. They regularly went to the nightclub and ordered soft drinks. As they interacted with the people who attended the club, they had opportunities to listen, counsel, show concern, and pray. Before long they became Mom and Pop to these wayward young adults. By building relationships with the regulars, these parents began to have opportunities to introduce them to Jesus Christ.

God may call you to invest time, energy, and resources to reach one person for Christ. As you develop a caring relationship with the person, he or she becomes more responsive to receive the message of Christ when you share it. This relationship, however, is not just a means of manipulating a decision. It should become a relationship of love that continues as a person grows in Christ.

I (Claude) was visiting in the home of a retired business executive in Texas. I had been teaching in his church about the Great Commission, and he was struggling to understand how he could get involved in reaching people for Christ. Because he lived on a golf course, I asked him about his golf game. He and several of his Christian friends got together two or three times a week to play golf, but sometimes they had trouble forming a foursome. I suggested that these men begin building bridges of relationship to other retirees living near the golf course. They could regularly start with three and ask the Lord to help them reach out to a fourth person who needed to know Christ. The man became excited when he realized how easily he could obey the Great Commission as he went about his normal routine.

8 **Read the following ways you can cultivate relationships. Check any you would choose to build a bridge of relationship with someone. Use the margin to write notes or to list additional ideas that come to mind.**
- ❑ Developing an interest and participating in the same hobby or recreational activity
- ❑ Spending time with the person over lunch or breaks
- ❑ Inviting the person into your world for an event or a special activity
- ❑ Inviting the person into your home for dinner
- ❑ Expressing interest during times of joy or celebration, such as marriage, the birth of a baby, graduation, or a job promotion
- ❑ Working together on a common project or for a common cause
- ❑ Sending cards (birthday, anniversary, sympathy) or writing notes
- ❑ Vacationing, camping, or picnicking together with each other's family
- ❑ Demonstrating love by meeting needs

9 **Review your lists in "My Circles of Influence" on pages 196–99 in the Made to Count Tool Kit. Ask the Lord to guide you to build a bridge of relationship with one or more people so that you can bring them across that bridge to a relationship with Jesus Christ. If a person comes to mind, write his or her name below, along with a way you can building a bridge to him or her.**

_____

We want to ask you to consider making a pledge to the Lord. Would you be willing to commit yourself to win one person to Christ this year in obedience

OTHER IDEAS

_____
_____
_____
_____
_____
_____
_____
_____
_____
_____

MY PLEDGE

_____

_____

_____

_____

_____

_____

_____

_____

Signed _____

Date _____

to the Great Commission? Although only God can draw people to His Son, He has called us and given us His Spirit to be His witnesses. You will not be alone. God's Spirit is present to empower you. And you have a spiritual family, the body of Christ, to work with you and encourage you. Your *Made to Count* small-group members could commit to support one another as they each try to win one person to faith in Christ.

10 **If you are willing to obey the final command of our Lord and become partners with Christ to seek to lead at least one person to faith in Christ this year, write your commitment in the margin. Then sign your name and record the date. If you are not ready to make such a pledge, don't. God knows your heart. According to Scripture, "It is better not to vow than to make a vow and not fulfill it" (Ecclesiastes 5:5).**

We pray that you've chosen to be intentional about your obedience to the Lord. As we continue this study together, we want to help equip you to fulfill that mission to make a life-changing difference in one life.

11 **If you made the pledge, tell the Lord about your dependence on Him for power, boldness, wisdom, and direction. Ask Him to give you love and compassion like Christ's for those who are yet to believe. If you were not ready to make the pledge, pray and give God permission to change your heart. Ask Him to give you boldness to accept His calling as His ambassador to your world.**

12 **Review today's summary ideas and respond to God in prayer. Ask Him to flow through your life to touch others with His love, hope, mercy, and grace.**
  • To be on mission with God to the people around you, you may need to cultivate new or closer relationships through which God can work.
  • Paul became a servant and a slave to others in order to win them to faith in Christ.
  • Paul identified himself with other people and shared the gospel in terms they could understand.
  • Paul's primary tool was to preach Christ and to allow God to demonstrate the Spirit's power to change lives.
  • God may call you to invest time, energy, and resources to reach one person for Christ.

DAY 4

Introducing Jesus Christ

Read and think about "Today's Word on Work" in the margin and respond to the Lord in prayer.

God's ultimate purpose is to reconcile people to Himself through Jesus Christ. You have been commissioned to be an ambassador for Christ to carry out that purpose. Use the following suggestions to find one or more ways you can best introduce Jesus Christ to the people in your circles of influence.

1 **As you read the following suggestions, underline or draw a star beside those you have used or would like to use to introduce Jesus to others. Write notes in the margins as thoughts or people come to mind. As you read the suggestions, pray that God will help you develop a customized approach to witnessing that is well suited to your personality.**

1. ***Personal testimony.*** If you have come to saving faith in Christ, you have a personal testimony. You can tell others about the way you placed your faith in Christ. You can testify to the difference life in Christ makes. You can tell about your personal relationship with Him. That's what a witness does. He or she describes a personal experience with Jesus Christ. Think about what you would say to (1) describe what life before Christ was like, (2) how you recognized your need for a Savior, (3) how you heard and responded to the gospel, and (4) the difference Jesus has made in your life.

2 **Turn to pages 202–3 in the Made to Count Tool Kit and use "Preparing My Story" to write your testimony. Check here when you have finished this activity:** ❏

2. ***Gospel tract.*** A tract is a leaflet or a booklet that tells the gospel and explains what God says about salvation in the Bible. It usually guides the person to consider Christ's claims on his or her life. You can carry tracts in your pocket or purse to share with someone you encounter during the day. You may provide the tract with a word of explanation and let the person read it in the privacy of his or her home. Better still, you can read through the tract with the person and answer questions he or she may have. Using

TODAY'S WORD ON WORK

"In your hearts set apart Christ as Lord. Always be prepared to give an answer to everyone who asks you to give the reason for the hope that you have. But do this with gentleness and respect."
I Peter 3:15

RESPONDING PRAYER

Lord, thank You for the hope I have because of Christ. Teach me how to answer those who need to know how to trust Christ and follow Him. Then encourage people to ask. I will respond. Amen.

NOTES

_____

_____

_____

_____

_____

_____

_____

_____

_____

_____

GOSPEL TRACTS

- Four Spiritual Laws
- Steps to Peace with God
- The Passion of the Christ
- How to Have a Full and Meaningful Life
- The Bridge to Life
- Discover the Answer to Life's Ultimate Question
- www.christianbook.com
- www.tractleague.com
- www.atstracts.org
- www.lifeway.com

MARKED NEW TESTAMENTS

- Share Jesus Without Fear New Testament
- Here's Hope New Testament

CHRISTIAN VIDEOS

- www.jesusvideo.org
- www.christianbook.com
- http://shop.wwp.org/retail/
- www.lifeway.com

NOTES

_____
_____
_____
_____
_____
_____
_____
_____
_____
_____
_____

a tract along with your testimony can be an effective witness when God is already working to draw the person to Jesus. Tracts should be available at your church or at a local Christian bookstore.

3. *Evangelistic book.* Many books have been written to present the gospel and invite people to respond to the claims of Jesus Christ. Prepare a testimony to go with your presentation of the book to those who are yet to believe. One such book is *Meet Jesus Christ: Discover the Purpose of His Passion* by Claude V. King. Page 204 in the Made to Count Tool Kit provides guidance for using this book to share your faith.

4. *Marked New Testament.* Christian bookstores sell inexpensive New Testaments that are designed for believers to use in sharing the gospel. They guide readers to key verses of Scripture that present God's plan of salvation. Usually a footnote explains the Scripture and directs the reader to the next verse. After reading the Scriptures, a person is invited to pray a prayer of repentance and faith in Christ.

5. *Video, movie, or television special.* Today we are blessed with many quality presentations of the gospel through movies. *Jesus* is a video about the life of Christ that uses the Gospel of Luke as the primary dialogue. Millions of people worldwide have been introduced to Jesus through this film. Throw a movie party and invite the people you most want to know Christ. Let God use the movie to help introduce your friends to Jesus.

6. *Church Bible class and worship.* Jesus said, " 'Everyone who listens to the Father and learns from him comes to me' " (John 6:45). Invite people to join you for Sunday School, Vacation Bible School, and/or worship at your church. As they hear God's Word taught and preached, God's Holy Spirit can bring conviction of sin and draw them to the Savior. Special presentations at Easter and Christmas are ideal times to invite people to church.

7. *Business program and meal.* Work with other Christ-followers to plan a breakfast, luncheon, or dinner for work associates, business contacts, and other business acquaintances. Invite a noted Christian businessperson or a well-known leader to address the group on a topic that will interest your guests. Ask the speaker to include a personal testimony of what a relationship with Jesus Christ means to him or her. Offer a tract, book, marked New Testament, video, or another resource to those who are interested in learning more about a relationship with Jesus Christ. Prepare a response card that can be left on tables so that people can record their decisions.

3 **The previous methods should be nonthreatening for you as a witness and for the person with whom you share. Which one(s) do you think might be effective for the people you most want to know Jesus? Check any that apply.**

❏ Personal testimony

❏ Gospel tract

❑ Evangelistic book
❑ Marked New Testament
❑ Video or movie
❑ Church Bible class and worship
❑ Business program and meal

8. ***Memorized plan of salvation.*** Many churches, denominations, and para-church groups offer courses that teach you how to share a detailed plan of salvation with others. They may use one of the methods I've already mentioned. Some help you memorize an outline and Scriptures to share the gospel. They may help you understand how to answer common questions about salvation and the Christian life. Classroom training is usually coupled with on-the-job training with an experienced witness. At first glance this approach may seem mechanical. However, after you have mastered the message, you can share the essentials of the gospel in a natural, appealing way. The FAITH Sunday School Evangelism Strategy, a 16-week course, equips believers to share a witnessing outline that can be adapted to a variety of witnessing situations.

9. ***Outreach Bible study.*** People who express an interest in learning more about Christ can be invited to an outreach Bible study. You can either use a prepared course of study or guide a study of one of the Gospels. The informality of a workplace, home, or apartment clubhouse reduces the fear of church for those who do not have church backgrounds. A couple or team can host this study, cultivate relationships with participants, share their own life stories, and answer questions of those who are seeking Christ. Many churches use this approach to start new minichurches (small churches within churches) as people come to faith in Christ. One church has more than one hundred groups meeting in apartments, homes, and other places outside the church building. Often a layperson serves as a Bible teacher and a lay pastor to the participants. A variety of resources are available for outreach Bible study.

4 **Do you know of places or people groups in your community that you could target with an outreach Bible study? A team from your church or workplace could plan and conduct it together. Check any of the following that God seems to be impressing you to reach.**

❑ Office complex   ❑ Business
❑ Apartment complex   ❑ Assisted-living facility
❑ Neighborhood   ❑ Government housing project
❑ Jail/prison   ❑ Nursing home
❑ College/university   ❑ Other: _____

EVANGELISM COURSES
• FAITH Sunday School Evangelism Strategy (www.lifeway.com/faith)
• Share Jesus Without Fear
• Learning to Share My Faith
• www.lifeway.com

OUTREACH BIBLE-STUDY RESOURCES
• www.serendipityhouse.com

NOTES
_____
_____
_____
_____
_____
_____
_____
_____
_____
_____
_____
_____
_____
_____
_____

10. *Prayer evangelism.* Many Christians find that prayer for a person yet to believe creates openness to the gospel. Many people who are broken and hurting will ask you or allow you to pray for their needs. After prayer they may be open to hear the gospel or receive a tract or a New Testament. When God answers the prayer, people have a living demonstration of His love and power. Some people use prayer evangelism with relatives, neighbors, coworkers, and others yet to believe. Tell people of your interest in praying for their needs, perhaps something like "How can I pray for you?" or "I'm a Christian, and I'm trying to take a greater interest in our neighborhood [or family, company, people around me]. I'm starting a prayer list to help me regularly pray for you and your family. Is there a special way I can pray for you today?" Pray for whatever they express as a need. Ask, "Would you mind if I prayed right now?" Then pray. You may be surprised by the ways prayer opens doors and allows you to reveal God's love by meeting needs. Follow up with a call, a visit, or a meal.[2]

SHARING THE FAITH

Congressman Jim Ryun represents the second district in Kansas. A lifelong runner, in 1965 Jim set the male high-school mile record—a mark that stood for 36 years. He ran in the 1964, 1968, and 1972 Olympic Games, winning a silver medal in the 1,500-meter run in 1968. Jim also held the world record in the mile, 1,500 meters, and 880 yards. He achieved legendary status as the first high-schooler ever to run a sub–four-minute mile.

Jim did something that he advises every Christian to do to share his or her faith. He developed a personal tract that tells his story and gives the plan of salvation. "When you talk to people who are interested in something more, you can't always share at that moment, but you have something to give them that they can read later. It's a good way to present the gospel in a nonobtrusive manner."[3]

One group invited Ron Anderson, the famed advertising guru responsible for "Got Milk?" and "Pork—the Other White Meat," to speak on creative advertising techniques. He concluded by describing his relationship with Jesus Christ and his work with the Billy Graham Evangelistic Association. On the lunch tables were copies of the tract *Steps to Peace with God* with Ron's autograph.

Realtor Jenny Pruitt sees her business as an opportu-

nity to be on call to meet spiritual needs. Here are some practical ways she implements that philosophy.

1. *Business talks.* Because of Jenny's success she is often asked to give business talks. But she will accept the invitation only if she is allowed to share the importance of faith in her life. "If they say no, then I tell them to find another speaker. That's the only way I'll do a talk, and so far I've never had anybody turn me down. It all goes back to a covenant I made with God when He gave me this company. I promised Him, 'Lord, I'll go anywhere you send me to talk about your love for me from this day forward.' "

2. *Office dedication.* With each new opening of a real-estate office, Jenny invites a local Christian leader to come and participate in the dedication. She knows firsthand how powerful a prayer of dedication can be.

3. *Prayer breakfast.* Every December Jenny hosts an inspirational prayer breakfast. "We focus both inside our company and the outside business community. For 22 years now we've had over four hundred people attend the breakfast each year. It's amazing how God has used this event to touch the lives of so many—and many have entered a personal relationship with Christ!"[4]

⑤ **The previous three ideas require more active participation, but they can bring very rewarding results. As you read these methods, which one(s), if any, did you sense that God may be leading you to participate in?**
❏ Memorized plan of salvation
❏ Outreach Bible study
❏ Prayer evangelism

⑥ **Read "Sharing the Faith" on page 114. Examine the other ideas in "Introducing Jesus Christ" on pages 204–5 in the Made to Count Tool Kit. Talk to the Lord about ways He would like for you to introduce His Son to those in your circles of influence. Pray for the people in "My Circles of Influence," pages 196–99 in the Made to Count Tool Kit, to meet Jesus.**

DAY 5

To the Ends of the Earth

Read and think about "Today's Word on Work" in the margin and respond to the Lord in prayer.

TODAY'S WORD ON WORK

" 'You will receive power when the Holy Spirit comes on you; and you will be my witnesses in Jerusalem, and in all Judea and Samaria, and to the ends of the earth.' "
Acts 1:8

RESPONDING PRAYER

Father, reveal anything in me that would get in the way of my being filled with Your Spirit. Fill me. Open my eyes to see and my ears to hear Your call beyond my own Jerusalem all the way to the ends of the earth. Let me clearly know my part. I choose to obey You. Amen.

God's assignment to His followers is to be His witnesses to the ends of the earth. Every Christ-follower and every church has a part to play in this world mission. World mission assignments are the greatest adventures to be filled in your service to your King. Whether you stay at home in a support role or go to the front lines of service, you can be a part of God's worldwide mission strategy. Let's look at three ways you can participate in God's world mission.

Missions Awareness

One place to begin is by becoming aware of God's work in other areas. We will use the term *missions* for God's work through the body of Christ to reach a lost world with the gospel of Jesus Christ. This could include home missions (in your country) and international missions (in other countries of the world). When you begin to learn about missions, God may guide you to be involved in specific ways through your support or personal participation. Use these suggestions to seek to obey Jesus' final command.

MISSIONARY BIOGRAPHIES
- Your church library
- A Christian bookstore
- www.lifeway.com

1 **Read the following suggestions for developing missions awareness. Check those you are willing to do to increase your awareness of God's work in the world.**

❏ a. Read a missionary's biography. Many missionaries say that they first sensed God's call to missions while reading biographies of missionaries like William Carey, Adoniram Judson, David Brainerd, John "Praying" Hyde, David Livingstone, Jim Elliott, Hudson Taylor, Bertha Smith, Amy Carmichael, William Booth, C. T. Studd, and Lottie Moon.

❏ b. Read about the history of missions in a missions group, a denomination, a parachurch group, a people group, or a country.

❏ c. Watch a video or documentary that tells the story of a missionary or a particular missions effort.

❏ d. Read or listen to news reports and updates from the mission field, as reported in missions magazines, Christian radio, Christian television, newsletters from missionaries, e-mail groups, and Web sites.

❏ e. Attend a missions conference at which missionaries report on their work.

❏ f. Listen to testimonies of people who have been touched by missions.

2 **What will you do to increase your missions awareness?**

_____

_____

_____

_____

_____

Missions Support

Missions awareness prepares you to hear what God may want to do through you. As you become aware of God's activity in a missions area, you can begin to identify ways He is inviting you to join Him in missions support or involvement. Missions support is helping others who are involved in missions work. This is a beginning step in obeying Jesus' final command. Just as Paul received support from churches in the areas of finances, coworkers, and prayers, today's missionaries need the support of other believers.

3 **Read the following suggestions for providing missions support. Check one or more that you are willing to do to provide support for missions work either outside or through your local church.**

❏ a. _Prayer for missions and missionaries._ Pray for—
- a missionary, his or her family, and his or her work;
- missionaries on their birthdays;
- specific requests given by missionaries or organizations;
- missions organization, administrators, and staff;
- gateway cities, countries, and areas where missionaries serve;

- an unreached people group (your church can even adopt one);
- God to call people to missions involvement;
- conversion of people in a non-Christian religion;
- governments and leaders whose laws may grant freedom or hinder missions work in their countries;
- national leaders (Christian workers in their own country or culture);
- missions events, crusades, or outreach efforts;
- use of media like the *Jesus* film, Gideon Bibles, or Christian radio to reach people for Christ.

❑ b. *Encouragement.* Send letters, cards, e-mails, and gifts that encourage missionaries in their work. Be careful, however, not to let your contacts become a hindrance by taking too much of the missionary's time.

❑ c. *Financial support.* Obey the Lord's scriptural directions to support missions by giving money to—
- your church for missions causes;
- individual missionaries and their projects;
- organizations that send missionaries;
- schools that train and equip missionaries for service;
- emergency requests for disaster relief or hunger projects;
- volunteers for short- or long-term mission trips;
- Bible societies or missions radio and television;
- churches or organizations that support national pastors and missionaries in other countries.

❑ d. *Material support.* You may have material you can give either from your personal property or through your company, such as medical supplies, food for disaster relief, clothes, blankets, bicycles, cars, Christian books or literature, Bibles, and radio or video equipment. Don't send material, however, without knowing a specific need.

❑ e. *Logistical support.* Your work or company may be able to provide logistical help for missionaries by coordinating travel, shipping goods, transferring data, providing technical training, and so forth.

❑ f. *Your children.* Parents and grandparents are sometimes the greatest hindrance to individuals who sense God's call to missions. If your children or grandchildren feel called to missions, give them your blessing. Send them off with your encouragement. Provide all the support at your disposal. Your greatest contribution to Jesus' final command could be godly children who respond to God's call.

4 **What will you do to support missions at home and/or abroad?**

_____

_____

_____

_____

> Your work or company may be able to provide logistical help for missionaries.

> You don't have to be a career missionary to get involved in missions.

Missions Involvement

You can also obey Jesus' final command by getting involved in missions and taking the gospel to the ends of the earth in person. You don't have to be a career missionary to get involved in missions. Nearly everyone can become personally involved.

5 **Read the following suggestions for missions involvement. Check one or more that you are willing to do to be involved in missions work beyond or through your local church.**

❑ a. Go as a volunteer on a short-term missions trip. Possibilities include—
- evangelism projects;
- Bible distribution;
- construction projects;
- medical/dental clinics;
- discipleship training for people and churches;
- ministry to missionary children while their parents are involved in meetings or events;
- music, dramatic presentations (individual or group);
- community health projects such as drilling water wells, building ponds/reservoirs, and water purification;
- disaster-relief efforts;
- prayerwalking (praying on site with insight), particularly in countries with limited access for missionaries;
- feeding projects;
- teaching business skills or English as a second language;
- ministry to orphans or lepers;
- agricultural projects;
- sports clinics or demonstrations.

❑ b. Minister to people in your area who could carry the gospel home with them. These people might be—
- international students at a university;
- foreign exchange students;
- international tourists at local attractions;
- international athletes in training or at sports events;
- employees who are temporarily working in your area.

❑ c. If God should call you, go as a career or long-term missionary—
- through your denomination's sending agency;
- through your church or a group of churches;
- for tentmaking (you provide your income through employment while volunteering in missions);
- as part of a parachurch group assignment (you usually raise your support before going and periodically as the need arises).[5]

MEDICAL MISSIONS AS RELATIONAL EVANGELISM

A group of medical doctors and other health-care professionals in Middle Tennessee have formed a missions organization to coordinate medical mission trips to such places as India, Mexico, South America, and Africa. They have found that many health-care professionals who have yet to believe in Christ nonetheless want to use their skills to help meet human needs. A 7- to 10-day trip provides many opportunities for Christ-followers to reveal Christ and talk about faith and eternal matters. Seeing a spiritual impact in the lives of needy people and watching others trust God for daily needs can have a powerful influence in introducing people to the Savior.[6]

6 What will you do to obey Jesus' final command by becoming personally involved in missions? Remember that God is your Master. He is the One who calls people to missions. What do you presently sense that God may be calling you to do?

_____

_____

_____

7 Are there ways your company might make a difference in meeting humanitarian needs, assisting missionaries logistically, or providing training or resources for community development? Write any ideas.

_____

_____

_____

8 Read "Medical Missions as Relational Evangelism" on this page. Review any activities you have decided to undertake to obey Jesus' final command. Take time to pray. Surrender your life to be available to God for whatever He asks and wherever He leads. Consider David Livingstone's prayer as your own:

Lord, send me anywhere, only go with me.
Lay any burden on me, only sustain me.
Sever any tie but the tie that binds me to Thyself.[7]

[1]Authors' interview, 17 June 2003.
[2]Claude V. King, *Final Command Action Manual* (Murfreesboro, TN: Final Command Resources, 2001), 74–78. Used by permission.
[3]Authors' interview, 5 June 2003.
[4]Authors' interview, 6 August 2003.
[5]King, *Final Command,* adapted from 93–97. Used by permission.
[6]Authors' interview.
[7]Henry Blackaby and Claude V. King, *Experiencing God: Knowing and Doing the Will of God* (Nashville: LifeWay Press, 1990), 135.

WEEK 7

God Reveals His Mission, Part I

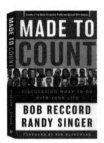

THIS WEEK'S SUPPLEMENTARY READING

Chapters 11–12, *Made to Count*

Archie grew up in Oklahoma, where he accepted Christ when he was 10. The first in his family to attend college, Archie graduated with a degree in geological and petroleum engineering and left college with an obligation to the Marine Corps. After completing his tour of duty, he earned an MBA and went to work for Continental Oil Company (Conoco).

Archie's rise was steady, fast, and promising but not fast enough for him. "I had a comfortable life, but I was not satisfied. I was firmly in control of my life, my family, and my career. I wanted more responsibility, and I wanted it now!"

Archie served as the chairman of a church land-acquisition committee. While he was attempting to help his church buy land (and getting nowhere fast!), an elderly deacon asked, "Archie, are you really asking God and trusting Him to do this, or are you trying to do it with your business skills?"

Archie told the deacon that he was indeed praying and asking God for help, but in his heart he knew it wasn't true. His prayer was perfunctory at best. He thought he had the skills to pull this off, but he couldn't get around the roadblocks. And things were no better in his business life. Archie recalls sitting outside his Houston home one night, coming to the end of his rope, and praying: "Lord, if You want me to stay in hot, humid, mosquito-infested Houston, I'll do it and be content. I'm turning my career and my family over to You!"

Within a few weeks of his surrender, the church had the land it so critically needed. A few months later Archie was elected the executive vice-president of a major Conoco subsidiary in San Clemente, California. There he and his wife, Linda, got involved in a local church, teaching young adults what it meant to follow and trust God with every aspect of their lives.

Archie would have a chance to test those lessons two years later when the phone rang. The president of Conoco told Archie that he'd been tapped to return to Houston to lead a project to build

the first campus-style headquarters in corporate America. As Archie listened, he was overwhelmed with the opportunity, but something deep in his heart told him that he shouldn't accept it.

After talking and praying with Linda for days, Archie called the president and graciously declined. An executive vice-president and a vice-president from Houston intervened and persuaded the president to extend the opportunity for another week. But Archie's unsettled feeling did not go away. Regardless of how much he prayed, the answer remained the same: "This is not for you." Once again he called the president to politely decline an opportunity that had amazing potential. As Archie hung up the phone, he wondered, "Is this the end of the road for me?"

Six months later Archie Dunham received his answer. He was elected the president of Conoco's California subsidiary, one of the best and most enjoyable jobs in his career. But it would be another 20 years before Archie learned the main reason God had kept him in San Clemente.

The commandant of the Marine Corps invited Archie and Linda to Washington, D.C., for an

event honoring a head of state. As they were being escorted off the parade ground, a Marine major approached them and said that the executive officer wanted to see the Dunhams. "In fact, he knows you," said the young officer. But when the major mentioned his colonel's name, Archie didn't recognize it.

The Marine colonel pulled a small Bible from his dress uniform, opened it, and took out a list of couples neatly typed on a piece of paper. It was the list of every couple who had been in Archie and Linda's Bible-study class in San Clemente 20 years before. "You may not remember, but my wife and I came to talk to you and Linda about whether to leave the Marine Corps. You shared with us your own journey and what you had learned about trusting God with your career as well as with your life. You prayed with us and taught us how to pray, seeking the Lord's call and leadership in our decision. Now I'm in Washington D.C., and I'm the commander of the President's Marine guard. Thank you for investing in me!"

Suddenly the reason God had not allowed Archie to move to Houston was clear.[1]

Have you surrendered control of your life, family, job, and future to the Lord's direction? If not, why not now? Pause to pray and give God full control and access to your life.

DAY 1

Principle 5: God Reveals His Mission

TODAY'S WORD ON WORK

" 'You are my friends if you do what I command. I no longer call you servants, because a servant does not know his master's business. Instead, I have called you friends, for everything that I learned from my Father I have made known to you. You did not choose me, but I chose you and appointed you to go and bear fruit— fruit that will last. Then the Father will give you whatever you ask in my name. This is my command: Love each other.' "
John 15:14-17

RESPONDING PRAYER

Jesus, I want to do what You command and to be called Your friend. You have chosen me to bear lasting fruit. I pray that You will make known to me my Master's business and invite me to be a part. Amen.

Read and think about "Today's Word on Work" in the margin and respond to the Lord in prayer.

Let "Today's Word on Work" sink in. Think about what Jesus said:
- If you do what Jesus commands, you will be His friend.
- Jesus reveals to His friends what He has learned from His Father.
- Jesus chose you and appointed you to go and bear lasting fruit.
- When you allow Jesus to bear fruit through your life, His Father will answer your prayers offered in His name and character.
- Jesus reminds us of a command we must obey: love one another.

Doesn't that sound like a life that has been made to count? This week we will continue our study of eight principles for a life that counts by focusing on principle 5.

Principle 5:	God reveals His mission through His Word, His Spirit, wise counsel, and His work in circumstances around you.
Your response:	Receive God's assignments and begin obeying by faith.

1 **Read principle 5 several times, giving special attention to the words that are bold and underlined.**

God reveals His mission through His **Word**, His **Spirit**, wise **counsel**, and His work in **circumstances** around you.

2 **Now personalize the principle by rewriting it. Change *you* to *me*.**

_____

_____

3 **Fill in the blanks below with the missing words and review all eight principles for a life that counts.**

1. God prepared a unique _____ and _____
   for your life even _____ you were born.

2. God calls you to a life-changing _____ with Him
   through _____ _____.

3. God calls you to partner with Him in a _____ that
   is _____ than you are.

4. God calls you to be on _____ with Him right where
   you are—starting _____.

5. God reveals His mission through His _____, His _____,
   wise _____, and His work in _____
   around you.

6. God repeatedly brings you to a crossroads of **choice** as He **forges**
   you for His mission.

7. God **guides** and **provides** for your mission one **step** at a time.

8. When you **answer** God's call, you experience His **pleasure** and **change**
   your world.

Jesus is the Author and the Finisher of our faith (see Hebrews 12:2). He chose you. He created you for a purpose. He prepared a unique plan and calling for your life even before you were born. When you entered a life-changing relationship with God through His Son Jesus Christ, you became a partner with Him in a mission that is bigger than you are. Because this mission is God's, He cares about its accomplishment more than you do. He assumes the responsibility of convincing you of His will to carry out the mission.

Although we often talk about discovering God's will, the process is more accurately understood as receiving what God wants to reveal. If He doesn't reveal it, you can do nothing to discover it. But as you seek Him and seek to please Him, He will reveal to you what He wants to do with your life. God doesn't hide His will. He reveals it. Your job is to keep your life in a right relationship with God so that you are prepared to hear the message clearly and receive it.

> "… looking unto Jesus the author and finisher of our faith."
> Hebrews 12:2, KJV

4 **Which of these statements is true? Mark it with a *T*.**

____ a. God's will, His mission for me, is hidden and hard to find. I must
   diligently work to search for and discover His will.

____ b. God wants me to know and do His will. As I spend time with Him
   and in His Word, He will reveal His mission and my part in that
   mission.

We saw the big picture of God's will in week 6 as we studied the Great Commission. God's ultimate purpose is to reconcile the world to Himself

NOTES

_____
_____
_____
_____
_____
_____
_____
_____
_____
_____
_____
_____
_____
_____
_____
_____
_____
_____
_____
_____
_____
_____
_____
_____

through Christ. Because He has already given this message and ministry to us, we have already been commissioned to go and make disciples.

As we spend time with God and in His Word, He will reveal the specific assignments of the mission He has for us to carry out. And as we go about that mission, God will reveal more specific assignments that contribute to the coming of His kingdom rule on earth as it is in heaven.

⑤ As you read the following specific areas in which God may reveal assignments, check the one(s) in which you have already experienced God's leadership. Write a note about that experience in the margin.

❑ 1. *A career, a profession, a vocation, a calling.* God may reveal His mission on a large scale through the whole of your work life. He calls people to careers like pastor or missionary, but He also calls others to medicine, media, education, government, business, law, and service industries. His call and His presence are the elements that make your career sacred. He called Peter to be a fisher of men (see Mark 1:17).

❑ 2. *A location.* Sometimes *where* God places you is more important than what you are doing. He may call you to a specific company, city, place of ministry, or country. Your presence there may be to influence the people or groups you come in contact with or to complete an assignment that must take place in that locality. He called Philip to go down to the road heading toward Gaza so that he would be in the right place to meet the Ethiopian official he would lead to Christ (see Acts 8:26-40). God called Jonah to go to the city of Nineveh (see Jonah 1:1).

❑ 3. *A person or group of people.* God's assignments are sometimes people-specific. These people-specific assignments may be short-term or long-term. God's mission may be for you to affect a person's coming to Christ, equip the person to grow and mature in Christ, influence the person to answer a call to service, or meet a humanitarian need. For example, God called Peter to go to Cornelius's home (see Acts 10:20). God's assignment may be a person in your home. He used a godly mother, Susannah Wesley, to provide an environment to rear sons John and Charles for their leadership in the evangelical awakening in England. Or God may call you to work with a specific group of people like prisoners, an ethnic group, or an unreached people group.

❑ 4. *A message.* The assignment God reveals may be a message. This may be a brief message like Jonah's message to Nineveh (see Jonah 3:4), a life message like that of John the Baptist (see Luke 1:76-77), or a message of correction like the one God entrusted to Ezekiel (see Ezekiel 3:16-21).

❑ 5. *A process, an action, or a ministry activity.* God may reveal a specific process you are to guide or an action you are to take. He may not tell you the reason for your call at the beginning of the assignment. He may use the result to bring glory to Himself or to accomplish a purpose He has in mind. An example of this assignment is when God guided Aquila and Priscilla to host a church in their home.

❏ 6. *Preparation.* Often the mission God has prepared for you requires preparation. He may need to develop your character, provide you with information or a skill, introduce you to an ethnic or cultural group, or sensitize you to a need. This is an important step in your mission assignments. Don't get in a hurry and bypass God's preparation phases.

❏ 7. *Others.* God is sovereign. We dare not put Him in a box and limit what He may reveal or what He may do. God may reveal any number of other aspects of a mission or assignment.

6 Review principle 5 and your response in the margin. What response should you make when God reveals an assignment?

_____

_____

In many of the stories we profile in this study, a breakthrough occurs when someone acts in obedience to God. God isn't looking for those who want to debate. He's looking for those who are committed to obey Him. As God reveals His mission to you, no matter what the assignment is, receive it and obey His will for your life.

7 Spend some time in prayer. Promise God that you will do whatever He asks without question or delay. Pledge to Him your willingness to obey as He reveals His mission.

8 Review today's summary ideas and respond to God in prayer. Ask the Lord to reveal His mission to you on His timetable and in His way.
- Jesus chose you and appointed you to go and bear lasting fruit.
- God reveals His mission through His Word, His Spirit, wise counsel, and His work in circumstances around you.
- Because this mission is God's, He cares about its accomplishment more than you do.
- God doesn't hide His will. He reveals it.
- As we spend time with God and in His Word, He will reveal the specific assignments of the mission He has for us to carry out.

PRINCIPLE 5
God reveals His mission through His Word, His Spirit, wise counsel, and His work in circumstances around you.

YOUR RESPONSE
Receive God's assignments and begin obeying by faith.

DAY 2

God Reveals His Mission Through His Word, Part 1

TODAY'S WORD ON WORK

"All Scripture is inspired by God and is useful to teach us what is true and to make us realize what is wrong in our lives. It straightens us out and teaches us to do what is right. It is God's way of preparing us in every way, fully equipped for every good thing God wants us to do."
2 Timothy 3:16-17, NLT

RESPONDING PRAYER

Father, thank You for the Scriptures, which train and equip me for Your divine purposes. Speak to me through Your Word so that I may know You and Your calling on my life. Amen.

"Paul, a servant of Christ Jesus, called to be an apostle and set apart for the gospel of God—the gospel he promised beforehand through his prophets in the Holy Scriptures regarding his Son. ... Through him and for his name's sake, we received grace and apostleship to call people from among all the Gentiles to the obedience that comes from faith."
Romans 1:1-5

> **Read and think about "Today's Word on Work" in the margin and respond to the Lord in prayer.**

In week 1 we saw that God interrupted Saul's personal agenda with His mission to carry the gospel to the Gentiles. When God spoke through Ananias, Paul immediately began to preach. Beginning today and continuing through week 8, we will examine ways God revealed His mission to Paul. We will see that Paul's life illustrates all of the avenues by which God reveals His mission, as identified in principle 5.

1 **Fill in the blanks to complete principle 5, which you learned yesterday. Look back at page 122 if you need to.**

God reveals His mission through His _____, His _____, wise _____, and His work in _____ around you.

By observing the way God used these avenues to reveal His mission to Paul, we can learn a lot about the way God reveals His assignments to believers today. Let's look at one way God revealed His mission to Paul.

2 **Read Romans 1:1-5 in the margin and underline the words that describe the way Paul learned about the gospel God had promised before Christ.**

God revealed the gospel of Jesus through the prophets in the Holy Scriptures, God's Word. Paul had studied the Jewish Scriptures under the teacher Gamaliel (see Acts 22:3). When Paul met Jesus, he realized that Jesus was the Messiah God had promised. Paul's knowledge of Scripture prepared him to preach about Christ convincingly. After Paul preached in Damascus and Jerusalem, the Jewish leaders were ready to kill him, so the disciples "took him down to Caesarea and sent him off to Tarsus" (Acts 9:30). God had called Paul, but Paul did not immediately head off to Gentile territory. He went through a time of private preparation.

3 **What is one way God revealed His mission to Paul?**

Through _____

Principle 5 teaches us that God reveals His mission through His Word, His Spirit, wise counsel, and His work in circumstances around you. Today we want to focus on how God reveals Himself and His work through the Holy Scriptures—God's Word.

Every vehicle has an owner's manual. The recommendations in the owner's manual are there for two interrelated reasons: to keep the vehicle operating at maximal effectiveness and to avoid major breakdowns. Unfortunately, too many of us wait to read the owner's manual until our vehicle has broken down. Isn't it strange that we do the same thing with the Bible? God gave it to us so that we can use its principles to keep our lives operating at maximal effectiveness and to prevent major breakdowns. Yet too often we don't turn to the Bible until we've experienced a significant breakdown.

4 **If you had to choose only one, which of these two reasons would cause you to read and study God's Word more frequently? Check one.**

❑ a. So that my life can operate at maximal effectiveness and fruitfulness—so that my life can count for God

❑ b. So that I can avoid major breakdowns in relationships and in my spiritual vitality that are caused by sin

Either one is a good reason to spend time with God in His Word. Fortunately, you can use both reasons to live in His Word. If we are to fulfill God's call in our individual lives, we must get a strong grip on the importance of reading God's Word on a regular basis. God made it very clear that His Word will work in us.

5 **In the margin read again 2 Timothy 3:16-17, Today's Word in Work, this time in the Amplified translation. Underline the benefits or values that come from applying Scripture to your life.**

God says that if we pay attention to His Word and follow it in our daily living, it will—

1. teach us the right way to walk;
2. give us a stab of conviction when we're not walking that way;
3. show us how to get back on the right path to do the right thing;
4. show us how to stay on that path;
5. make us thoroughly equipped and ready to fulfill God's call, live His plan, and receive His provision. This is the ultimate purpose for studying and applying God's Word.

"Every Scripture is God-breathed (given by His inspiration) and profitable for instruction, for reproof and conviction of sin, for correction of error and discipline in obedience, [and] for training in righteousness (in holy living, in conformity to God's will in thought, purpose, and action), so that the man of God may be complete and proficient, well fitted and thoroughly equipped for every good work."
2 Timothy 3:16-17, AMP

6 Read again those five benefits that come from applying God's Word in your life. Circle the number of each benefit that you believe you don't need in your life in Christ.

Did you circle anything? We hope not. God loves you so much that He gave His Word to help you experience life at its best. Avoiding any one of these benefits is a plan for a breakdown. God uses His Word to reveal His mission to you and to help you implement that mission.

God has revealed His will to us from one end of Scripture to the other. The Bible is full of truths and practical ways of living that every Christ-follower can apply. When you put those truths into practice, God's call on your life comes alive. That's the promise God made to His followers in the Old Testament: " 'Take to heart all the words I have solemnly declared to you this day, so that you may command your children to obey carefully all the words of this law. They are not just idle words for you—*they are your life*' " (Deuteronomy 32:46-47, italics added). Jesus said almost the same thing in the New Testament when He declared to His followers, " 'The words I have spoken to you are spirit and *they are life*' " (John 6:63, italics added).

God will never ask us to do anything that contradicts His will as expressed in Scripture. If we claim to hear God's voice but claim that God has asked us to do something that is inconsistent with Scripture, we are really claiming that God is a liar. God does not change. And He does not tell us one thing through His Word, only to give us another set of directions through another means. God's plan for our lives will always be consistent with Scripture. Always. Every time. Therefore, Scripture is always a reliable guide to God's will for our lives.

7 Read Malachi 2:14-16 in the margin and check the statement that is consistent with the Scripture.
- ❏ a. Because my wife refuses to go on mission with me, I'll have to get a divorce and find someone else who will go with me.
- ❏ b. Because my wife refuses to go on mission with me, I need to keep praying and discussing with her what God is saying. Perhaps I'm off base or this isn't God's timing. I have to trust God to convince my wife. Since we're one flesh, we have to move together.

8 Read Hebrews 11:6 and 2 Corinthians 5:6-7 in the margin and check the statement that is consistent with Scripture.
- ❏ a. I'm confident that God is guiding me in this direction, so I must start taking actions of obedience even though I don't yet see how He will provide the resources.
- ❏ b. I'm confident that God is guiding me in this direction, so I am still going to wait about taking any action until every resource is in place.

"The Lord is acting as the witness between you and the wife of your youth, because you have broken faith with her, though she is your partner, the wife of your marriage covenant.

"Has not the Lord made them one? In flesh and spirit they are his. And why one? Because he was seeking godly offspring. So guard yourself in your spirit, and do not break faith with the wife of your youth.

"I hate divorce," says the Lord God of Israel. ...

"So guard yourself in your spirit, and do not break faith."
Malachi 2:14-16

"Without faith it is impossible to please God."
Hebrews 11:6

"We are always confident. ... We live by faith, not by sight."
2 Corinthians 5:6-7

You probably agree that 6. *b* and 7. *a* are consistent with God's Word. The real challenge comes in knowing when God is speaking or in discerning what He is saying when different Scriptures might point you in different directions. This is why a close, personal relationship with God is so critical. Ultimately, He alone can provide the clarity you need.

The following guidelines can help you discern God's direction and His will as you spend time reading and studying His Word.

9 **As you read the following suggestions for seeking God's guidance in His Word, write any questions in the margin. You will have an opportunity to discuss these in your small-group session.**

1. *Spend regular times reading and studying God's Word so that you become familiar with what He has already made clear in His Word.* Follow a plan that will encourage balanced reading throughout the Bible rather than focus only on your favorite passages.

2. *Pray as you begin reading and invite God to speak through His Word.* Then listen for words of correction, instruction, direction, and warning.

3. *Be prepared to obey what God says to you in His Word.* When the instruction is clear, obey it. Don't debate it.

4. *Pay attention to verses that seem to jump off the page and grab your attention.* Write these down. Meditate on them. Consider memorizing the ones that are particularly meaningful. Pray and ask God to make clear the meaning and personal application of these verses. Sometimes God may plan for a verse to be applied at a future time, but He wants you to start thinking about the topic now so that He can get your attention when the right time comes.

5. *Search the Scriptures when you have a particular question or an issue on which you want God's counsel.* Be careful, however, not to look only for verses that support your preconceived idea of what you want God to say. Be open to change your mind in light of what you find. When different Scriptures can point you in different directions, take the matter to God in prayer for specific guidance. For example, you might be guided to submit to people in authority over you (see 1 Peter 2:13-14) in one situation but to obey God rather than people (see Acts 5:29) in another.

6. *Pay attention to times when God's Holy Spirit quickens your spirit.* *To quicken* means that God makes your spirit come alive, active, aroused, or sensitive. This quickening may be perceived as emotion. When you get emotional about a Scripture, take it to the Lord in prayer and verify that the emotion is from Him.

7. *Pay attention if several unrelated people point you to the same passage in Scripture or to a similar theme.* When people claim to have a word for you from God, pay attention. Listen. Then take what they have said

QUESTIONS

_____
_____
_____
_____
_____
_____
_____
_____
_____
_____
_____
_____
_____
_____
_____
_____
_____
_____
_____
_____
_____
_____
_____
_____
_____
_____
_____

If you are unsettled, keep praying and seek the wise counsel of others.

and talk to the Lord about it. If it is His Word for you, He will affirm it in a way that you will recognize.

8. ***When you sense that God has revealed something through His Word and you have taken it to Him in prayer, watch for a sense of either peace or discontent.*** If you are unsettled, keep praying and seek the wise counsel of others.

10 Have you ever sensed that God revealed His will or mission to you in a specific way through His Word or gave you guidance about how to do something? If so, describe the experience, referring to or quoting the Scripture God used to speak to you.

_____
_____
_____
_____
_____
_____

11 Review today's summary ideas.
- God gave the Bible to us so that we can use its principles to keep our lives operating at maximal effectiveness and to prevent major breakdowns.
- If we are to fulfill God's call in our individual lives, we must get a strong grip on the importance of reading God's Word on a regular basis.
- God's plan for our lives will always be consistent with Scripture. Always. Every time. Therefore, Scripture is always a reliable guide to God's will for our lives.

12 Respond to God in prayer. Talk to Him about the value you see in His Word and invite Him to speak to you through it as He reveals His will and His purpose for you.

DAY 3

God Reveals His Mission Through His Word, Part 2

Read and think about "Today's Word on Work" in the margin and respond to the Lord in prayer.

1 **Review principle 5 for a life that counts and your response by filling in the blanks.**

Principle 5: God reveals His mission through His _____,
His _____, wise _____, and His work
in _____ around you.

Your response: Receive God's _____ and begin
obeying by _____.

Principle 5 emphasizes that God reveals His mission through His Word, His Spirit, wise counsel, and His work in circumstances around you. Yesterday and today we are focusing on God's Word as a source of His will for our mission and purpose. Reading and meditating on God's Word has no substitute. God speaks through His Word and guides you to walk in His ways.

2 **Turn to "God's Word on Work," page 206 in the Made to Count Tool Kit. Follow the instructions to learn how God's Word can give specific guidance on work matters. Begin by praying that the Lord will reveal Himself and His ways to you as you read the suggested Scriptures.**

3 **If you or your company and its employees applied the Scriptures from "God's Word on Work" to your work and work environment, what are some things you would change? What would you do differently?**

_____

_____

4 **Spend time praying. Talk to the Lord about your work, your career, your profession, and your workplace. Ask Him to reveal ways you can make a difference in the lives of others through your work.**

TODAY'S WORD ON WORK

"I meditate on your precepts
    and consider your ways.
I delight in your decrees;
    I will not neglect your word."
Psalm 119:15-16

RESPONDING PRAYER

Lord, I recognize that Your Word, Your decrees, Your precepts, and Your ways are important for me to know and follow. I will not neglect Your Word. Amen.

DAY 4

God Reveals His Mission Through His Spirit, Part I

TODAY'S WORD ON WORK

" 'When he, the Spirit of truth, comes, he will guide you into all truth. He will not speak on his own; he will speak only what he hears, and he will tell you what is yet to come.' "

John 16:13

RESPONDING PRAYER

Father, thank You for sending the Spirit of truth to guide me into all truth. I pray that You will guide me to know clearly Your will and purposes in every matter. I want to do Your will. Amen.

PRINCIPLE 5

God reveals His mission through His Word, His Spirit, wise counsel, and His work in circumstances around you.

> **Read and think about "Today's Word on Work" in the margin and respond to the Lord in prayer.**

" 'Ask and it will be given to you; seek and you will find; knock and the door will be opened to you. For everyone who asks receives; he who seeks finds; and to him who knocks, the door will be opened' " (Matthew 7:7-8). If you read those verses in the original language, you would discover that Jesus was talking about *persistent* asking, *continuous* seeking, and *relentless* knocking. You must do everything in your power to know and understand His will. He wants you to persevere, to finish what you begin, especially in asking and searching for the clarity of His call and the direction of His plan.

What an amazing promise God gives for those who do just that. If we ask, He will answer! God invited Jeremiah, " 'Call to me and I will answer you and tell you great and unsearchable things you do not know' " (Jeremiah 33:3). God doesn't promise that He will always give the answer we want to hear, but He promises always to answer with what we need to hear.

When we interact with God in prayer, the Holy Spirit is involved. We learned in week 3 that prayer is not just religious activity but a relationship with God—the Holy Spirit. When God reveals His mission to us through the Holy Spirit, prayer is taking place.

1 **Review in the margin principle 5 for a life that counts. In addition to using His Word, what is another way God reveals His mission to us?**
Through _____

Today we will continue our look at the life of Paul to observe the way God revealed His mission to him through the Holy Spirit.

In the early days of Christianity, when the gospel began to be preached to Greek-speaking Jews, word got back to Jerusalem that many in Antioch were turning to the Lord. Barnabas went and saw God's work in Antioch and realized that he needed Saul's (Paul's) help. For a year Barnabas and Paul worked in Antioch, where the disciples were first called Christians (see

Acts 11:26). Paul knew all along that his calling was to the Gentiles, but he awaited God's revelation about the timing of and direction for his calling. He served where God had placed him until he received the next specific assignment. God chose to reveal this next step during a church prayer meeting.

2. Read Acts 13:1-3 in the margin and answer these questions.
   a. Who spoke to these believers and told them to send Barnabas and Paul on their missionary assignment? _____
   b. What were these leaders doing when the Holy Spirit spoke?

   _____

   c. After the Holy Spirit spoke, what did the group do?

   _____

> "In the church at Antioch there were prophets and teachers: Barnabas, Simeon called Niger, Lucius of Cyrene, Manaen (who had been brought up with Herod the tetrarch) and Saul. While they were worshiping the Lord and fasting, the Holy Spirit said, 'Set apart for me Barnabas and Saul for the work to which I have called them.' So after they had fasted and prayed, they placed their hands on them and sent them off."
> Acts 13:1-3

While a group of leaders (and perhaps the whole church) was worshiping the Lord and fasting, the Holy Spirit revealed God's will to send Paul and Barnabas to the Gentiles. Paul and Barnabas knew about God's calling. Now they knew God's timing. They had depended on God to speak through the body of Christ to help them know God's will and timing. The fact that the group was fasting may indicate that this was a specially called prayer meeting to seek the Lord's counsel. The Holy Spirit spoke to the church to reveal God's timing for the missionary ventures of Paul and Barnabas.

The Bible doesn't tell us how the leaders at Antioch knew the speaker was the Holy Spirit. It doesn't tell us whether He spoke in an audible voice that no one doubted or whether He simultaneously bore witness in their minds and hearts that this was what He wanted. But the observers knew that God had spoken. They believed Him, and they knew what to do. It's exciting to realize that the Holy Spirit in the New Testament era is the same Holy Spirit whom God has given to Christ-followers today!

How would your church respond if the leaders called a prayer meeting to fast, worship, and pray together to seek the Lord's directions for those God wanted to call into ministry and send on mission?

3. As you seek God's calling for your involvement in His mission, how would you respond to an invitation to fast, worship, and pray with a group of other believers to seek the Lord's direction? Check one.
   ❑ a. I'd jump at the chance. This is too significant a decision to make alone. I need help from others.
   ❑ b. You don't know the people of my church. I can't trust them to help me make such an important decision.
   ❑ c. God doesn't work like that anymore. He expects me to use my own reasoning and wisdom to devise a plan.
   ❑ d. I'm too busy right now. I won't be able to make it.
   ❑ e. Other: _____

If you've never experienced God speaking through His Holy Spirit in a prayer meeting, such an invitation might make you a little apprehensive. Perhaps as your small group meets, you'll experience God's Spirit speaking. Pray that you will. Once you've experienced Him that way, prayer meetings take on a new appeal. He promises, " 'Where two or three come together in my name, there am I with them' " (Matthew 18:20). Is it time to call a prayer meeting? He's waiting for you there!

Learn to pray together with other Christ-followers. Jesus promised an extra measure of His presence when two or three gather in His name (see Matthew 18:20). To that group He makes a huge promise: " 'If two of you on earth agree about anything you ask for, it will be done for you by my Father in heaven' " (Matthew 18:19).

The agreement God is looking for is not for believers to agree with one another. God wants us to come into agreement with Him. What God wants to do is far more important than what we want Him to do for us. As we gather to pray as a group, we can agree that more than anything else we want to hear from God; we want to know His will in the matter at hand.

As we pray about a topic, the Holy Spirit guides our prayer according to the Father's will. Spiritually, he distributes interlocking pieces of a spiritual vision God has for us. When you pray, I may adjust how I pray. Another prays, and we sense a witness to our spirits that God directed that prayer. As the pieces of the picture begin to come together, we reach an aha moment when we sense what God has in mind. Then we ask together, "God, would you do that?" And His answer to the prayer of agreement is yes.

> **God wants us to come into agreement with Him.**

4 **If you have ever experienced God speaking to you or your group, family, or church through the Holy Spirit in a prayer meeting, briefly describe that experience.**

_____

_____

_____

_____

_____

_____

_____

Many of us fervently pray for God's guidance, then wonder why we are still so confused. One reason may be that we've forgotten prayer is a two-way conversation. It's not just asking; it's also listening. Understanding this, the early Christians practiced the spiritual discipline of meditating on God's Word and listening for His guidance—waiting on the Lord.

The question is not whether God still speaks. The question is whether we're still listening—and whether we will be able to recognize His voice when

He speaks. We are a nation of multitaskers addicted to noise. But God's Word says the same thing to us that it did centuries ago to the agrarian nation of Israel: "Be still, and know that I am God" (Psalm 46:10, NKJV).

How long has it been since you've been still and listened to God? Are your devotional and prayer times filled with lots of requests, but little time is spent listening? Do you need to come apart from your crushing schedule, earnestly pray for God's guidance, and then take time to listen for a response?

If you feel that it's been a long time since you've heard from God, then we urge you to do two things.

1. Break your normal routine and listen.

2. Focus on strengthening your walk with Christ.

Don't approach God as a celestial guide dog. Worship Him as God and snuggle close to Him in His love. Let Him become your loving Shepherd, who walks with you day by day. Then when He speaks, you will know His voice, and you will follow (see John 10:3-5).

5 **How would you describe your relationship with God, and how well do you know His voice? Check an answer or write your own.**

❑ a. I spend a lot of time with God, and I've learned to recognize His voice when He speaks.

❑ b. I pray, but it feels like a long-distance call. I don't really know His voice.

❑ c. I spend very little time with Him, and my prayers are one-sided, with me doing the talking.

❑ d. Other: _____

_____

6 **Review today's summary ideas and spend some unhurried time with God in prayer sometime today.**

• God doesn't promise that He will always give the answer we want to hear, but He promises always to answer with what we need to hear.

• Prayer is not just religious activity but a relationship with God— the Holy Spirit.

• God reveals His mission through His Spirit.

• Jesus promised an extra measure of His presence when two or three gather in His name.

• God wants us to come into agreement with Him.

• Prayer is a two-way conversation. It's not just asking; it's also listening.

• "Be still, and know that I am God" (Psalm 46:10, NKJV).

" 'The watchman opens the gate for [the shepherd], and the sheep listen to his voice. He calls his own sheep by name and leads them out. When he has brought out all his own, he goes on ahead of them, and his sheep follow him because they know his voice. But they will never follow a stranger; in fact, they will run away from him because they do not recognize a stranger's voice.' "
John 10:3-5

DAY 5

God Reveals His Mission Through His Spirit, Part 2

TODAY'S WORD ON WORK

"The Spirit helps us in our weakness. We do not know what we ought to pray for, but the Spirit himself intercedes for us with groans that words cannot express. And he who searches our hearts knows the mind of the Spirit, because the Spirit intercedes for the saints in accordance with God's will."
Romans 8:26-27

RESPONDING PRAYER

I agree, Lord, that my great weakness is that I don't know what to pray for. I thank You for sending the Holy Spirit to pray with and for me according to Your will. Teach me to pray. Amen.

NOTES

_____
_____
_____
_____
_____
_____
_____
_____
_____
_____

Read and think about "Today's Word on Work" in the margin and respond to the Lord in prayer.

The Holy Spirit plays a direct role in your prayer life. He joins you in prayer, guides you in prayer, and prays for you according to God's will. As you pray and seek God's will for your mission, use the following suggestions to hear what He wants to reveal through the Holy Spirit.

1 As you read these suggestions, underline ideas that you think are most helpful. Write notes or questions in the margin.

1. Position yourself to hear from the Holy Spirit as you pray. This requires confessing and turning from your sin. Reconcile broken relationships and forgive offenses.
2. Schedule unhurried times with God—early mornings, late nights, or half- or full-day retreats. This will require major commitments and adjustments.
3. Cultivate an attitude of prayer throughout the day. Paul commanded, "Pray without ceasing" (1 Thessalonians 5:17, KJV). Be conscious of God's presence so that you can speak with Him at any time and so that He can get your attention when He chooses to speak.
4. Pray about all things. "In every thing by prayer and supplication with thanksgiving let your requests be made known unto God" (Philippians 4:6, KJV). Pray about problems that need solutions, people who need to change, relationships that need mending, direction, strategy, decisions, deliverance, needs, stewardship of resources, investments—everything.

2 Try an experiment before going to work. Pray and ask God to help you be aware of His presence throughout the day. Remembering that He is present with you, take time to pray silently and talk to Him. Seek His guidance, counsel, wisdom, or strength. You may even want to begin keeping a spiritual journal about experiencing God in your workplace. Be prepared to share your experience in your next small-group session.

5. Pray for new things. Ask God to bless others through you. Pray for discoveries, breakthroughs, new business, increased productivity, inventions, and new things you don't know to ask for by name.

6. Keep the Scriptures before you as you pray. Pray Scriptures that relate to the matters you are praying about. Seek scriptural promises, guidelines, or examples that guide and shape your prayers. Pay special attention when God seems to bring a Scripture to mind. Read it and meditate on what God may want to say through it. Write it down for study and review.

7. Pay attention to your spirit as you pray. Do you sense a peace and confident assurance of God's presence and guidance? Or do you feel uneasy, awkward, distanced, disoriented, or confused? Talk to the Lord about those feelings. If He needs to correct or discipline, let Him. If He needs to redirect your thinking and praying, let go and follow. If He's trying to warn you about a potential problem if you maintain your present course, talk about it. Don't ignore the negative feelings; they may be God's way of getting your attention for a divine purpose.

8. Be careful about giving God deadlines. We do not direct His schedule. He has no obligation to adjust to ours. He may wait one day past your deadline just to see if you are going to trust Him, wait on Him, and allow Him to be Lord or if you are going to retake control of your life. If you do not hear a direction, be patient with God. Wait on Him. Learn to rest on His timetable. Don't jump to your own conclusions if God hasn't spoken.

9. Suppose others have given you a deadline, and you are praying for an answer. What do you do if God doesn't speak on time? You cannot make God speak on your schedule. God knows the issues. If He hasn't spoken when others expect an answer, assume He is saying no. Don't try to manipulate an answer, presuming that you know what He wants. God may have another plan you won't know about until the deadline passes.

3 **Write principle 5 for a life that counts and your response.**

Principle 5: _____

_____

Your response: _____

4 **Thank God for speaking to you through His Word and His Holy Spirit. Ask Him to help you diligently seek His will in these ways.**

5 **Plan an unhurried time of prayer today. Focus on your relationship with Him and listen more. Then describe in the margin your time with Him.**

———
[1]Authors' interview, 27 May 2003.

NOTES

MY TIME WITH GOD

WEEK 8

God Reveals His Mission, Part 2

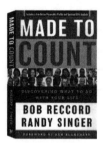

**THIS WEEK'S
SUPPLEMENTARY READING**

Chapter 13, *Made to Count*

Kathy grew up in a Christian home in Wichita Falls, Texas. Through the years she made several decisions for Christ at church camps. But "the head knowledge of Christ took its precious time to travel to my heart," she recalls. During her first year in college, she finally let go and invited Jesus Christ to take control of her life. She found the assurance of her salvation for which she had been searching.

Before Kathy had settled her relationship with the Lord, God had already begun to shape her life and passions for her future assignments. At the age of 12 she received a book by Art Linkletter that included letters written to President Nixon. She became fascinated with politics and the presidency. At 15 she worked in her first political campaign, stuffing envelopes and calling voters. She developed deep convictions about the importance of voting and being involved in the political process.

No one, including Kathy, would have planned the career path she has taken into politics and government. At each turn in the road, she has sensed God's direction and provision for her unique mission assignments. She describes her journey this way:

My journey looks glamorous on the outside and is sometimes glamorous on the inside but often lonely as well. Uprooting my life every few years, making new friendships, finding a new cleaner, a new hair salon, new doctors, and learning new directions can get lonely and tiring. I have never focused on the bumps in the road; I have chosen to lift my feet and soar above them. Sometimes I feel like a bird in flight. I often have to work my wings hard to move ahead, other times I let go and soar, and still other times I am the bird you rolled your eyes at that ran full throttle into your sliding glass door. I've hit a lot of glass doors in my journey, but I so enjoy the flying that it's always worth going up again.

Today Kathy Wills serves in Washington, D.C., as an adviser to the Secretary of State and as the White House liaison at the U.S. Department of State. But her career path has included serving as the receptionist for the first President Bush, working in the U.S. Department of Transportation, and serving as the vice-president of public affairs for a conservative organization in Washington, D.C. With these political/governmental positions she has mixed religious jobs, serving as the director of marketing for Thomas-Nelson Publishers and the director of communications at Dallas Theological Seminary. If Kathy were relying on her human wisdom alone, she probably would not have chosen such a mixture of political and religious jobs for her career path. When we asked Kathy how God revealed His assignments to her, she replied:

Thankfully, God knows us better than we know ourselves and calls us according to His purpose and not our own. My own purpose would have kept me from following God's most recent call. In fact, I would have been extremely happy if my job in Washington had fallen through.

Determining your calling is much easier with closed doors. Open doors require a lot of prayer and soul searching. Just because you are comfortable and everything feels right doesn't mean you are in your calling. I often find that my calling is a little uncomfortable.

Determining my calling has always been a process. Even when the opportunity coming to me is attractive, I still don't avoid the road I need to travel to determine if this opportunity is *my* calling. Since the callings are not always in the same direction I am moving, it behooves me to stay alert. I do this by maintaining a relationship with God and supporting that relationship by studying His Word and talking to Him.

My steps usually include plenty of prayer, intentional listening to God, and seeking wise counsel from people I explicitly trust to give me their advice. Some are family, some are friends, but all have something in common: they know me well, they love me, and they have no selfish agenda when giving me advice.[1]

Ask the Lord to give you sensitivity to Him as He reveals His assignments to you through His Word, His Spirit, wise counsel, and His work in circumstances around you.

DAY I

God Reveals His Mission, Part 2

TODAY'S WORD ON WORK

"Where there is no vision, the people perish."
Proverbs 29:18, KJV

"Where there is no revelation, the people cast off restraint."
Proverbs 29:18, NKJV

RESPONDING PRAYER

Father, as one of Your people, I do not want to perish. "Cast off restraint" sounds so rebellious. I don't want that either. I want Your vision—Your revelation of the mission You have for my life. I want to receive Your calling and to fulfill my mission—my destiny. Would You open my eyes to see what You are doing around me? Would You open my ears to hear the wise counsel of others? I would be grateful. I will obey. Amen.

> **Read and think about "Today's Word on Work" in the margin and respond to the Lord in prayer.**

Many people quote Proverbs 29:18 to focus on a vision, a mission, or a purpose statement that guides behavior and actions toward a goal. As you can see, having a vision is important, and not having a vision is dangerous. But many go astray at this point. They seek visions of their own. They dream their own dreams. They set their own goals and then ask God to bless what they have planned. The New King James Version gives a better understanding of what we need to look for: we need divine revelation from God.

Without divine revelation, people do what is right in their own eyes and live their own plans. They "cast off restraint" (Proverbs 29:18, NKJV). They live their lives according to their own views of right and wrong. The consequences can be costly. In Scripture God was not pleased when "everyone did what was right in his own eyes" (Judges 17:6, NKJV). Instead, He commended those who did "what was right in the eyes of the Lord" (1 Kings 15:5).

1 **Which of the following is what God wants from you? Check one.**
   ❑ a. God wants me to understand what He reveals of His mission. Then He wants me to do what pleases Him.
   ❑ b. God wants me to come up with my own vision and do what is right in my own eyes.

We must learn to wait for the Lord to reveal His mission. Then we can spend our lives doing what is significant and what pleases Him rather than going our own way (*a*). Last week we began studying ways God reveals His mission.

2 **Review principle 5 for a life that counts by filling in the blanks with the missing words.**
   God reveals His mission through His _____,
   His _____, wise _____, and His work
   in _____ around you.

Last week we studied the first two ways God reveals His mission—through His Word and His Spirit. This week we will focus on the other two ways— wise counsel and His work in circumstances around us. Let's start by examining the way God worked in the life of an early Christ-follower.

The church in Jerusalem chose Philip as a servant (deacon) so that the apostles could devote themselves to prayer and the ministry of the Word. Therefore, he was a layman. When the church scattered due to the persecution following the death of Stephen (another deacon of the church), Philip went to Samaria, where he "preached the word" and "proclaimed Christ" (Acts 8:4-5). Yes, laymen can do that!

So many people responded to Philip's message that word got back to Jerusalem. The church there sent Peter and John to check out what was happening. In the middle of this big response, God revealed a mission assignment to Philip.

3 As you read Philip's story in the margin, watch for ways Philip was guided in this mission assignment. Underline clues you see.

Although we don't read in the Bible anything more about this important Ethiopian official, he may well have been the person responsible for carrying Christianity to North Africa. What a mission assignment God gave Philip. In one day he had the privilege of touching a nation and perhaps a continent for Christ.

4 How did God reveal this mission to Philip? Check all that apply.
❑ His Word   ❑ His Spirit
❑ Wise counsel   ❑ His work in circumstances

First, an angel told Philip to go to a specific location. When he arrived, he saw and heard a man reading Scripture. Then the Spirit impressed Philip to go near the man's chariot. Knowing he was there by God's revelation, Philip asked a gently probing question, the door opened, and Philip led the official to place his faith in Christ. God revealed the mission through His Spirit and the work He was doing in the circumstances around Philip. Even God's Word played a role in this encounter.

As you look for God's work in your life, don't jump to the conclusion that your thinking or reasoning automatically leads you to God's will. People can think of ideas that do not come from God. Even Christ-followers can allow their human plans and desires to become substitutes for God's plans and desires. Not every open door comes from God, and not every closed door means that God is discouraging you from going in that direction. When you sense that God has spoken to you, spend time with Him to make sure that the message is from Him and that you've heard Him clearly. When you

"An angel of the Lord said to Philip, 'Go south to the road—the desert road—that goes down from Jerusalem to Gaza.' So he started out, and on his way he met an Ethiopian eunuch, an important official in charge of all the treasury of Candace, queen of the Ethiopians. This man had gone to Jerusalem to worship, and on his way home was sitting in his chariot reading the book of Isaiah the prophet. The Spirit told Philip, 'Go to that chariot and stay near it.'

"Then Philip ran up to the chariot and heard the man reading Isaiah the prophet. 'Do you understand what you are reading?' Philip asked.

" 'How can I,' he said, 'unless someone explains it to me?' So he invited Philip to come up and sit with him.

"The eunuch asked Philip, 'Tell me, please, who is the prophet talking about, himself or someone else?' Then Philip began with that very passage of Scripture and told him the good news about Jesus.

"As they traveled along the road, they came to some water and the eunuch said, 'Look, here is water. Why shouldn't I be baptized?' And he gave orders to stop the chariot. Then both Philip and the eunuch went down into the water and Philip baptized him."
Acts 8:26-31,34-38

> When you think you sense God's direction, test your impression against the four ways God reveals His mission.

think you sense God's direction, test your impression against the four ways God reveals His mission, as identified in principle 5.

1. Learn whether your sense of direction is consistent with God's Word.
2. Pray to learn whether the Holy Spirit confirms this impression in your spirit.
3. Submit the idea to other Christ-followers for their evaluation and counsel.
4. Consider what God is doing through circumstances around you to determine whether the direction agrees with His activity. God does not work at cross-purposes with His own plans and activities.

5 **As you read the statements about receiving God's revealed mission or assignments, mark each one *T* for *true* or *F* for *false*.**

___ a. I should test what I'm sensing to make sure it is in line with what God has already said in His Word.

___ b. God will not lead me contrary to His Word.

___ c. Once I have a sense of direction, I don't need to listen to the counsel of anybody else.

___ d. God doesn't lead in personal ways anymore. He expects me to use my own intelligence to figure out what I am to do.

___ e. God's Holy Spirit in me can confirm or correct a sense of direction I have. I should trust Him to do so.

If you marked the statements a. *T*, b. *T*, c. *F*, d. *F*, e. *T*, you probably have a good understanding of the ways to confirm God's direction in your life.

6 **Review today's summary ideas and respond to God in prayer. Ask the Lord to give you keen spiritual sensitivity to Him as He reveals His mission to you.**

- We need divine revelation from God.
- We must learn to wait for the Lord to reveal His mission.
- Don't jump to the conclusion that your thinking or reasoning automatically leads you to God's will.
- When you sense that God has spoken to you, spend time with Him to make sure that the message is from Him and that you've heard Him clearly.

DAY 2

God Reveals His Mission Through Wise Counsel

Read and think about "Today's Word on Work" in the margin and respond to the Lord in prayer.

TODAY'S WORD ON WORK

"Plans fail for lack of counsel,
    but with many advisers they succeed."
Proverbs 15:22

When we last looked at Paul's story, God had instructed a group of believers at prayer to tell Paul and Barnabas it was time for them to go on their mission (see Acts 13:1-3). Trusting God to reveal His will through the church can remove a heavy burden from you. God intends for you to be a part of the body of Christ. Christ-followers need one another. His intention is more about trusting in God's ability to speak through people than about trusting in your fellow Christ-followers. The believers in Antioch were relatively new Christians; most had been believers for about a year. Yet God used them to make history by launching the missionary journeys of the Apostle Paul. Learn to value the counsel of others in whom the Spirit of Christ dwells.

Don't avoid a prayer meeting for God's mission because you think God isn't calling you to a mission now. Keep in mind that your presence may not be for you. God calls the body of Christ to be on mission through its members. The body needs members who stay as a support base as well as members who go. Others were present in the Antioch prayer meeting. Paul and Barnabas needed to hear what God was saying to the church in order to better know their part in the mission.

RESPONDING PRAYER

Lord, I surely don't want my plans to fail because I act in pride and refuse to seek and receive the wise counsel of others. Show me the people around me from whom I should seek counsel when I need it. Amen.

1 Complete the blank in principle 5 to identify another way God reveals His mission.

God reveals His mission through His Word, His Spirit, wise _____, and His work in circumstances around you.

As this biblical account illustrates, God reveals His mission through the wise counsel He gives through others.

Paul relied on others' wise counsel more than once. Three years after his conversion, he went to Jerusalem to meet with Peter (see Galatians 1:18-19).

"Then after three years, I went up to Jerusalem to get acquainted with Peter and stayed with him fifteen days. I saw none of the other apostles—only James, the Lord's brother."
Galatians 1:18-19

Then 14 years later Paul and Barnabas went to Jerusalem "in response to a revelation and set before them the gospel that I preach among the Gentiles. But I did this privately to those who seemed to be leaders, for fear that I was running or had run my race in vain" (Galatians 2:2). After describing the work God had done through them, Paul and Barnabas were affirmed in their calling to the Gentiles:

> They saw that I had been entrusted with the task of preaching the gospel to the Gentiles, just as Peter had been to the Jews. For God, who was at work in the ministry of Peter as an apostle to the Jews, was also at work in my ministry as an apostle to the Gentiles. James, Peter and John, those reputed to be pillars, gave me and Barnabas the right hand of fellowship when they recognized the grace given to me. They agreed that we should go to the Gentiles, and they to the Jews (Galatians 2:7-9).

God loves us enough to send mature, seasoned, and integrity-filled believers into our lives. We watch them model wisdom and godly living. We see first-hand the impact they make. It doesn't take us long to determine that we want to have relationships and influence as they do.

We encourage you to seek wise counsel from those people, but first heed this warning: wise counselors may be godly, but they are not God. Like all of us, they have a sin nature and are only one step away from disobedience. If they are truly godly, they would be the first to tell you not to put your faith in them. Put your faith in Christ. Look to others for counsel but not for salvation. Men and women will disappoint. Only Christ is perfectly faithful.

You may seek wise counsel in two different ways. In one case you may seek a mentor to share general wisdom with you about God's will and your work, family, or career. You want to learn from that person's experience and wisdom gained over the years. Older, more mature Christ-followers are valuable assets for you to consult. See the questions in the margin to understand the type of direction you would request from a mentor.

QUESTIONS TO ASK A MENTOR

- How did God reveal His call and His plan for your life?
- Did God give you a passion that corresponded with His call?
- What are some ways God helped you hear His call on your life and understand His plan for your future?
- How did God use your temperament, talent, spiritual gifts, and experiences to reveal His call and plan?
- What would you do differently if you were going through the journey again?

2 **Define a mentor in your own words. A mentor is ...**

_____

_____

_____

3 **Do you know someone who might be a valuable mentor for you or is already your mentor? If so, who is it?**

_____

④ **Read James 1:5 in the margin and answer these questions.**

a. Where does godly wisdom come from? _____

b. To whom is this wisdom available? _____

"If any of you lacks wisdom, he should ask God, who gives generously to all without finding fault, and it will be given to him."
James 1:5

When you seek to clarify God's direction for specific ministry or mission assignments, you will seek wisdom in a different manner. In this case you share the direction you sense that God is leading or what you sense that He is saying. The questions in the margin identify areas of spiritual wisdom God can give through others in the body of Christ. You might call these people spiritual counselors.

A spiritual counselor and a mentor may be the same person. But you may find someone who has an intimate prayer life and walk with Christ but doesn't have many years of experience. Although he or she may not make a good mentor, this person may be a good spiritual counselor.

⑤ **Define a spiritual counselor in your own words. A spiritual counselor is ...**

_____

_____

_____

QUESTIONS TO ASK A SPIRITUAL COUNSELOR
1. Is this direction in line or consistent with Scripture?
2. Do you sense the Spirit's confirmation of this direction?
3. Do circumstances indicate that this is God's direction and timing?
4. Do I need to consider other factors that I haven't considered?

⑥ **Do you know someone who might be a valuable spiritual counselor for you or is already your spiritual counselor? If so, who is it?**

_____

⑦ **Review today's summary ideas and respond to God in prayer.**
- Learn to value the counsel of others in whom the Spirit of Christ dwells.
- God calls the body of Christ to be on mission through its members.
- You may seek a mentor to share general wisdom with you about God's will and your work, family, or career.
- When you seek to clarify God's direction for specific ministry or mission assignments, you will seek wisdom in a different manner.

⑧ **Pray Paul's prayer in the margin for yourself and for others in your church and in your small group.**

"I keep asking that the God of our Lord Jesus Christ, the glorious Father, may give you the Spirit of wisdom and revelation, so that you may know him better."
Ephesians 1:17

DAY 3

Evaluating the Counsel of Others

TODAY'S WORD ON WORK

"We have not stopped praying for you and asking God to fill you with the knowledge of his will through all spiritual wisdom and understanding. And we pray this in order that you may live a life worthy of the Lord and may please him in every way: bearing fruit in every good work."

Colossians 1:9-10

RESPONDING PRAYER

Lord, I want to live a life that is worthy of You. I want to please You and bear fruit in the good works for which You have created me. I pray that You will fill me with the knowledge of Your will through spiritual wisdom and understanding. Lord, do the same for those in my small group. Amen.

> **Read and think about "Today's Word on Work" in the margin and respond to the Lord in prayer.**

When the apostle Paul prepared to return to Jerusalem after his third missionary journey, a man named Agabus warned Paul not to go. Agabus grabbed Paul's belt, tied his own hands and feet with it, and prophesied that the owner of the belt would be bound by the Jews in Jerusalem and handed over to the Gentiles. Paul's response? " 'Why are you weeping and breaking my heart? I am ready not only to be bound, but also to die in Jerusalem for the name of the Lord Jesus' " (Acts 21:13).

Then Luke, the writer of the Book of Acts, made an interesting comment: "When he would not be dissuaded, we gave up and said, 'The Lord's will be done' " (Acts 21:14).

Did you catch that? "The Lord's will be done." Against the advice of his friends, Paul went to Jerusalem knowing that was the Lord's will. Agabus was right; Paul was bound and delivered to the Gentiles. He was tried in the Roman legal system, eventually appearing before Caesar himself. Because he went to Jerusalem, Paul was able to present the gospel to the Gentile rulers, including Caesar's household. Because he went to Jerusalem, Paul wrote the Book of Romans. Because he went to Jerusalem, Paul was able to faithfully fulfill his mission to take the gospel to " 'Gentiles, kings, and the children of Israel' " (Acts 9:15, NKJV).

Don't discount the advice of friends, but use it wisely. Seek wise counsel on God's purpose for your life. Ask those you respect how God worked in their lives. When you sense that God has given you a mission, an assignment, or direction, invite other Christ-followers to help you evaluate it to seek confirmation from the Lord. Just remember that God's calling is personal. He will use others to help you, but ultimately, you must receive your final word from Him.

1 **Mark these statements *T* for *true* or *F* for *false*.**

___ a. Because I have to get final direction from God, I don't need to seek the counsel of others.

___ b. When others are unanimous in what they sense that I should do, I should submit to their wishes even if I sense that the Lord is directing otherwise.

___ c. God's counsel is never personal. I can know God's will in general terms that apply to everybody.

You no doubt discovered that all of these statements are false. God speaks through the wise counsel of others, but ultimately, you must obey His personal direction to you.

> God speaks through the wise counsel of others, but ultimately, you must obey His personal direction to you.

2 **Take a moment to review principle 5. What are four ways God may use to reveal His mission to you?**

a. _____

b. _____

c. _____

d. _____

What is your response to principle 5? Refer to page 122 if you don't remember.

_____

_____

3 **Read "Serendipities" on page 148. Ask the Lord to teach you how to watch for and respond to His invitations to join His work. Ask Him to make you sensitive to every opportunity to serve Him.**

4 **Review today's summary ideas and respond to God in prayer.**

• Don't discount the advice of friends, but use it wisely.

• When you sense that God has given you a mission, an assignment, or direction, invite other Christ-followers to help you evaluate it to seek confirmation from the Lord.

• God's calling is personal. He will use others to help you, but ultimately, you must receive your final word from Him.

SERENDIPITIES

In 1999 Ralph Reed traveled with an elite group of political consultants and strategists to the Holy Land, a trip sponsored by the American Israeli Public Affairs Committee. As he walked where Jesus walked, Ralph searched for a way to gracefully and tactfully share his faith. But at every turn the doors seemed strangely and abruptly closed. Ralph decided not to exercise forced entry into any conversation, circumstance, or event.

Then it happened. As his group gazed awestruck over the gorgeous Sea of Galilee from the spot many believe was the location of Jesus' Sermon on the Mount, the door pushed open a crack. But it wasn't Ralph's hand that pushed open the door; he knew it was an invisible one. A tour guide invited Ralph to read the Sermon on the Mount from Matthew 5–7.

"I didn't preach or deliver any message at all—I simply read the passages as requested. Then I looked up and saw tears in the eyes of so many hardened veterans of many political battles. It was one of the most amazing and beautiful moments I've ever had. We all experienced the unique feeling of hearing those words on the very ground where they were spoken by Christ. I sensed each of us drawing closer to the God who had brought us there!"

Ralph said it was remarkable how many doors then opened in private conversations to talk about the truths of that famous sermon and the One who originally delivered it.[2]

Are you on the lookout for the serendipities God brings your way that could be entry points to transforming encounters? If you aren't, you'll miss them.

DAY 4

God Reveals His Mission Through His Work in Circumstances

Read and think about "Today's Word on Work" in the margin and respond to the Lord in prayer.

Our friend Henry Blackaby has helped many Christ-followers look at God's will from a very different perspective. In his book *Experiencing God* Henry urges us to find where God is working and to join Him in His work. This type of thinking helps keep our focus where it should be—on God. As Henry explains it, "Once I know God's will, then I can adjust my life to Him. In other words, what is it that God is purposing where I am? Once I know what God is doing, then I know what I need to do. The focus needs to be on God, not my life!"[3]

1 **Review principle 5 for a life that counts by filling in the blanks with the missing words.**

God reveals His mission through His _____,
His _____, wise _____, and
His work in _____ around you.

The fourth way God reveals His mission is through His work in circumstances around you. Paul's life illustrates the way God works this way. On one occasion Paul saw the rejection of the gospel as an indication to make a move (see Acts 18:6-7). When Paul made a move next door, "Crispus, the synagogue ruler, and his entire household believed in the Lord; and many of the Corinthians who heard him believed and were baptized" (Acts 18:8).

Perhaps Paul's most famous experience of God's leadership involves God's work in circumstances around him. Although we don't know all the details of what God did or how Paul knew what God was doing, we are told that Paul and his companions were "kept by the Holy Spirit from preaching the word

TODAY'S WORD ON WORK

"We know that in all things God works for the good of those who love him, who have been called according to his purpose. For those God foreknew he also predestined to be conformed to the likeness of his Son, that he might be the firstborn among many brothers."
Romans 8:28-29

RESPONDING PRAYER

Father, You have predestined me to become like Your Son Jesus. What an awe-inspiring thought that is—to be like Jesus. Please work in circumstances around me to mold and shape me into a tool You can use for Your glory. Amen.

"When the Jews opposed Paul and became abusive, he shook out his clothes in protest and said to them, 'Your blood be on your own heads! I am clear of my responsibility. From now on I will go to the Gentiles.'

"Then Paul left the synagogue and went next door to the house of Titius Justus, a worshiper of God."
Acts 18:6-7

in the province of Asia. ... They tried to enter Bithynia, but the Spirit of Jesus would not allow them to" (Acts 16:6-7). In Troas, waiting and praying but not understanding, Paul had a vision in the night of a man begging, " 'Come over to Macedonia and help us' " (Acts 16:9). They immediately headed for Macedonia, "concluding that God had called us to preach the gospel to them" (Acts 16:10). Somehow God worked through circumstances around Paul to turn him away from Asia and Bithynia and turn him toward Macedonia. From there the gospel entered Europe and eventually Rome.

2 **Throughout our study of principle 5, we have seen that God revealed His mission to Paul through His Word, His Spirit, and wise counsel. What is another way God revealed His mission to Paul?**
Through _____

When we recognize that God works through circumstances, we are not talking about a call to bandwagon Christianity. Believers are not always called to join the largest and fastest-growing church, to go to the most fruitful mission field, or to pursue occupations where God is doing a great work. Some of us are called to be pioneers and to labor faithfully in arenas where we'll never personally see much fruit. Remember that God is at work just as much in the sowing as in the reaping.

3 **In your opinion, what is one arena in our society in which God's activity is not evident on the surface?**

_____

God may be calling you to a career or a place that the church has spurned as a secular arena in which God is not at work. But perhaps the reason we see no fruitfulness in that arena is because Christ-followers have abandoned the field. When you look for God at work in the circumstances around you, don't focus exclusively on where God is bringing in the harvest. God is at work when He—
- breaks our hearts over a need;
- creates new opportunities to share the good news;
- helps us establish meaningful relationships;
- gives us a platform of credibility or success that can be used to increase the effectiveness of our sharing.

As you evaluate God's work in the circumstances around you and determine to join Him in what He's doing, keep in mind that He may not be calling you to be part of a great movement that's already bearing visible results. Instead, God may be calling you to the quiet and thankless job of planting shade trees under which you will never sit.

God may be calling you to the quiet and thankless job of planting shade trees under which you will never sit.

4 **Read "Running a Good Race" and "Seeking Divine Appointments" on this page. Have you been nudged or forced into unusual or unexpected circumstances that God can use for divine purposes? Think about activities in your life. Is God inviting you to join Him in a place to which He has taken you? Have you recently been involved in an activity through which you sensed God's leading in a new direction or to a particular ministry action? Spend time meditating about your life circumstances. Ask God to reveal anything about your circumstances that represents His invitation or direction for you to join Him.**

5 **Review today's summary ideas and respond to God in prayer.**
- The fourth way God reveals His mission is through His work in circumstances around you.
- Believers are not always called to join the largest and fastest-growing church, to go to the most fruitful mission field, or to pursue occupations where God is doing a great work.
- Some of us are called to be pioneers and to labor faithfully in arenas where we'll never personally see much fruit.
- God is at work just as much in the sowing as in the reaping.

RUNNING A GOOD RACE

In high school Jim Ryun achieved legendary status as the first high-schooler ever to run a sub–four-minute mile. While running through Kansas in 1996 with the Olympic torch, God gave Jim a vision for a whole new race. The second-district seat in Kansas was open, and Jim felt God calling him to run for that office.

"At first I was hesitant because of the changes it would bring to our family life if I were elected. My wife had wanted me to be in public service for some time, so she was fully supportive as we prayed about it. Our children were so excited. Our daughter told me to remember that evil abounds when good men do nothing. So it seemed that as I spent time praying and listening to my family, it really did point to the fact that this was the Lord's doing. So we put my name on the ballot, and God gave us a victory."

Since then Jim has been reelected every two years and has used this platform to influence the lives of those around him.[4]

SEEKING DIVINE APPOINTMENTS

Jeanine Allen lives with her husband and two daughters in Lawrenceville, Georgia. When Jeanine developed breast cancer, Her commitment to make a difference for Christ even during the tough times led Jeanine to ask her husband not to accompany her to her cancer treatments. Jeanine would have none of it. She believed that other women receiving cancer treatments would be more open to talk with her if her husband wasn't there.

She told her husband: "I love you, Honey. And I really appreciate your wanting to go with me and support me. But maybe God's allowing me to have this difficult time so that I can help someone else who's going through the same thing. And who knows? Maybe God has a divine appointment for me while I'm sitting in a chemo-treatment chair!"[5]

DAY 5

God Uses Circumstances

TODAY'S WORD ON WORK

"Great and marvelous are
your deeds,
　　Lord God Almighty.
Just and true are your ways,
　　King of the ages.
Who will not fear you, O Lord,
　　and bring glory to your name?
For you alone are holy.
All nations will come
　　and worship before you,
for your righteous acts have been revealed."
Revelation 15:3-4

RESPONDING PRAYER

Yes, Lord! Your deeds are marvelous. Your righteous acts have been revealed! Bring glory to Your name, Sovereign Lord! Amen.

> **Read and think about "Today's Word on Work" in the margin and respond to the Lord in prayer.**

Jesus watched to see what His Father was doing and then joined the Father where He was at work (see John 5:17-20). That is the way you should function also. Watch to see where God is working around you, and when He shows you, join Him.

But how do you recognize God at work around you? Only God can reveal His activity in such a way that you know He is the Author of it. You need Him to open your spiritual eyes to see what He is doing. You should anticipate that He will do just that. When He shows you His activity, join Him.

1 **Review principle 5 for a life that counts by filling in the blanks. Then record your response to the principle.**
God reveals His mission through His _____,
His _____, wise _____, and
His work in _____ around you.

Principle 5 has taught us that God reveals His mission through His Word, His Spirit, wise counsel, and His work in circumstances around us.

The following guidelines describe ways God works in circumstances around us.

2 **As you read the following insights about how God may work through circumstances around you, underline thoughts that are particularly helpful or meaningful. If you have experienced God working in one of these ways, write a note in the margin. Also write questions you have.**

1. *Often, circumstances help you understand God's timing.* When God has given direction through His Word, His Spirit, and even the wise counsel of others, you may still face the inability to make things happen to accomplish the assignment. Like Moses, who kept coming back to the Lord in Egypt to get His direction in the face of closed doors, you need to stay

in a close relationship with God and be patient for His timing. He may reveal His timing through circumstances—by providing needed resources, by sending a human invitation, by creating an opportunity, or by connecting a Scripture with an opportunity for action. The method God chooses to work is not the key. The key is the confirmation from His Spirit that this is His action.

2. ***Not every open door indicates God's calling.*** Satan can open doors and keep you busy doing something that is not God's plan for your life. Don't depend on opportunities or needs alone to indicate a calling. Otherwise, you will wear yourself out doing everything that comes along. Connect open doors with what God is saying in His Word, in prayer, and through the counsel of others in the body of Christ.

3. ***Not every closed door indicates that the direction is not God's calling.*** Remember the closed door Moses faced in the form of the Red Sea after the people had escaped from Egypt? When an opportunity seems to end, take the circumstance to the Lord in prayer. You cannot know the truth of the circumstance until you have heard from the Truth. Sometimes a closed door confirms that this is not God's plan. Sometimes opposition or hindrance is a divine stall until the timing is right. At other times God may use opposition or a closed door to discipline or correct you before He allows you to move forward. Sometimes, as with Moses and the Israelites at the Red Sea, God wants you to stop and seek His face so that He can perform an unusual work that brings glory to Himself. Again, go to your relationship with God in prayer and seek a word from Him on the truth of the circumstance.

4. ***Connect circumstances with your prayers.*** Too often we pray and never expect an answer. Then, when God's answer comes, we miss it because we are not paying attention. Or we pray and have a preconceived idea of what the answer will look like. Then we miss God's answer because it is different from our expectations. Pay attention to what you are praying and watch the circumstances or activities around you that may be God's work to answer your prayer. Keep your relationship right with God so that your spirit will be keenly sensitive to His "still small voice" (1 Kings 19:12, NKJV).

5. ***Connect unusual circumstances in which a need and the resources that meet the need come together in a short period of time.*** On these occasions, which the world calls coincidences, you can connect a piece of information with a need in order to provide guidance, answer a question, solve a problem, or confirm a direction God has already given. Allowing you to make this connection at precisely the time you need the information may represent God's work around you! For example, read "Just in Time" on the following page.

6. ***Sometimes God may orchestrate circumstances around you that are out of your control.*** You may have no idea why you are going through

NOTES

_____
_____
_____
_____
_____
_____
_____
_____
_____
_____
_____
_____
_____
_____
_____
_____
_____
_____
_____
_____
_____
_____
_____
_____
_____
_____
_____
_____
_____
_____

JUST IN TIME

Hugh Hewitt discovered that the writings of C. S. Lewis in *Mere Christianity* had originally been read as part of a radio show during World War II in Britain. Lewis's writings had greatly influenced Hugh's life. Learning this bit of information at a time he was hosting a late-night radio talk show on KFI in Southern California gave Hugh an idea. "If it was good enough for Lewis, it's good enough for me," Hugh decided. For six straight weeks he did nothing but read *Mere Christianity* on a secular radio station that dominated the Los Angeles market. The results? Six full boards of incoming calls, week after week.[6]

NOTES

_____

_____

_____

_____

_____

_____

_____

_____

_____

_____

"Praise be to the God and Father of our Lord Jesus Christ, the Father of compassion and the God of all comfort, who comforts us in all our troubles, so that we can comfort those in any trouble with the comfort we ourselves have received from God."
2 Corinthians 1:3-4

the experience. It may make no sense to you. God doesn't always tell you in advance what He is doing. Remember Job? He had no idea what was taking place in heavenly realms, but in the end he could see God's handiwork. God may do work this way in order to move you to a job or a location you never would have chosen. He may do things to refine your life and prepare your character for a coming assignment. Only when you look back and see God's fingerprints on the path you've taken or the experience you've had do you realize that God has used the circumstances to direct you to just the right place and time to do His will.

7. ***God may use circumstances to get your attention.*** He may use a season of silence to intensify your seeking Him so that you won't miss the message when it comes. He may use circumstances to correct you or to stop you from going in a direction or to a place you don't belong. He may sensitize you to a need through one circumstance to prepare your heart or experience to minister to needy people in similar circumstances. Sometimes circumstances prepare you for future ministry (see 2 Corinthians 1:3-4). For instance, a person who has lost a child in death and has been comforted by God through the experience is equipped to minister to others who are going down a similar path.

③ **Have you experienced God's comfort in a circumstance that He could now use as a ministry to others? Read these examples and check any that apply to your experience. Then write your own experience.**
❑ Cancer survivor or family member of a cancer patient
❑ Lost a spouse, child, or parent in death
❑ Reared a special-needs child
❑ Victim of a crime
❑ Grew up in the home of an alcoholic or abusive parent
❑ Victim of injustice, oppression, or discrimination
❑ Laid off work for an extended period
❑ Recovered from significant financial debt

My experience: _____

_____

_____

_____

_____

_____

_____

_____

4 **Take a few minutes and review what you have learned in weeks 7 and 8 about the ways God reveals His mission.**

5 **Review principle 5 for a life that counts by filling in the blanks. Then record your response to the principle.**

God reveals His mission through His _____,
His _____, wise _____, and His work
in _____ around you.

Your response: _____

_____

6 **If you sense that God has made clear a part of His mission assignment to you, write a summary of that call.**

_____

_____

_____

_____

_____

_____

7 **Close with a time of prayer. Accept the assignments God has made clear. Ask Him to continue to perfect His will and work in your life.**

____

[1]Authors' interview, summer 2003.

[2]Response to authors' questionnaire, 2003.

[3]Henry Blackaby and Claude V. King, *Experiencing God: Knowing and Doing the Will of God* (Nashville: LifeWay Press, 1990), 14.

[4]Authors' interview, 5 June 2003.

[5]Authors' interview, spring 2003.

[6]Authors' interview, 3 July 2003.

WEEK 9

God Forges, Guides, and Provides

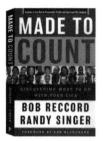

SUPPLEMENTARY READING

Chapters 14–15, *Made to Count*

Born in the Bronx of New York City, Vernadette was reared in an inner-city Puerto Rican barrio by parents without a high-school education. She was one of five children in a poor immigrant family. But they had a massive faith in God!

> Though I began with a weak foundation in many ways, economically, socially, demographically—I can credit what has happened in my life to basically four major things— a faith in a living God, the love of an intact family (however poor), a strong education, and a hard work ethic. I grew up in a home with a message that resonated deep within my heart—I was created by a loving God who found me personally significant. That message created a personal desire to succeed and a faith that would undergird it. That was the catalyst. That was the key. That was the answer!

As you take a bird's-eye view of Vernadette's journey, you can see the impact of this faith. Graduating from high school with honors, she was awarded a scholarship to Yale University. After graduating from Yale, she was accepted at Harvard Law School and later graduated. After marrying, Vernadette Ramirez Broyles began a law practice in Atlanta, Georgia. That practice took her into commercial litigation and then on to an assistant district-attorney position for the Fulton County district attorney's office.

While making an unsuccessful bid for secretary of state in Georgia, Vernadette grew to believe that God was calling her to a special role:

> I feel called to be an advocate … someone willing to speak out for godly principles, godly truths, and God's people. And it really is a call to be an advocate in the public sector, which is basically government. Government touches everything and is desperately in need of a biblical worldview and voice. I read in my Bible that when the righteous prosper, the city rejoices.

It is clear to me from my study of the Word of God that His people are to remain on earth to infiltrate every avenue of life, to be on mission for Him while serving others. God intended His people to infiltrate every sphere of life. We're to be salt—a preserving element—and light, illuminating God's principles in practical living.

Because we need to infiltrate every area of life as we serve our Lord and Master, we need to understand that too often the world considers the church irrelevant, and they would prefer to marginalize us. It's much more difficult to do that when Christians are actually a part of the fabric of everyday living. It is especially difficult to do it when Christians who are a part of that everyday fabric do what they do in the marketplace, in whatever realm, with excellence and high performance.

Today God has opened a door for me to be a national consultant in faith-based initiatives. In addition, the *Atlanta Journal-Constitution* has invited me to write a regular column in which I'm able to inject biblical principles on any subject I'm writing about. My background in politics, law, the district attorney's office, and even Yale and Harvard has been an amazing steppingstone toward being able to bring biblical influence in ways I never dreamed possible.

Vernadette offers a practical perspective on hearing God's call:

• Spend time quieting your life. Look inward to see what God is saying in your heart through His Word and your prayers, interests, passions, and abilities. That should be a clue as to what God created you for.

• Go before God and ask Him to provide clarity about specific direction and timing for your future direction.

• If God seems to be quiet or slow, be careful about taking matters into your own hands and running ahead of God in your way and your timing. If you err in any direction, err in waiting on God rather than running ahead of Him.

• Be willing to lay your hopes and dreams on the altar—to let them die. It's not until you're willing to let your calling die that you can ever be certain that you're not just following your own desires.[1]

Be quiet and look inside. What has God been saying to you through His Word and your prayers, interests, passions, and abilities? Ask God to reveal His mission, direction, and timing for you to be involved in His work. Acknowledge to God your willingness to lay down your hopes, dreams, and plans for His will.

DAY 1

Reviewing God's Process for Making Your Life Count

TODAY'S WORD ON WORK

"His divine power has given us everything we need for life and godliness through our knowledge of him who called us by his own glory and goodness. Through these he has given us his very great and precious promises, so that through them you may participate in the divine nature and escape the corruption in the world caused by evil desires."

2 Peter 1:3-4

RESPONDING PRAYER

Lord, I realize that I am a work in progress. I've got a distance to go to godliness. I pray that You will guide me to take full advantage of Your promises so that I can escape corruption in the world that is caused by evil desires. Transform me to be like You and provide everything I need to follow You. Amen.

> **Read and think about "Today's Word on Work" in the margin and respond to the Lord in prayer.**

As we began our look at eight principles for a life that counts, we divided these eight principles into three stages. Let's review them.

1 **Review the three stages in God's process by filling in the blanks below. If you need to review, look back at pages 17–24.**

1. Get ready: Cultivate Your _____

2. Get set: Receive God's _____

3. Go: Fulfill Your _____

STAGE 1: CULTIVATE YOUR RELATIONSHIP

Principle 1: God prepared a unique plan and calling for your life even before you were born.

Your response: Seek to recognize, understand, and participate in God's plan.

Principle 2: God calls you to a life-changing relationship with Him through Jesus Christ.

Your response: Enter the relationship and submit to God's transforming work in your life.

---

2 **How would you evaluate your life-changing relationship with God? Check your response or write your own.**

❏ a. I certainly haven't arrived, but God has done a good work in my life. I sense a closeness to Him in prayer and worship.

❏ b. God has begun a good work in me, but I'm far from what I need to be. I know Him, but I don't sense much closeness to Him yet.

❏ c. My life doesn't really reflect that my life has changed because of my relationship to God through Jesus Christ. I'm questioning whether I have that relationship at all.

❑ d. Other: _____

_____

Your relationship with the Lord is foundational to all that God wants to do in and through your life. The life-changing part will be a lifelong process. You will never arrive at complete Christlikeness this side of heaven, but you should be making progress. Your closeness to the Lord should increase as you allow Him to transform you more and more into the image of Christ. If you have come to the conclusion that you don't yet have a relationship with God, this would be a good time to turn away from your old, sinful life and turn to Christ by faith in what He has done for you on the cross.

> **Your closeness to the Lord should increase as you allow Him to transform you more and more into the image of Christ.**

As God cleanses and prepares you, He invites you to join His mission to reconcile the people of the world to Himself. He calls you to faithful service and reveals His assignments to you one step at a time.

STAGE 2: RECEIVE GOD'S ASSIGNMENTS

Principle 3: God calls you to partner with Him in a mission that is bigger than you are.

Principle 4: God calls you to be on mission with Him right where you are—starting now.

Principle 5: God reveals His mission through His Word, His Spirit, wise counsel, and His work in circumstances around you.

Your response: Receive God's assignments and begin obeying by faith.

---

③ **Use the following questions to review what God has been revealing about His mission for you.**

a. In what way(s) has God already given you a mission assignment in which you've partnered with Him and experienced Him working through you to bear spiritual fruit?

_____

_____

b. In what ways have you been able to join God's work right where you are in your home, in your neighborhood, at work, or with relatives?

_____

_____

c. Has God been revealing a new mission assignment for you? If so, what do you sense that He's been revealing in the following ways?

• Through His Word: _____

_____

• Through His Spirit: _____

_____

_____

• Through the wise counsel of other Christ-followers: _____

_____

_____

• Through His work in circumstances around you: _____

_____

d. How have you sensed that God is calling you to obey His Great Commission to make disciples of all people, beginning at home and going to the ends of the earth?

_____

_____

_____

_____

4 **If you sense that God has clearly revealed His mission assignment to you for the present time, describe what that mission assignment is and how He has guided you to that understanding.**

_____

_____

_____

_____

5 **Read the following principles and responses in stage 3 and pray that God will help you recognize and fulfill your part of His mission.**

STAGE 3: FULFILL YOUR MISSION

Principle 6: God repeatedly brings you to a crossroads of choice as He forges you for His mission.

Your response: Seek His direction at every crossroads and pay the price for the adjustments required.

Principle 7: God guides and provides for your mission one step at a time.

Your response: Depend on God for guidance and provision as you continue your walk of faith.

Principle 8: When you answer God's call, you experience His pleasure and change your world.

Your response: Obey Him and give Him glory when He accomplishes His work through you.

DAY 2

Principle 6: Crossroads of Choice

Read and think about "Today's Word on Work" in the margin and respond to the Lord in prayer.

Today we begin stage 3 in God's process, "Fulfill Your Mission," by studying principle 6 for a life that counts.

Principle 6:	God repeatedly brings you to a crossroads of choice as He forges you for His mission.
Your response:	Seek His direction at every crossroads and pay the price for the adjustments required.

1 **Read principle 6 several times, giving special attention to the words that are bold and underlined.**

God repeatedly brings you to a crossroads of **choice** as He **forges** you for His mission.

2 **Now personalize the principle by rewriting it. Change *you* to *me*.**

_____

_____

3 **Fill in the blanks with the missing words and review all eight principles for a life that counts.**

1. God prepared a unique _____ and _____
   for your life even _____ you were born.
2. God calls you to a life-changing _____ with Him
   through _____ _____.
3. God calls you to partner with Him in a _____ that
   is _____ than you are.

TODAY'S WORD ON WORK

" 'Seek first the kingdom of God and His righteousness, and all these things shall be added to you.' "
Matthew 6:33, NKJV

RESPONDING PRAYER

Lord, I choose to seek first Your kingdom rule in my heart and life. I want to see Your kingdom come and Your will done. Lord, I long to be filled with Your righteousness. I am going to trust You to be my Provider for everything You know I need. Amen.

4. God calls you to be on _____ with Him right where you are—starting _____ .
5. God reveals His mission through His _____, His _____, wise _____, and His work in _____ around you.
6. God repeatedly brings you to a crossroads of _____ as He _____ you for His mission.
7. God **guides** and **provides** for your mission one step at a time.
8. When you **answer** God's call, you experience His **pleasure** and **change** your world.

Not long after Jesus' crucifixion and resurrection and the Holy Spirit's filling of the church on the day of Pentecost, Peter and John went to the temple to pray. They encountered a beggar asking for money. But instead of money, Peter healed the man in the name of Jesus Christ. When a crowd gathered, Peter took advantage of the opportunity to tell the people about Jesus and to call them to repentance and salvation. "Many who heard the message believed, and the number of men grew to about five thousand" (Acts 4:4).

The priests, the temple guard, and the Sadducees were disturbed by the miraculous healing, the message, and the crowd's response. This group, which had recently crucified Jesus, arrested Peter and John, commanding them not to speak or teach in the name of Jesus. After further threats they let them go.

> This group, which had recently crucified Jesus, arrested Peter and John, commanding them not to speak or teach in the name of Jesus.

4 **A group that had cruelly crucified your leader commands you never again to speak in His name and threatens you. What would most people do?**
❏ a. Leave town and find a safer place to serve.
❏ b. Protect their lives by hiding in fear and keeping their mouths shut.
❏ c. Try to mobilize public opinion in their favor and challenge the leaders to change their orders.
❏ d. Pray for God to wipe out the opposition.
❏ e. Pray for boldness, power, and an increase in the demonstration of God's miraculous powers through Jesus' name.

If you had stood by the cross and watched Jesus die an agonizing death, as John had, or if you had denied with cursing that you even knew Jesus, as Peter had, you would probably choose to leave town, hide in fear, or give up preaching. Human reason, pride, or anger might prompt you to accept the challenge and see if you could mobilize public opinion in your behalf. Few of us would respond as Peter and John did. They prayed for great boldness and asked God, " 'Stretch out your hand to heal and perform miraculous signs and wonders through the name of your holy servant Jesus' " (Acts 4:30). The result? "The place where they were meeting was shaken. And they were all filled with the Holy Spirit and spoke the word of God boldly" (Acts 4:31).

Peter and John came to a time of testing—a spiritual crossroads. Their decision at this point would affect their future witness for Christ. Had they chosen to back down at this point, their future witness would have been weakened or compromised. Instead, they chose to obey Christ's final command to make disciples and to be His witnesses.

(5) **Read their response in Acts 4:19-20 in the margin and underline their decision.**

Filled with God's Holy Spirit and forged by such life-changing choices, Peter and John became pillars of the church who would turn the world upside down. They chose to pay the price to obey.

(6) **Read "Something Worth Dying For" on this page. Then read Luke 9:23 and 1 John 3:16 in the margin and answer the following questions.**
   a. If you want to follow Jesus, what two things are required?
      (1) Deny _____ (2) Take up _____
   b. What did Jesus do for you to demonstrate His love?
   _____

" 'Judge for yourselves whether it is right in God's sight to obey you rather than God. For we cannot help speaking about what we have seen and heard.' "
Acts 4:19-20

"Then [Jesus] said to them all: 'If anyone would come after me, he must deny himself and take up his cross daily and follow me.' "
Luke 9:23

"This is how we know what love is: Jesus Christ laid down his life for us. And we ought to lay down our lives for our brothers."
I John 3:16

SOMETHING WORTH DYING FOR

Sometimes you attend a day-long meeting at which you think somebody tampered with the clock to make its gears go more slowly—one of those meetings at which you cram 30 minutes' worth of work into eight hours.

But this meeting was different. Ideas about college evangelism—how to reach the next generation—flew around the room. We had gathered the experts—campus ministers, youth-group leaders, popular youth speakers. And they didn't disappoint.

Everyone was engaged. Well, almost everyone. Popular youth speaker Louie Giglio, a dynamic speaker and worship leader for the next generation, was conspicuously quiet. He didn't seem to laugh when several of us joked about getting fired from our jobs if we implemented some of the cutting-edge ideas being tossed about the room. "I'd try this," someone might say, "except I don't have a death wish."

At Bob's urging, Louie spoke. "I've just been listening and learning," he said. "This has been great—a ton of good ideas."

"What do you think it will take to reach the next generation?" Bob prodded.

Louie became pensive. And then he nailed us. "Well," he said at last, "we've talked about some ideas we like, but then we've jokingly said that we didn't like them enough to die for them. My read of the next generation is that they're looking for precisely that—something important enough to die for—and they're willing to follow someone who will put his life on the line for that cause."

Ouch! We immediately knew Louie was right. And not just about the next generation. Men and women everywhere, of all ages, have longed to be part of something bigger than themselves. Something permanent. Something that matters. And in their best moments they're willing to lay down their lives for that cause.

It's almost as though God created us that way—which, of course, He did!

The Great Commission—a transcendent cause. Is there anything more worth dying for?

c. What did John say we ought to do in response?

_____

d. Have you come to the point in your spiritual life at which, in your desire to love and follow Jesus, you are willing to give yourself fully to His kingdom purposes? ❏ Yes ❏ No

7 **To conclude today's study, reread the Scriptures in the margin on page 163 and meditate on what obedience might mean in your life and place of service to your King. Talk to the Lord about your love relationship with Him and pray, as Peter and John did, for courage and boldness.**

DAY 3

Crossroads Choices

TODAY'S WORD ON WORK

" 'I have set before you life and death, blessings and curses. Now choose life, so that you and your children may live and that you may love the LORD your God, listen to his voice, and hold fast to him. For the LORD is your life.' "
Deuteronomy 30:19-20

RESPONDING PRAYER

Wow, Lord! You ask me to take up my cross and follow You. You want me to be willing to lay down my life for my brothers. But You command me to choose life. Lord, You are my life—whether I live or die. I choose You. I choose to love You, listen to Your voice, and hold fast to You. I choose to obey You, whatever You ask. Amen.

Read and think about "Today's Word on Work" in the margin and respond to the Lord in prayer.

If you reviewed the stories of biblical heroes like David or Daniel and their climactic victories, you would find that their heroic moments were preceded by choices made at lesser crossroads. Before these heroes were ready for their high-profile stands, God forged and equipped them at a crossroads of choice. Most of the time, the crossroads occurred on an issue of lesser importance in the eyes of the world, but from God's eternal perspective it was a moment that determined a destiny. God says, " 'You have been faithful with a few things; I will put you in charge of many things' " (Matthew 25:21).

1 **Write principle 6 and your response. Look back at page 161 if you need to.**

Principle 6: _____

_____

Your response: _____

_____

This principle teaches that as God prepares us for our mission, He continually bring us to a crossroads of choice. Let's learn some things about the crossroads choice to which God brings us in His work to prepare us for His mission.

The Crossroads Choice Is a Tough Choice

There is nothing easy about choosing God's way at the crossroads. Even the first crossroads we encounter in our spiritual lives is a tough one.

2 **Remember principle 2? It describes the first crossroads we encounter with God. Write that principle here.**

_____

_____

The second principle taught us that God calls us to a life-changing relationship with Him through Jesus Christ. This critical decision, whether to accept Christ or reject Him, is the first and most important spiritual crossroads we encounter. Observe the way Christ described it: " 'Enter through the narrow gate. For wide is the gate and broad is the road that leads to destruction, and many enter through it. But small is the gate and narrow the road that leads to life, and only a few find it' " (Matthew 7:13-14).

This first crossroads isn't the only tough choice we encounter. The road is seldom smooth and broad, with lots of amenities and fellow travelers. Instead, it may be a rocky and forbidding road, with few companions, that we can travel only through the power of the Holy Spirit. We need to determine in advance that when we encounter a crossroads, we will choose God's way no matter what the cost.[2]

The Crossroads Choice Is a Crisis Choice

A crossroads choice often comes without warning, requiring you to make an instinctive decision without a lot of time for planning or seeking counsel. Crossroads choices are choices made from the heart, reflecting the depth of our character.

From David we can learn a key principle that will help us make the right call when the pressure is on:

> I have hidden your word in my heart
> that I might not sin against you (Psalm 119:11).

It wasn't enough for David to be familiar with God's Word or to know it in a vague or general sense. He had hidden God's Word in his heart. David understood the importance of memorizing and meditating on God's Word, of allowing it to become a part of his fiber and being. Over and over again David would meditate on God's law and memorize God's Word until it

> Crossroads choices are choices made from the heart, reflecting the depth of our character.

Blessed are they whose ways are blameless,
    who walk according to the law
    of the Lord.
Blessed are they who keep his statutes
    and seek him with all their heart.
How can a young man keep his way pure?
    By living according to your word.
I have hidden your word in my heart
    that I might not sin against you.
I meditate on your precepts
    and consider your ways.
I delight in your decrees;
    I will not neglect your word.
Your statutes are my delight;
    they are my counselors.
Oh, how I love your law!
    I meditate on it all day long.
I have kept my feet from every evil path
    so that I might obey your word.
Your word is a lamp to my feet
    and a light for my path.
My heart is set on keeping your decrees
    to the very end.
Psalm 119:1-2,9,11,15-16,24,97,101,105,112

"Samuel replied:
    'Does the Lord delight in burnt offerings
    and sacrifices
as much as in obeying the voice
    of the Lord?
    To obey is better than sacrifice,
    and to heed is better than the fat
    of rams.
For rebellion is like the sin of divination,
    and arrogance like the evil of idolatry.
Because you have rejected the word
    of the Lord,
    he has rejected you as king.' "
1 Samuel 15:22-23

became as natural to him as breathing. David not only got into God's Word, but he also made sure that God's Word got into him. When a crossroads came and there was no time to take an eight-week Bible study or to make an appointment with a spiritual counselor, David instinctively knew the right path because God's Word had become a part of who he was.

3 Read in the margin David's verses about God's Word. Underline the ideas or phrases that seem most important to you.

How about you? Are you hiding God's Word in your heart, preparing for the next crossroads of choice? A crossroads choice is usually an unexpected choice. But that doesn't mean you cannot prepare for it. When you go around a turn and a crossroads suddenly appears, God will help you recall the precise verses of Scripture that will illuminate His choice, as long as you've done your part and hidden His Word in your heart ahead of time.

The Crossroads Choice Is a Life-Changing Choice

Certain crossroads choices in life will determine our destiny, changing every step we take thereafter. These choices will make a permanent mark on us, defining who we are and where we're going. And most of the time we're not given a second chance at that crossroads. Ignoring God's path can have lasting, devastating consequences.

In 1 Samuel 15 we read about a mission that God gave to King Saul. In God's eyes Saul's partial obedience was disobedience. God considered it rebellion. Look at what Saul's disobedience cost him.

4 Read 1 Samuel 15:22-23 in the margin and underline the cost of Saul's disobedience.

Saul's choice at this crossroads was a poor one. He didn't understand that obedience is more important to God than sacrifices. His rebellion cost him his position as king.

Your personal history will be affected in unchangeable ways by your choices at certain crossroads. Although God sometimes gives second chances, He has no obligation to do so. Do not lightly shrug off the path that God is directing you to follow. We never know when an act of disobedience at this crossroads will permanently alter our future in negative ways. We have no way of knowing where it will lead or how many lives it will change. We know only this: if it weren't the best path for us, He wouldn't call us to take it. Your choices at crossroads are life-changing.

The Crossroads Choice, Though Sometimes Low-Profile, Is Always a Significant Choice

The choices that determine our destinies are not always the choices that make the headlines. In fact, Satan entices us to walk down the wrong road by claiming: "It's not that big a deal. The other road is tough and dangerous. Don't you think you're entitled, just this once, on such a small matter, to take a road that's smooth and comfortable?"

But to God, there are no insignificant crossroads choices. Each choice shows our character and tests our obedience. Each time we must choose either God's way or our own way. And although the issue might seem insignificant to us at the time, it may be God's way of forging our lives for a time of much greater impact farther down the road.

5 **Read in the margin some crossroads choices you can make to choose God's plan for your life.**

Be patient as God prepares you for your calling. Don't worry if you're struggling to figure out what to do. Pray for insight. Then be ready to show unquestioned obedience at the crossroads, even if it means that a lifelong battle looms ahead.

6 **As you read "Staying in Law to Serve the Lord" on page 168, watch for the times Sealy had to make a choice. Write a C beside each choice.**

7 **Review today's summary ideas and respond to God in prayer.**
- We need to determine in advance that when we encounter a crossroads, we will choose God's way no matter what the cost.
- Crossroads choices are choices made from the heart, reflecting the depth of our character.
- David not only got into God's Word, but he also made sure that God's Word got into him.
- Certain crossroads choices in life will determine our destiny, changing every step we take thereafter.
- To God, there are no insignificant crossroads choices.

CROSSROADS CHOICES
1. Choose to obey God's laws and follow His standards, not your own.
2. Choose to obey the Holy Spirit's leadership every time He speaks.
3. Choose to submit to God's character building in you in order to become like Christ.
4. Choose to pay the price of adjustments and obedience.
5. Choose to take risks as you follow Christ's leadership.
6. Choose right over wrong.
7. Choose to obey in the little things.
8. Choose to walk by faith and not by sight.

STAYING IN LAW TO SERVE THE LORD

Sealy Yates was depressed, and he didn't understand why. Three months earlier he had become a lawyer, something he had dreamed about since the age of 17. The story continues in Sealy's words:

I began to ask myself why I felt that way emotionally. After praying about it for two months, I came to the conclusion that I was far from God, working in the practice of law. He was just nowhere on my daily agenda. No one talked about God, and I did not find Him in my office or in the halls of the courthouse. I was miserable because I had concluded that I had been running from God and His call on my life. I did not want to live the rest of my life running from Him. I had to go where I could find God. I had to go to seminary and prepare for some kind of full-time Christian ministry.

I found myself on the horns of a dilemma. My wife, Susan, had sacrificed and worked so very hard to get us through law school. We now had a child, and she was ready for me to start providing for the family financially. She would be crushed if I told her that I had to leave the legal profession and go to seminary. I just couldn't do that to her. I had no good place to go. I was stuck.

One week at church I learned how to share my faith actively and overtly with others. We were given our first homework assignment: "We want you to pray about your schedule [for tomorrow] and ask the Holy Spirit to show you someone in your day whom you can share the *Four Spiritual Laws* with."

The next day I had an appointment with my very first client. I had worked on firm clients before, but this was the very first person coming into my office for my legal services. I decided this was the person the Lord had put into my schedule so that I could share the *Four Spiritual Laws* and my personal faith in Christ.

After I gave her my best legal advice, I asked her if she had just a few more minutes so that I could share something that might help her in the difficult days ahead. She agreed, and I went to the other side of my desk, sat down next to her, and shared the *Four Spiritual Laws*.

I do not know what happened to that woman spiritually, but I know what happened to me! Sharing the gospel with her in the context of my law practice changed my life forever. I realized that the ministry God had been calling me to was serving Him in the profession I had come to love. My depression was gone, and I never looked back. I finally realized that God had not been in my daily law practice because I hadn't taken Him there. Now God was there because I brought Him into my professional business world.

That was 35 years ago. Today Sealy is a highly successful lawyer and agent. But that's not where he finds his contentment. The most rewarding things he does is to take Christ into every situation in the service of his clients and to share the truth with those he finds on his daily schedule.[3]

DAY 4

Principle 7: God Guides and Provides One Step at a Time

> **Read and think about "Today's Word on Work" in the margin and respond to the Lord in prayer.**

Today we turn to the next principle for a life that counts.

Principle 7:	God guides and provides for your mission one step at a time.
Your response:	Depend on God for guidance and provision as you continue your walk of faith.

① **Read principle 7 several times, giving special attention to the words that are bold and underlined.**

God **guides** and **provides** for your mission **one step** at a time.

② **Now personalize the principle by rewriting it. Change *your* to *my*.**

_____

_____

③ **Fill in the blanks below with the missing words and review all eight principles for a life that counts.**

1. God prepared a unique _____ and _____ for your life even _____ you were born.
2. God calls you to a life-changing _____ with Him through _____ _____.
3. God calls you to partner with Him in a _____ that is _____ than you are.
4. God calls you to be on _____ with Him right where you are—starting _____.
5. God reveals His mission through His _____, His _____, wise _____, and His work in _____ around you.

TODAY'S WORD ON WORK

"The steps of a [good] man are directed and established of the Lord when He delights in his way [and He busies Himself with his every step]."
Psalm 37:23, AMP

RESPONDING PRAYER

Lord, I delight in Your way. I want You to direct every step I take. I will busy myself and follow every step You guide me to take. Use my life for Your honor and glory. Amen.

6. God repeatedly brings you to a crossroads of _____ as He _____ you for His mission.

7. God _____ and _____ for your mission one _____ at a time.

8. When you **answer** God's call, you experience His **pleasure** and **change** your world.

When God reveals His mission to us, He usually gives us the big picture of His purposes. But He seldom gives us a detailed road map of how to get there. He loves us and wants a love relationship with us. If He gave us all the details we needed in advance, we would leave that relationship and go off on our own to get the job done, only to find that we couldn't do it without Him.

God told Moses to lead the Israelites out of Egypt to the promised land. God did not tell him about the 10 plagues or the crisis at the edge of the Red Sea. Instead, at each step along the way, Moses talked to the Lord, and God told him what to do. Had Moses seen in advance all the challenges he would face, he probably would have stayed in the desert herding sheep.

We see a similar pattern with Paul. God told him that his mission was to carry the gospel to the Gentiles, but Paul had to remain in communion with God to know the timing for his mission. At Troas Paul had to wait for further directions. And God normally didn't tell him about the stoning and the beatings that awaited. Paul followed one day at a time as the gospel made its way to Rome and beyond.

God typically gives you the details on a need-to-know basis. If He hasn't revealed the details yet, you don't need to know yet. You don't have to get impatient with God. He is God, and this is His work. He cares more about its accomplishment than you do. As long as your relationship with Him is right and you are ready to obey when He gives you the next step to take, God will not allow you to miss His will (see Philippians 2:13; 4:19). And God's timing is always right.

"God is working in you, giving you the desire to obey him and the power to do what pleases him."
Philippians 2:13, NLT

"My God will meet all your needs according to his glorious riches in Christ Jesus."
Philippians 4:19

4 **Mark each statement *T* for *true* or *F* for *false*.**

___ a. I can expect God to give me all the details about where we are going, how we will get there, and what we will face along the way before I get started.

___ b. Once God gives me an assignment, He expects me to go off and do it on my own.

___ c. God cares more about His work's being done than I do, and He will make sure I don't miss the assignment.

___ d. I must remain in a close relationship with God to receive the day-by-day direction, encouragement, and support I need along the way.

___ e. God gives me only the main objective, and He leaves up to me all the details of how to do it.

God reveals the details as you stay in a close relationship with Him and obey His direction step by step. Did you mark *c* and *d* true and *a*, *b*, and *e* false?

You cannot accomplish God's purposes in your own strength or ways. You need Him and His guidance. But God promises to guide your steps.

5 **Read the Scriptures in the margin. Then match each Scripture reference on the left with the key truth it teaches on the right.**

____ 1. Isaiah 30:21   a. God's ways are very different from human ways.

____ 2. Psalm 32:8   b. God will personally guide you and counsel you in the way you should go.

____ 3. Isaiah 55:9   c. Even when someone makes his own plans, God determines his steps.

____ 4. Proverbs 16:9   d. God's voice will tell you when to turn right or left.

These Scriptures show that God's ways are not like ours; yet he personally guides us in the way we should go. The correct answers are 1. *d*, 2. *b*, 3. *a*, 4. *c*.

Paul sensed an urgency to reach Jerusalem by the day of Pentecost. He explained to church leaders in Ephesus: " 'Compelled by the Spirit, I am going to Jerusalem, not knowing what will happen to me there. I only know that in every city the Holy Spirit warns me that prison and hardships are facing me' " (Acts 20:22-23).

Does that make sense? God sent Paul to Jerusalem so that he could go to prison. Paul's companions didn't think so. They tried their best to change his mind. Yet Paul's imprisonment in Jerusalem eventually led him to the place where he would stand before Caesar himself in Rome and touch the highest levels of world leadership.

God doesn't promise that His guidance will always make sense to us. We can't possibly think on the grand scale that He thinks. Nor does God promise that the steps He orders will be exactly where we would have chosen to go. Sometimes God directs our steps for reasons that we may not understand until we meet Him in heaven. Often God's plan unfolds in a way that makes no sense at the time, but in hindsight His wisdom is obvious to everyone, and we marvel. We need to celebrate those moments, allowing them to buttress our trust and confidence in God's amazingly intricate plan, even when He asks us to take steps we don't understand.

6 **Write principle 7 and your response below. Look back at page 169 if you need to review.**

Principle 7: _____

_____

Your response: _____

_____

"Your ears will hear a word behind you, saying, 'This is the way; walk in it,' when you turn to the right hand and when you turn to the left."
Isaiah 30:21, AMP

"I will instruct you and teach you in the way you should go;
   I will counsel you and watch over you."
Psalm 32:8

" 'As the heavens are higher than the earth, so are my ways higher than your ways and my thoughts than your thoughts.' "
Isaiah 55:9

"In his heart a man plans his course, but the Lord determines his steps."
Proverbs 16:9

7 **Check one box to indicate the extent to which you are depending on God for guidance and provision for your walk of faith.**

❑ I'm afraid I depend on God only when I am in trouble.

❑ I depend on God for direction at every step of my life.

❑ I sometimes forget to depend on God until I have become frustrated trying to do things myself.

8 **Talk to God about your level of dependence on Him. Commit to depend on Him for every step in discovering and carrying out His mission.**

9 **Review these summary ideas and respond to God in prayer.**

- God typically gives you the details on a need-to-know basis.
- He is God, and this is His work. He cares more about its accomplishment than you do.
- As long as your relationship with Him is right and you are ready to obey when He gives you the next step to take, God will not allow you to miss His will.
- God's timing is always right.
- God promises to guide your steps.
- God doesn't promise that His guidance will always make sense to us.

DAY 5

God Provides One Day at a Time

TODAY'S WORD ON WORK

"May the God of peace, who through the blood of the eternal covenant brought back from the dead our Lord Jesus, that great Shepherd of the sheep, equip you with everything good for doing his will, and may he work in us what is pleasing to him, through Jesus Christ, to whom be glory for ever and ever. Amen."

Hebrews 13:20-21

> **Read and think about "Today's Word on Work" in the margin and respond to the Lord in prayer.**

Yesterday we began looking at principle 7 for a life that counts.

1 **Fill in the blanks to complete principle 7 and your response.**

Principle 7: God _____ and _____ for your mission _____ _____ at a time.

Your response: Depend on God for _____ and _____
as you continue your walk of _____.

When God calls you to carry out a mission for Him, He not only guides you one step at a time but also provides everything you need to accomplish His purposes. His provision often comes one day at a time. That's the way God provided manna for the Israelites in the wilderness. And Jesus instructed us to pray, " 'Give us today our daily bread' " (Matthew 6:11). This daily need and provision ensure that we stay in close communion with our Provider.

Not only does God provide material resources, but He provides Himself through His Holy Spirit. Because God's Spirit is within you, He can give you every gift and all the power you need to accomplish the task He has assigned. Sometimes we think about gifts as finite and unchangeable. But the Holy Spirit is the Gift (see Acts 2:38). "To each one the manifestation of the Spirit is given for the common good" (1 Corinthians 12:7). As Paul described spiritual gifts, he said, "All these are the work of one and the same Spirit" (1 Corinthians 12:11). A spiritual gift is God's Holy Spirit working in and through you to accomplish the assignment God has given you.

As our friend Henry Blackaby once said to Bob, "In Scripture God didn't call the qualified; He qualified the called!" When God calls you, you can depend on Him to be everything you need Him to be. God's calling to an assignment is the first thing you need to understand clearly. Then you can trust Him to provide the spiritual gift(s) necessary to accomplish the work.

When God called Moses at the burning bush, Moses argued with the Lord because he didn't see the needed gifts in his life. But once the call was clear, Moses obeyed, and God gave him every gift he needed to accomplish the assignment. When asked for His name, God said to Moses, " 'I AM WHO I AM' " (Exodus 3:14). Essentially, God said, "I will be everything you need Me to be." And He was! God is still the I AM. You can trust Him to be everything you need Him to be.

2 **What one gift does God give to everyone who enters a faith relationship with Jesus Christ? Check one.**
❑ a. The gift of preaching
❑ b. The gift of hospitality
❑ c. The gift of the Holy Spirit
❑ d. The gift of administration
❑ e. The gift of healing

Once God has given you His Holy Spirit, He can manifest Himself and His power to accomplish every mission assignment He gives you. Sometimes God calls you to an assignment that requires a similar gift to one you already have. But be careful not to build a box around God and tell Him that He can give

RESPONDING PRAYER

This is my prayer too, Lord. You are the One who possesses resurrection power. I need You to equip me with everything good for doing Your will. Work in and through me what is pleasing to You for Your glory through Jesus Christ. Amen.

"Peter replied, 'Repent and be baptized, every one of you, in the name of Jesus Christ for the forgiveness of your sins. And you will receive the *gift of the Holy Spirit.*' "
Acts 2:38, italics added

you only an assignment that requires the same gifts He has used before. As God did with Moses, He may call you to an assignment that will require you to walk with Him by faith in new experiences of His Spirit. You can trust Him to be all you need.

According to Scripture, "Without faith it is impossible to please God, because anyone who comes to him must believe that he exists and that he rewards those who earnestly seek him" (Hebrews 11:6). Faith is trusting God when your human senses cannot see the way. "Faith is being sure of what we hope for and certain of what we do not see" (Hebrews 11:1). Faith requires that you—

- trust that God is present even when you do not sense that He is near;
- trust in God's purpose even when you don't understand or when the objective seems impossible;
- trust in God's protection when you are under attack and want to turn to purely human means for protection;
- trust in God's provision when you do not see where the resources (human and/or material) or abilities will come from;
- trust in God's ways even when your human reason would call the ways foolish or tell you to do things differently.

> **Faith is trusting God when your human senses cannot see the way.**

3 **As you think about your work life, in which of the following areas do you seem to have difficulty trusting God? Check all that apply.**

☐ a. I have trouble believing that God is present in my workplace.

☐ b. I have trouble believing that God can change and redeem the people and the environment where I work.

☐ c. I have trouble believing that God will protect me when I do what is right.

☐ d. I have trouble believing that God will provide for my needs and that He will enable me to accomplish His work.

☐ e. I have trouble believing that God's ways are the right ways to accomplish kingdom work.

☐ f. Actually, I have trouble believing that God cares about my workplace and will do something of value through me.

If you find yourself weak in faith, keep the following truths in mind.

1. *A little faith is enough to accomplish much.* Jesus said: " 'I tell you the truth, if you have faith as small as a mustard seed, you can say to this mountain, "Move from here to there" and it will move. Nothing will be impossible for you' " (Matthew 17:20). The amount of your faith is not the problem. Either you have faith, or you practice unbelief. With a little faith you can see mountains move.

2. *When your faith is weak, you can turn to God for help.* On one occasion the disciples asked Jesus, " 'Increase our faith!' " (Luke 17:5). You too can

ask Christ to increase your faith. A father once asked Jesus to heal his demon-possessed son. Jesus said, " 'Everything is possible for him who believes' " (Mark 9:23). The father needed faith, but he realized that his faith was weak. So he said, " 'I do believe; help me overcome my unbelief!' " (Mark 9:24). Jesus helped him and then healed his son. If your faith is weak, you can ask Christ to help you overcome your unbelief.

3. ***Christ works greater things through those who trust Him.*** Jesus said to His disciples: " 'Anyone who has faith in me will do what I have been doing. He will do even greater things than these, because I am going to the Father. And I will do whatever you ask in my name, so that the Son may bring glory to the Father. You may ask me for anything in my name, and I will do it' " (John 14:12-14).

4. ***Christ begins and perfects your faith.*** When you surrender to Him as Lord and fix your attention on Him, Christ strengthens your faith. The writer of Hebrews said it this way: "Let us fix our eyes on Jesus, the author and perfecter of our faith" (Hebrews 12:2).

④ **Review principle 7 and your response in the margin.**

⑤ **Review today's summary ideas and respond to God in prayer. Talk to Him particularly about your faith in His guidance and provision for each step in His plan for you.**
- Because God's Spirit is within you, He can give you every gift and all the power you need to accomplish the task He has assigned.
- "God didn't call the qualified; He qualified the called!"
- When God calls you, you can depend on Him to be everything you need Him to be.
- Faith is trusting God when your human senses cannot see the way.
- A little faith is enough to accomplish much.
- When your faith is weak, you can turn to God for help.
- Christ works greater things through those who trust Him.
- Christ begins and perfects your faith.

PRINCIPLE 7
God guides and provides for your mission one step at a time.

YOUR RESPONSE
Depend on God for guidance and provision as you continue your walk of faith.

---

[1]Authors' interview, 4 April 2003.
[2]For a more thorough discussion, see Bob Reccord, *Forged by Fire* (Nashville: Broadman & Holman, 2000).
[3]Authors' interview, 10 June 2003.

WEEK 10

God Makes Your Life Count

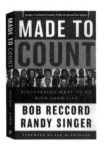

THIS WEEK'S SUPPLEMENTARY READING
Chapters 16–18, *Made to Count*

Fred's parents were gravely disappointed when he told them he wanted to be in television. They believed he should be a minister. Fred was hearing a call, though he wasn't sure how it could be that God wanted him to go into television instead of to seminary. He answered the call and, after graduating from college in 1951, moved to New York to help other people who also felt called to work in television.

Remembering his parents' desire and encouragement for seminary, Fred attended classes during his lunch breaks from television. It took him eight years to finish seminary, but they were eight wonderfully deepening years of his message and personality. Fred's program, at first titled "Misterogers," was only 15 minutes, relying heavily on the use of puppets. But the show grew into "Mr. Rogers' Neighborhood" and went national in 1968 with the theme song "It's a Beautiful Day in the Neighborhood" emanating from every broadcast.

Fred admired the way television began with wholesome, healthy messages, but the larger the audience grew and the greater the amount of money involved, the more the values began to implode. That very dilemma stirred Fred to explore the idea of developing a children's program. He didn't like the values being reflected through the screen and being brought into living rooms. So rather than sit back and curse the darkness, Fred Rogers lit a candle.

An ordained Presbyterian minister, Fred went on to get his master's degree in child development. All along the way, he was greatly troubled that children seemed to be catapulted into the adult world of demanding schedules, busy agendas, many activities, and very little time for quiet character development. His lanky and unshakable presence, together with children's songs and animated puppet fantasies, brought character qualities alive to children by teaching them what's really important in life. His daily promise was "Yes, I'll be

your neighbor!" And millions of children found tremendous comfort and security in those words.

Every weekday Fred would shuffle into his "house," take off his suit jacket and don a sweater, change his shoes from dress shoes to canvas Dockers, and welcome viewers to his neighborhood!

For 35 years Fred had an impact on the world of families as he hosted "Mr. Rogers' Neighborhood" on PBS stations across North America. Before his death from stomach cancer at age 74, Fred had received every major television award, from Emmys to the Peabody. Four years before his death, he was inducted into the Broadcasting Hall of Fame.

Day after day Fred gave children the opportunity to be children. He never forced them into adult topics or hurried childhood. He let them enjoy the journey of just being kids.

More than 870 episodes aired in millions of homes. Fred declared about his desire to influence an audience with the healthy principles and values grounded in Scripture: "Every time I walk into the studio I say to myself [as a prayer], 'Let some word that is heard be Yours.' The Holy Spirit translates our best efforts into what needs to be

communicated to that person in his or her place of need. The longer I live, the more I know it's true."

Each day millions of children watch "Mr. Rogers' Neighborhood" as episodes are rebroadcast. Their parents, who watched Fred when they were children, find themselves delightedly humming along, "It's a Beautiful Day in the Neighborhood."[1]

Maybe there's an area of the media that you don't like, and you find it easier to criticize what's wrong than to step forward and do something positive. Has God given you gifts and talents that you could use in the media or to influence those who work in the media? Start praying today that God will use you to make a difference in this critical realm of our culture.

Pray now that God will bring about a spiritual transformation in the lives of those involved in various types of media. Pray for those who follow Christ to influence those around them through a godly lifestyle and a bold and timely witness. Ask God how He might want you involved.

DAY 1

Your Divine Network

TODAY'S WORD ON WORK

"To him who is able to do immeasurably more than all we ask or imagine, according to his power that is at work within us, to him be glory in the church and in Christ Jesus throughout all generations, for ever and ever! Amen."
Ephesians 3:20-21

RESPONDING PRAYER

Lord, how exciting for me to be a part of Your church, where You can do more than I can imagine. Please help me and my church become a church that will bring You glory because of the power You manifest in and through us to the world. Amen.

> **Read and think about "Today's Word on Work" in the margin and respond to the Lord in prayer.**

You are part of a team, not a loner. You are one member of the body of Christ in your local church, and you are a part of the larger kingdom of Christ. When a body of Christ is healthy, every member does his or her mission assignment in cooperation with the rest of the body. Assignments in the body are different for different people. Some are more public, while others are unseen ministries. Some may work on the front lines of ministry, and others may serve in supportive roles through prayer, giving, or other forms of service. Some work assignments may lay a foundation for someone else to come along and complete the work.

Paul described assignments in the body of Christ this way: "Neither he who plants nor he who waters is anything, but only God, who makes things grow. The man who plants and the man who waters have one purpose, and each will be rewarded according to his own labor. For we are God's fellow workers" (1 Corinthians 3:7-9).

Because you are part of a team and not a loner, assignments in the kingdom are different for different people. Some may plow, plant, water, or harvest. As God's fellow workers, the part of the process you are assigned doesn't matter. God is the One who gets the credit. He will reward you for your labor. You might call this team your divine network.

① 📖 **Turn to "Identifying My Divine Network" on pages 207-8 in the Made to Count Tool Kit. Read and work through the activities to begin identifying the people God may place in a divine network with you. Place a check here when you finish. ❑**

A local church is the body of Christ functioning in the world. Christ's commission to the church was to go into all the world. This assignment is not just for missionaries and Tuesday-night visitation. Imagine the impact for the kingdom if every church member saw his or her workplace as a personal mission field. God wants all members of the body to function where He has placed them so that the whole body will be built up. Think of your church as a diplomatic corps with ambassadors to the high school, the hospital, the manufacturing plant, restaurants, government agencies, the unemployment office, and every other workplace in your community.

Let's look at several ways your church can facilitate or support your work in your mission field.

2 **As you read the following suggestions of ways your church can facilitate or support your work in your mission field, underline particularly helpful ideas. In the margin jot down other ideas that come to mind.**

1. Your church can equip every member to understand his or her mission for Christ's kingdom work. It can also encourage members to join God on mission in their respective workplaces. Our prayer is that this *Life Planner* will help.

2. Pastors can preach sermons about applying kingdom principles in the workplace. He would probably welcome your questions or suggestions for sermon topics that are practical for your work life as a Christ-follower.

3. Study, discussion, and support groups can provide a forum for problem solving and decision making in kingdom ways. Your small group could suggest ways your church can provide practical help and encouragement for workplace missionaries.

4. Testimony times can encourage Christ-followers and glorify God as unordained daily-life ministers share the results of God's activity in their lives and workplaces.

5. The church can commission teams of lay missionaries to carry the light of the gospel to the local factory or any other business or work environment. Consider periodically having a commissioning service for those completing a study of *Made to Count Life Planner*. Commission schoolteachers, government employees, service-industry employees, attorneys, and others.

6. Church members can function as a house of prayer to support lay missionaries in their work. Just as Paul asked for prayer, marketplace missionaries need prayer too.

The ways your church can support the missions of Christ-followers are almost endless. Christ Himself, as the Head of your church, can direct you to join Him in kingdom purposes in ways you would never think of. We challenge you to seek the Lord's directions about involving more Christ-followers in studies of *Made to Count Life Planner*. Then do everything He guides you to do.

NOTES

_____

_____

_____

_____

_____

_____

_____

_____

_____

_____

_____

_____

_____

_____

_____

_____

_____

_____

_____

_____

_____

_____

_____

(3) **Review your notes and the following summary ideas. Then spend time praying for your church, your small group, and your pastor and staff.**

- You are one member of the body of Christ in your local church, and you are a part of the larger kingdom of Christ.
- When a body of Christ is healthy, every member does his or her mission assignment in cooperation with the rest of the body.
- Assignments in the body are different for different people.
- Imagine the impact for the kingdom if every church member saw his or her workplace as a personal mission field.
- God wants all members of the body to function where He has placed them so that the whole body will be built up.
- Christ Himself, as the Head of your church, can direct you to join Him in kingdom purposes in ways you would never think of.

DAY 2

Principle 8:
Changing Your World

TODAY'S WORD ON WORK

"Stand firm. Let nothing move you. Always give yourselves fully to the work of the Lord, because you know that your labor in the Lord is not in vain."
I Corinthians 15:58

Read and think about "Today's Word on Work" in the margin and respond to the Lord in prayer.

Today we come to the last of the eight principles for a life that counts.

Principle 8:	When you answer God's call, you experience His pleasure and change your world.
Your response:	Obey Him and give Him glory when He accomplishes His work through you.

RESPONDING PRAYER

King Jesus, enable me to know Your will clearly and empower me to do it fully. Please help me stand firm in my service to You and Your kingdom. I trust Your Word that my labor in You will not be in vain. Thank You! Amen.

1 **Read principle 8 several times, giving special attention to the words that are bold and underlined.**

When you **<u>answer</u>** God's call, you experience His **<u>pleasure</u>** and **<u>change</u>** your world.

2 **Now personalize the principle by rewriting it. Change *you* to *I* and *your* to *my*.**

_____

_____

3 **Fill in the blanks below with the missing words and review all eight principles for a life that counts.**

1. God prepared a unique _____ and _____ for your life even _____ you were born.

2. God calls you to a life-changing _____ with Him through _____ _____.

3. God calls you to partner with Him in a _____ that is _____ than you are.

4. God calls you to be on _____ with Him right where you are—starting _____.

5. God reveals His mission through His _____, His _____, wise _____, and His work in _____ around you.

6. God repeatedly brings you to a crossroads of _____ as He _____ you for His mission.

7. God _____ and _____ for your mission one _____ at a time.

8. When you _____ God's call, you experience His _____ and _____ your world.

4 **Review the eight principles. Based on what you sense that God has been doing in your life during this study, where are you in this process? Write the number of the principle: _____**

Based on what you sense that God has been doing in your life during this study, where are you in this process?

God wants to change the world. He wants people to get right with Him everywhere. If our world is going to change, we need an explosion of Christ-followers who follow God's call into our institutions of higher education, into the practice of law, into journalism, and into politics. We need Christ-followers who follow His call to work in Hollywood, on Broadway, on Madison Avenue, and on Wall Street. As we've seen, God is the only One who has the right to tell you where He wants you to serve. So don't shy away from mission assignments to these places. They are mission fields. A call to these fields honors God just as much as a call to China or India.

These professions—media, art, law, and finance—have an enormous impact on our culture. A call into any of these professions is not more valuable in God's eyes, but a Christ-follower in one of these professions has opportunities to change cultural dynamics that are dramatically leading our nation away from Christ. Currently, the professions that have the greatest impact on our culture are influenced by Christ-followers the least.

5 **Spend an extended time today praying that God will call people into His service in the places that will influence our world the most. Talk to Him about your role in that work.**

DAY 3

Living to Please God

TODAY'S WORD ON WORK

"We make it our goal to please Him."
2 Corinthians 5:9

"We are not trying to please men but God."
I Thessalonians 2:4

RESPONDING PRAYER

Father, I want to please You. I confess that I am often tempted to please people, but I pray that You will give me the strength and courage to obey You always. Continue to reveal to me what I can do to please You most. Amen.

> **Read and think about "Today's Word on Work" in the margin and respond to the Lord in prayer.**

Earlier we learned that God created Paul for a divine purpose. When Paul went into the sophisticated culture of Athens, he employed a threefold strategy. First, he preached in the synagogues. Then he reasoned in the marketplace daily with those who happened to be there. And third, he was given an opportunity to speak on Mars Hill to the cultural influencers, a group of philosophers—the gatekeepers in Athens. Paul shared the gospel with them, and Scripture records that "some mocked," others wanted to hear him again, while still others "joined him and believed" (Acts 17:32-34, NKJV).

1. **Pause to pray that God will call people into places of influence in our world and will give them His strategy for reaching those who will believe.**

2. **Fill in the blanks to complete principle 8 for a life that counts.**

   When you _____ God's call, you experience His _____ and _____ your world.

When we answer God's call, we experience His pleasure. Others may not understand that call, but this should never keep us from pursuing it. Paul said, "We make it our goal to please Him" (2 Corinthians 5:9) and "We are not trying to please men but God, who tests our hearts" (1 Thessalonians 2:4). Nothing pleases God more than watching you obediently pursue His mission for your life.

3. **Read the Scriptures in the margin. Circle the words *please* or *pleasing*. Underline the words describing what is pleasing or not pleasing to God.**

4. **Read "Running to Please God" on this page. If you can remember a time when you had to choose to please either people or God, describe it below. How did you respond?**

   _____

   _____

   _____

"I urge you, brothers, in view of God's mercy, to offer your bodies as living sacrifices, holy and pleasing to God. ... Do not conform any longer to the pattern of this world, but be transformed by the renewing of your mind. Then you will be able to test and approve what God's will is—his good, pleasing and perfect will." Romans 12:1-2

"A man reaps what he sows. The one who sows to please his sinful nature, from that nature will reap destruction; the one who sows to please the Spirit, from the Spirit will reap eternal life." Galatians 6:7-8

"We instructed you how to live in order to please God. ... You know what instructions we gave you by the authority of the Lord Jesus. It is God's will that you should be sanctified: that you should avoid sexual immorality; that each of you should learn to control his own body in a way that is holy and honorable." 1 Thessalonians 4:1-4

RUNNING TO PLEASE GOD

Scottish runner Eric Liddell was one of the best athletes ever to represent Great Britain in the Olympic games. A trained sprinter, Eric faced a crossroads of choice when he discovered that the finals for the one-hundred-meter dash in the 1924 Games in Paris would be held on Sunday. He made history when he refused to run in his main Olympic event for religious reasons and then shocked everyone by winning gold in the much longer four-hundred-meter dash, an event held on a different day.

Eric's story is chronicled in the Academy Award-winning film *Chariots of Fire*. A poignant scene in the movie occurs when Eric decides that he will join his parents on the mission field in China but that he first wants to train for and run in the Olympics. He knows this decision will be difficult for his sister to accept, because she believes that Eric should immediately depart for the mission field. As the two walk along the Scotland hillside, Eric takes her hands and says: "Jenny, you've got to understand. I believe that God made me for a purpose—for China. But He also made me fast, and when I run, I feel His pleasure. To give it up would be to hold Him in contempt. You were right; it's not just fun. To win is to honor Him."

Jenny silently walked away, displaying her disapproval, but Eric would not be deterred. His decision to honor God rather than men at the Olympics made headlines around the world, serving as a powerful testimony and example to others. Then Eric went to China and gave his life there in service to his King—Jesus Christ.

⑤ *Chariots of Fire* is a powerful testimony of Eric Liddell's passion to serve Christ and his willingness to make difficult choices to please the Lord. Plan to rent the movie and watch it with your family or with your small group. Ask the Lord to guide you to make a stand for right and to bring Him pleasure and honor.

⑥ What is your response to principle 8? See page 180 if you need a reminder.

_____

_____

⑦ Tell the Lord that you want to please Him. Ask forgiveness for times when you have made wrong choices. Pledge your faithfulness to Him. Pray the pray from Hebrews 13:20-21 in the margin for yourself and your small group.

"May the God of peace, who through the blood of the eternal covenant brought back from the dead our Lord Jesus, that great Shepherd of the sheep, equip you with everything good for doing his will, and may he work in us what is pleasing to him, through Jesus Christ, to whom be glory for ever and ever. Amen."
Hebrews 13:20-21

DAY 4

God Changes Your World

TODAY'S WORD ON WORK

" 'I send you out as sheep in the midst of wolves. Therefore be wise as serpents and harmless as doves.' "
Matthew 10:16, NKJV

RESPONDING PRAYER

Lord, that's a little bit scary. But I know that You are always with me. I need Your help to be gentle and wise in a world that doesn't want to follow Your ways or live by Your laws. Use me to make a difference in that world for Your honor and glory. Amen.

> **Read and think about "Today's Word on Work" in the margin and respond to the Lord in prayer.**

No one has had a more profound impact on the world than Jesus Christ. Yet in His humility He acknowledged that the glory belongs to His Father.

① Read the three Scriptures in the margin on page 185 and underline the words Jesus used to direct credit and glory to His Father.

Just as God the Father worked through His Son Jesus, God will work through you by His indwelling Holy Spirit. When you get to have a part in changing your world for eternal and spiritual purposes, God will be the One who does it.

2 **Fill in the blanks to review principle 8 for a life that counts. Also complete your response.**

Principle 8: When you _____ God's call, you experience His _____ and _____ your world.

Your response: _____ Him and give Him _____ when He accomplishes His work through you.

God created you and called you to a life-changing relationship with Him. He reveals His mission and invites you to be a part of it. Then He gives His Holy Spirit, a Gift of Christ, to accomplish things through you that you cannot do alone. Jesus said, " 'Apart from me you can do nothing' " (John 15:5). But when Christ works through you, He bears fruit through you.

3 **When you play a part in changing your world, which of the following is true? Check one.**
- ❏ a. I did it! I came up with a good plan, worked hard, used my best skills, and pulled it off.
- ❏ b. God did it. His wisdom, His guidance, and His gifts worked through me to do something I couldn't have done without Him. But what an adventure to be a part!

Did you check *b?* That is the way God works. You cannot change the world for kingdom good or make an eternal difference unless God does His work through you.

4 **Read "Bringing Change to Hollywood" on page 186. Then think about your corner of the world. What needs to change for good and for God where you are? In the margin, list some things that need to change in your community, at your workplace, in your profession, in your church, and in your home.**

5 **Use your list to begin praying. Pray that God will call people to make a difference in these places where change is needed. Give God permission to call you. Ask Him for wisdom and a strategy. If He speaks, obey Him and experience His pleasure.**

"Jesus answered them and said, 'My doctrine is not Mine, but His who sent Me.' " John 7:16, NKJV

"Jesus said to them, 'When you lift up the Son of Man, then you will know that I am He, and that I do nothing of Myself; but as My Father taught Me, I speak these things.' " John 8:28, NKJV

" 'Do you not believe that I am in the Father, and the Father in Me? The words that I speak to you I do not speak on My own authority; but the Father who dwells in Me does the works.' " John 14:10, NKJV

CHANGES IN MY WORLD

_____
_____
_____
_____
_____
_____
_____
_____
_____
_____
_____
_____
_____

BRINGING CHANGE TO HOLLYWOOD

Ted Baehr grew up around the studios and back lots of Hollywood, where his dad was an actor. Ted expected to become a well-known producer or a famous actor. Instead, his world was turned upside down at age 27 when he met a Man who radically changed his life—Jesus Christ.

Instead of acting or producing, Ted became involved in the financial side of Hollywood. After Ted had financed five feature films, God guided him in a direction he had never anticipated. Ted realized that those who really control Hollywood are not the studio moguls, the directors/producers, or even the actors. When he discovered that the ones who control Hollywood are the ticket-buying consumers, Ted knew that the best way to have an impact on box-office profits was to influence the quality of films and programs being produced.

Ted published *Ted Baehr's Movieguide and Media-Wise Family Tool Kit* to help moviegoing families make informed decisions about what they view. He established a special awards night for movies and television that reinforce Judeo-Christian values and ethics. The Faith & Value Awards Gala honors TV shows such as *Walker, Texas Ranger* and *Seventh Heaven* and movies such as *The Prince of Egypt, Gods and Generals,* and *Parent Trap 2.*

As a result, Ted has forged relationships in Hollywood that open doors for him to share Christ. Some in Hollywood say that successful films must filled with violence and sex. The bottom line contradicts this idea. Ironically, the most financially successful studio has not compromised its principles at all. Pixar has rolled out hit after hit, including *Toy Story; Toy Story 2; Monsters, Inc.;* and *A Bug's Life,* always keeping the movies clean and wholesome. Pixar's managers intend to keep them that way because Ted has helped them understand where mainstream society's heart is and why clean entertainment draws people to the movies.

Ted is also frequently invited to review scripts to judge their acceptability to the general public. "I've often said: 'You don't want to make this film. How many empty seats do you want in the theaters? You've got to change it, or it will never fly at the box office.' And the amazing thing is, they're starting to listen!"[2]

Ted grew up in Hollywood. When he came to faith in Christ, he began serving the Lord where he was. No matter where you live, God can use you to change your world for His purposes.

DAY 5

Find Us Faithful

Read and think about "Today's Word on Work" in the margin and respond to the Lord in prayer.

In Matthew 25 Jesus told a parable about a master who was going on a long journey. The master entrusted his property to His servants so that they could carry on his work in his absence. One day the master returned and required an accounting. He commended his faithful servant with the words recorded in Today's Word on Work.

1 **What do you think Jesus was teaching through this parable?**

_____

_____

_____

The master who was going on a long journey is like Jesus, who was going to heaven. As the master entrusted his property and responsibilities to His servants during his absence, Jesus entrusts us with His Spirit and His gifts to do His work. May Jesus find us faithful when He returns!

2 **Review this study by completing all eight principles for a life that counts.**

1. God prepared a unique _____ and _____ for your life even _____ you were born.

2. God calls you to a life-changing _____ with Him through _____ _____.

3. God calls you to partner with Him in a _____ that is _____ than you are.

4. God calls you to be on _____ with Him right where you are—starting _____.

5. God reveals His mission through His _____, His _____, wise _____, and His work in _____ around you.

6. God repeatedly brings you to a crossroads of _____ as He _____ you for His mission.

TODAY'S WORD ON WORK

" 'His lord said to him, "Well done, good and faithful servant; you were faithful over a few things, I will make you ruler over many things. Enter into the joy of your lord." ' "
Matthew 25:21, NKJV

RESPONDING PRAYER

Jesus, one day I want to hear those words from You. I want to be a faithful servant who has accomplished what pleases You. I want to enter Your joy. Help me, Lord, to discover the mission You have for me. Guide and provide for me to accomplish it to change my world for Your glory. Amen.

7. God _____ and _____ for your mission one _____ at a time.

8. When you _____ God's call, you experience His _____ and _____ your world.

③ Answer the following questions as you think about your experience in this study.

a. What has been the most meaningful insight you have gained?

_____

_____

_____

_____

b. What has changed in your relationship with the Lord? _____

_____

_____

_____

_____

c. What has God revealed to you about His mission where you are?

_____

_____

_____

_____

d. What have you begun to do in response to what God has shown you?

_____

_____

_____

_____

e. What crossroads of choice have you experienced or do you currently face?

_____

_____

_____

_____

f. How has God forged you for His mission? _____

_____

_____

_____

_____

> **What has God revealed to you about His mission where you are?**

g. How has God guided and provided for you as you have begun to partner with Him in His mission?

_____

_____

_____

_____

4 **Look over this list and begin praying about what the Lord may want you to do next to join Him on mission.**

❑ a. Continue meeting and praying with my small group to encourage and counsel one another.

❑ b. Start another *Made to Count* small group to help other people in my church discover God's purpose for them.

❑ c. Start another small group for my coworkers or for people in my profession to influence my workplace or profession for Christ.

❑ d. Begin introducing people to Jesus Christ by bringing one person to faith this year.

❑ e. Work with my pastor and church's approval to host a meeting in my home or community about starting a new church, as Aquila and Priscilla did.

❑ f. Other: _____

_____

_____

5 **Read principle 8 and your response in the margin. Give glory to God for the ways He has worked in and through you during this study. Tell Him that you are ready to answer His call. Pray for His guidance as you continue seeking His will for your life.**

---

[1]Compiled from public tributes.
[2]Authors' interview.

PRINCIPLE 8
When you answer God's call, you experience His pleasure and change your world.

YOUR RESPONSE
Obey Him and give Him glory when He accomplishes His work through you.

My Faith at Work Assessment

> **Describe your work and your work environment by completing the activities and answering the questions. If your workplace varies or if you have more than one job, describe your most typical workplace or type of work or the job in which you spend the most time. Or copy this assessment to evaluate multiple workplaces.**

1. What is your job title? _____

2. In one sentence state the primary nature or objective of your work. _____

   _____

   _____

3. If your company has a mission statement, what is it? _____

   _____

   _____

4. Describe the physical and social environments of your workplace. _____

   _____

   _____

   _____

5. Based on your knowledge of your coworkers, how would you describe their relationships with Jesus Christ?
   ❑ a. Most are followers of Christ.
   ❑ b. Many are followers of Christ.
   ❑ c. Few are followers of Christ.
   ❑ d. As far as I know, I am the only follower of Christ.
   ❑ e. I don't know much about their spiritual lives.

6. If an outside inspector observed persons in your kind of work, what would he observe that would most clearly distinguish a Christian worker (or Christ-follower) from one who does not have a relationship with Jesus Christ? List characteristics in the columns below.

Christian Worker   **Non-Christian Worker**

_____   _____

_____   _____

_____   _____

_____   _____

7. What are the most common practices or activities in your workplace or profession that do not reflect Christlike attitudes or behaviors?

_____

_____

8. What are the most common practices or activities in your workplace or profession that reflect Christlike attitudes or behaviors?

_____

_____

9. Who are some of the most obvious followers of Christ in your workplace, if any?

_____   _____

_____   _____

10. How do other employees view this person? _____

_____

11. In your opinion, which person, if any, most exemplifies Christlike behavior in your workplace or profession?

_____

12. What would you say is the greatest obstacle to your living your faith in your work or workplace?

_____

_____

13. In your opinion, which of the following activities, attitudes, or characteristics would most clearly identify a person who truly lives his faith in his work? If you have another idea, write your own.

❑ Honesty
❑ Integrity
❑ Excellence
❑ Productivity
❑ Wisdom in making decisions

❑ Praying for guidance
❑ Taking a stand for right, morality, ethics
❑ Applying biblical principles to decision making
❑ Sharing a verbal witness of Christ
❑ Other: _____

14. What action, attitude, or behavior have you observed from someone who claims to be a Christ-follower that was most contrary to the true Spirit of Christ? How did it make you feel?

_____

_____

15. If God drew only one person in your profession or workplace to Christ and the person really lived for Christ, which person would have the greatest influence on your work environment? Why do you think so?

_____

_____

16. If you could change only one thing about your work or workplace to make it a more Christlike activity or environment, what would you change?

_____

_____

17. If you could change several things about your work or workplace to make it a more Christlike activity or environment, what would you change?

_____

_____

18. Go back through the previous list and prioritize these changes. Write *1* beside the most important change needed, *2* beside the second most important change needed, and so on.

19. Circle a number to rate your knowledge of God's Word and His teachings about living your faith in your workplace or career. 1 = no knowledge and 10 = well informed.

   1   2   3   4   5   6   7   8   9   10

20. What are positive aspects of your work and workplace that encourage you to apply your faith at work?

\
\

21. What are negative aspects of your work and workplace that hinder or discourage you from applying your faith at work?

\
\

22. In what ways have you attempted to apply your faith to your work or in your workplace? Describe one or more experiences, using extra paper if necessary.

\
\

23. Did you experience a positive or negative response when you applied your faith to your work or in your workplace? Write a plus sign (+) beside the positive experiences above and a minus sign (-) beside the negative ones.

24. What do you believe are the most positive opportunities to live your faith in your work and your workplace?

\
\

25. If a faith-at-work consultant were available, what questions would you like to have answered about living your faith in your workplace or profession?

\
\

My Personal Prayer Guide

PRAYER FOR CLEANSING
Use the following questions to guide your personal prayer times about your spiritual life. Examine yourself before the Lord and allow Him to cleanse you for usefulness to His kingdom.

1. What are areas of sin in my life that hinder my usefulness for Your kingdom?

2. What commands have You given to me in Scripture or through prayer that I have failed to obey?

3. Have I offended anyone or any group and failed to ask for forgiveness and seek reconciliation?

4. Am I holding on to unforgiveness or bitterness toward anyone or any group who has offended or wounded me whom I need to forgive and let go of the offense?

5. Do I have any relationships with people, groups, or organizations that are impure or displeasing to You?

6. Have I become so tolerant that by accepting certain things or people, I have become a participant in sin?

7. What idols of the heart are present in my life (see Ezekiel 14:3)? Do I love something or someone too much, hindering my wholehearted love for You (see Matthew 22:37)? Has anything become a false god to me? Consider the following possibilities. None are necessarily bad or evil in themselves. The question is whether you love them too much. Do they get in the way of your loving God with all your heart?
   • Hobbies, collections
   • Computer games
   • Sports, recreation
   • Houses, real estate, time shares
   • Career, job
   • Vacations, trips, camping, travel
   • Money, material things, stocks, bonds, market accounts
   • Exercise, fitness
   • Shopping, buying, selling
   • Clubs, organizations
   • Internet activities, surfing the Web
   • Entertainment
   • Unhealthy eating habits, excessive dieting
   • Friendships, family relationships
   • Television, movies
   • Cars, boats, sport vehicles

8. If God reveals sin in any area, use this process to return to Him.
   • Confess: agree with God that you have sinned.
   • Repent: turn away from your sin and turn to God to live His way.
   • Seek the Lord's forgiveness and cleansing.
   • Show your repentance by a changed life/deeds.

PRAYER FOR CALLING AND WORKPLACE
Use the following suggestions to guide your personal prayer times about your spiritual growth, your workplace, your profession, and/or your place in Christ's larger mission to touch the world through you.

1. What would You like for me to do to improve my personal relationship with You?

2. Are there hurts or wounds in my past that keep me from experiencing Your love as my Heavenly Father? If so, please heal my spirit and reveal Your perfect and safe love to me in such a way that I'll know Your love for me by experience.

3. What is Your plan for my work and workplace that will bring glory to You and make a difference in the lives of people?

4. Who are the other Christ-followers in my church, my workplace, or my profession with whom I need to talk and pray about Your plans for our work? Whom have You placed in my divine network?

5. What would You like for me to do differently in my work so that my testimony would "make the teaching about God our Savior attractive" (Titus 2:10)?

6. Do I have any work habits, attitudes, or relationship issues that need to change in order to improve my life witness?

7. Are sinful activities, attitudes, policies, or practices present in my work environment? What do You want me to do to bring about change? How can I let You work through me to accomplish Your desire in these matters?

8. In my circles of influence, for whom do You want me to pray? To whom do You want me to witness? Bring someone across my path even today and give me open eyes to recognize Your divine appointments.

9. In what ways can I witness for You and also remain faithful to my employer's work expectations?

10. What would You like to do through me to be a blessing to my employer and cause him or her to prosper?

11. Who are the people around me who are hurting and need special ministry? How can I let Your love flow through me to meet their needs?

12. Do my coworkers or does my employer face problems for which You want to provide a solution or an answer through me? If so, reveal the details to me on Your timetable.

13. With whom would You like for me to intentionally cultivate a relationship as a channel for Your drawing them to Christ?

14. Where in our community or in the world could our company (my employer) be used by You for the sake of people in need? What would You have us do? How do I join You in that work?

15. What would You like to do in and through me today?

My Circles of Influence

The following pages provide lines for you to record the names of people in your circles of influence who do not yet know Christ and to identify God's work through you to reach them. These pages will guide you to survey your world, identify people for whom God gives you a special concern, and pray for those who do not yet believe in Christ.

FAMILY AND RELATIVES

List the people in your immediate family and relatives by blood or marriage who have not yet trusted Christ for salvation. Include the following.

- Husband or wife
- Mother and father
- Stepparents
- Children
- Stepchildren
- Grandchildren
- Sisters and brothers
- Grandparents
- Aunts and uncles
- Cousins
- Nieces and nephews
- In-laws

_____ _____

_____ _____

_____ _____

_____ _____

_____ _____

_____ _____

_____ _____

_____ _____

FRIENDS AND NEIGHBORS

Friends. List the names of people to whom you are particularly close—those you spend time with, care about, trust for counsel, confide in, or depend on in times of need. If you are close to the friend's family, include the names of family members as well. Include in-town friends and out-of-town friends. You may even want to include friends from your past whom you cared about deeply, even though you do not currently maintain contact.

Neighbors. List those who live near you on your street, in your neighborhood, in your apartment building or complex, in your dorm, and so forth. You may need to do research to discover the names of those who live near you. The Lighthouses of Prayer movement suggests that you begin praying for 5 families on your left, 5 on your right, and 11 across the street.

COWORKERS AND ASSOCIATES

List the names of your coworkers and associates—those you regularly see and interact with while performing your work duties. Include the following.

- Coworkers
- Students you teach
- Supervisors/management
- Teammates in sports or recreational activities
- Subordinates
- Fellow club members

- Clients
- Fellow volunteers with whom you regularly work
- Vendors
- Accountants/bookkeepers
- Other employees in your workplace

- Attorneys
- Fellow union members
- Other professionals with whom you work
- School classmates and teachers

_____   _____

_____   _____

_____   _____

_____   _____

_____   _____

_____   _____

_____   _____

_____   _____

_____   _____

_____   _____

_____   _____

_____   _____

ACQUAINTANCES

List the names of people you see only occasionally or for short periods. You may not know these people well, but you know their names or their faces. Include people you know from places like the following.

- Grocery or department store
- Library
- Gas station/market
- Barbershop or hair salon
- Doctor's/dentist's office
- Mall
- Club
- Restaurant
- Fitness center/gym
- Businesses you frequent
- School
- Public transportation
- Government offices

_____   _____

_____   _____

_____   _____

_____   _____

PERSON X

Person X is someone you don't know personally but for whom God gives you a special prayer concern. This list can also include persons you once met in passing and may never see again. These may be people who live either in your town or a long distance from you. Think of the following people you may have met.

- Civic or government leader
- Coach or athlete
- Schoolteacher or principal
- Someone in the news
- Business person/leader
- Law-enforcement officer
- Business owner you see in commercials
- Public servant/employee
- Media personality
- Beggar
- Entertainer
- Homeless person

_____   _____

_____   _____

_____   _____

_____   _____

Adapted from Claude V. King, *Final Command Action Manual* (Murfreesboro, TN: Final Command Resources, 2001), 27–41. Used by permission.

God's Activity Watch List

Read the following suggestions, keeping in mind the people you listed in your circles of influence. Pray and ask God to identify the people on whom He wants you to focus your prayers and attention. Those who come to mind are your most wanted. Write their names on the lines to the right.

_____

_____

_____

_____

1. Pray and ask God to reveal the people of His choosing—those God wants you to carry a special concern for in prayer and action. Do you have a special concern to see a particular person come to faith in Christ? Assume that this concern is from God and add the person to your circles of influence.

2. As you pray through your circles of influence, identify people for whom you develop a special concern during prayer.

3. Watch for spiritual interest or spiritual hunger in the lives of those for whom you are praying. Do people in your circles of influence show a special interest in spiritual things? Are they asking questions about spiritual matters?

4. As you pray, pay special attention to a person who surfaces in your circles of influence almost unexpectedly—someone who surprises you. Ask the Lord whether He has brought that person to your mind because of His work in his or her life.

5. Pray more intensely for people when you become aware of a special need they have. This may be God's invitation for you to show His love by meeting the need.

Do you know of special needs in the lives of any of those in your circles of influence? Pray and ask God whether He wants you to reach out to these people during their time of need.

6. Pay special attention to those around you when you experience a crisis together. A crisis may give you a special opportunity to share Christ, meet a need, or demonstrate Christ's peace or wisdom. Have you recently faced a significant crisis with anyone?

7. When you experience a broken relationship with another person, pray about how you can seek reconciliation in a way God can use for divine purposes in the person's life. Has anyone sinned against you to whom you can show God's mercy by forgiving him or her?

8. Watch for people who enter your circles of influence through unique or special circumstances. God may want to use you to introduce them to Christ. Did you add anyone to your circles of influence who has come into your world by unusual circumstances?

Adapted from Claude V. King, *Final Command Action Manual* (Murfreesboro, TN: Final Command Resources, 2001), 42–43. Used by permission.

Praying for Those Yet to Believe

Use this tool to pray for the people God has identified as your most wanted—those you most want to come to Christ. Read the following suggestions for ways to ask God to work in each person's life. Check those that are meaningful or applicable to the person's circumstances. Ask the Lord to guide you as you read this list. Then as you pray, write on the lines at the right additional ways or Scriptures God guides you to pray for those who need to place their faith in Jesus Christ as Savior and Lord. Start with I Timothy 2:1-4.

_____

_____

_____

_____

_____

_____

❑ Bring the person to recognize and understand his emptiness and purposelessness in life. Bring him to the end of himself so that he will turn to You.

❑ Cause him to hunger and thirst for more in life.

❑ Bring him to understand the truth of his condition without Christ and to understand what Christ has done to make his salvation possible.

❑ Bring conviction of sin. Allow the consequences of his sin to cause him to desire a different life. Let him become disgusted with his life as it is.

❑ Jesus, reveal the Father to him.

❑ Father, exalt Jesus in his eyes.

❑ Father, draw him to Yourself and to Your Son Jesus.

❑ Guide and create circumstances that create a need. Then show Your love by meeting needs through me or other Christ-followers.

❑ Bring godly people into his life that will influence him for Christ.

❑ Prepare circumstances in his relationships so that another Christian or I will have the opportunity to forgive him and thus reveal Your mercy.

❑ Open his ears to hear Your call.

❑ Allow him to see the unity and love of Your people in a way that convinces him that Jesus must be sent from You. Convince him that Jesus is indeed the Savior of the world.

❑ Prepare his life to receive the planting of Your Word.

❑ Protect him from Satan's attempts to blind him and steal the Word that has been sown.

❑ Reduce the cares of the world around him that could choke the planted seed.

❑ Raise up intercessors in behalf of this person. Guide my prayers for him.

❑ Reveal to me the time and the way for me to share a witness about You and the good news of salvation.

❑ Bring him under the hearing and influence of Your Word through teaching or preaching. Create in him an openness to listen.

❑ Create opportunities for him to hear a witness for Christ from several different trusted sources. Use the timing and diversity of these witnesses to convince him that You are the Author behind them all.

❑ Cause him to recognize his need for a Savior.

❑ Lord, do whatever it takes to cause this person to seek You. Break the hardness of his heart toward You.

Adapted from Claude V. King, *Final Command Action Manual* (Murfreesboro, TN: Final Command Resources, 2001), 49–50. Used by permission.

Preparing My Story

A witness is someone who testifies to what he or she has heard, seen, learned, or experienced. Your account of the way you placed your faith in Jesus Christ is a powerful tool because it is true. As you allow Christ's life to show through your life, God can use your testimony to convince others of their need for a relationship with Jesus Christ. Use the following suggestions to prepare your testimony.

IDENTIFY WITH SOMEONE IN SCRIPTURE WHO MET JESUS

Consider beginning your story with a brief example of a person in Scripture who came to faith in Jesus Christ.

1. Timothy grew up in a godly home with religious instruction prior to coming to faith in Christ (see 2 Timothy 1:5).
2. The Samaritan woman at the well had been through five failed relationships before recognizing that she needed a relationship with Jesus Christ, the Living Water (see John 4:7-42).
3. Zacchaeus was an influential but disrespected tax collector who responded to Jesus' invitation and changed his lifestyle (see Luke 19:1-10).
4. The demon-possessed man was out of control and in spiritual bondage until Jesus set him free (see Mark 5:1-20).
5. Thomas overcame doubts to follow Christ (see John 20:24-31).
6. Saul of Tarsus opposed Christianity until meeting Jesus and becoming a powerful preacher of the good news (see Acts 9:1-31).
7. Lydia was a business woman who was transformed when she came to know the truth about Christ (see Acts 16:13-15).
8. The Philippian jailer, at a time of crisis when his life could have been at stake, heard and believed the good news about Jesus (see Acts 16:16-34).

REVIEW YOUR EXPERIENCE WITH CHRIST

What have you experienced of life in Jesus Christ that would prompt someone else to want to know Him? What about your story could others identify with? With what need in your past might they identify? What in your life with Christ would they desire? Why would they want to know the Jesus Christ you have come to know? Consider these questions.

1. What was your life like before you met Christ?
2. What caused you to recognize your need for a Savior?
3. How did you learn about Jesus and the way you could receive His gift of eternal life?
4. What were your greatest challenges in choosing to follow Christ?
5. Who was the most influential person in pointing you to Jesus?
6. When and how did you choose to turn to Christ and follow Him? What Scriptures played a part in your decision?
7. What difference has Christ made in your life?
8. Why would you recommend that others meet Jesus Christ?

WRITE YOUR STORY

Use the lines below to write a beginning draft of your story. Don't glorify your past without Christ. Give the greatest focus to the difference Christ has made or the fullness of your life now because of Him. Refine your story so that you can tell others what Jesus means to you. Then use the following tool, "Introducing Jesus Christ," to share about Jesus.

_____

_____

_____

_____

_____

_____

_____

_____

_____

_____

_____

_____

_____

_____

_____

Introducing Jesus Christ

After you've prepared your story of what Jesus Christ has done in your life, you can begin obeying your mission assignment to be Christ's witness to the world. Combine your personal testimony with a tool that clearly presents the good news of Jesus Christ and explains how a person can place his or her trust in Christ's promise of salvation.

WITNESSING TOOLS

Here are some tools you can use to share the gospel.

1. Gospel tracts
   - *Four Spiritual Laws*
   - *Steps to Peace with God*
   - *The Passion of the Christ*
   - *How to Have a Full and Meaningful Life*
   - *The Bridge to Life*
   - *Discover the Answer to Life's Ultimate Question*
   - *www.christianbook.com*
   - *www.tractleague.com*
   - *www.atstracts.org*

2. Marked New Testaments
   - *Share Jesus Without Fear New Testament*
   - *Here's Hope New Testament*
   - *www.christianbook.com*

3. Christian videos
   - *www.jesusvideo.org*
   - *Jesus* film: *shop.wwp.org/retail/*
   - *www.christianbook.com*
   - *The Passion of the Christ*

4. Evangelism courses
   - FAITH Sunday School Evangelism Strategy: *www.lifeway.com/faith*
   - *Share Jesus Without Fear: www.lifeway.com*
   - *Learning to Share My Faith: www.lifeway.com*

5. Outreach Bible-study resources: *www.serendipityhouse.com*

6. *Meet Jesus Christ* by Claude King can be particularly helpful in sharing the gospel with those who are not familiar with who Jesus is or what He did. *Meet Jesus Christ* tells the accounts of men and women in the Bible who met Jesus and describes their responses to Him. Interactive questions and activities invite the reader to consider the benefits Jesus has to offer them. Each vignette moves readers toward a presentation of the plan of salvation and the way they can experience new life in Jesus Christ. Many people need more than a brief overview of what Jesus has done for us in order to make a life-changing decision. Others need more time to process a message that may require them to turn from their cultural religion and family traditions. This book will give them more time to make a decision. *Meet Jesus Christ,* an 80-page book, is available for bulk orders and mass distribution at *www.finalcommand.org.*

USING THE TOOLS

The following are nonthreatening ways to use the previously described witnessing tools to share the gospel with those in your circles of influence.

Live testimony. Share your personal testimony. Leave a tract or a copy of *Meet Jesus Christ* and say something like this: "Jesus Christ has made such a difference in my life that I'd like for you to meet Him too. I'd like to give you this little book so that you can find out what Jesus can do for you. If you ever have questions, give me a call. My phone number is inside the front cover."

Lighthouses of Prayer. Many people pray for their neighbors through Lighthouses of Prayer. After you have taken actions for prayer and care, deliver a tract or a copy of *Meet Jesus Christ* and use your personal testimony to begin the SHARE phase of your outreach to your neighborhood. For information about Lighthouses of Prayer, visit *www.hopeministries.org.*

Movie night. Invite people for whom you are praying in your circles of influence to your home for a movie such as *Jesus, The Passion of the Christ,* or a Billy Graham film. Share a brief testimony about what Jesus means to you and how the movie has been meaningful to you. Give your guests a tract or *Meet Jesus Christ* as they leave.

Christmas or Easter letter. Many families send out letters with their Christmas cards giving an update on family happenings over the past year. Prepare a Christmas letter explaining that the reason for the season is Jesus. Include your personal testimony of what Jesus has meant to you and your family. Enclose a tract or a copy of *Meet Jesus Christ.* Use the same idea at Eastertime. You could also use this format to invite your most wanted to a special presentation or service at your church around Christmas or Easter.

Church Christmas and Easter presentations. Work with your pastor and church to tell the story of Jesus through music, drama, or other special services around Christmas and Easter. The pastor can extend an invitation at the end of the presentation inviting people to meet the resurrected and living Jesus Christ. Give out tracts or copies of *Meet Jesus Christ.* Your *Made to Count* small group could underwrite the costs and encourage others in your church to pray for and invite the people in their circles of influence who have not yet believed.

Prayer station. Set up a table at local festivals, at sports events, at parades, at special events, or in places with large crowds of people like bus stops and transit stations. Have a banner over the table, brightly colored vests on intercessors, and volunteers at street corners handing out fliers and inviting people to share their prayer needs. After praying for people's needs, talk about their relationship with Jesus Christ. Give people tracts or copies of *Meet Jesus Christ.*

Lay-evangelism workshop. Use the resources in this tool kit to conduct a workshop that trains people to list and pray for the people in their circles of influence, watch to identify those in whose lives God is working, and share their testimonies and the gospel. Provide a variety of resources that participants can examine and use to present the gospel. Invite Christ-followers from your workplace or profession to attend. Spend time praying for God to influence your workplace and community.

Support-group evangelism. Many churches provide Christ-centered support groups to minister to people who are trapped in addiction or other needs that can be helped by group support. Support groups deal with such topics as chemical dependency, codependency, addiction to gambling or pornography, sexual addiction, sexual abuse, grief, divorce recovery, eating disorders, cancer, and other issues. In many cases participants join such a group because they have a felt need, but their deeper need is a relationship with Jesus Christ. *Meet Jesus Christ* can encourage people to come to Jesus for help. The stories of a crippled woman, a bleeding woman, a demon-possessed man, a sinful woman, and even a terrorist named Saul can help support-group participants realize what Jesus can do for them.

Business gift. Many companies provide a gift to patrons from time to time. If your company and its employees are known as Christ-followers, a marked New Testament, the *Jesus* video, *The Passion of the Christ,* or *Meet Jesus Christ* would be a meaningful gift for customers.

———
Adapted from *www.finalcommand.org,* © 2004 Final Command Resources. Used by permission.

God's Word on Work

As you read the following Scriptures, identify reasons to do your best on the job, as well as specific things you should do and should not do.

• Ephesians 6:5-9

Reasons to do my best: _____

_____

Things to do: _____

_____

_____

Things not to do: _____

_____

• Colossians 3:22-24

Reasons to do my best: _____

_____

Things to do: _____

_____

_____

Things not to do: _____

_____

_____

• Colossians 4:1

Reasons to do my best: _____

_____

Things to do: _____

_____

_____

Things not to do: _____

_____

• Titus 2:9-10

Reasons to do my best: _____

_____

Things to do: _____

_____

_____

Things not to do: _____

_____

_____

• 1 Peter 2:18-25

Reasons to do my best: _____

_____

Things to do: _____

_____

_____

Things not to do: _____

_____

_____

God can use the following Scriptures to develop your character and to guide you to act in Christlike ways as you interact with others and conduct your work as a means of bringing glory to God. Read and meditate on these Scriptures. Memorize meaningful ones. Use them for discussion topics during a break, lunch, or commute.

• 1 Chronicles 29:17
• Proverbs 3:5-6
• Proverbs 10:9
• Proverbs 29:7
• John 15:5
• Romans 12:1-2
• Romans 14:17-18
• 1 Corinthians 3:7-9
• 2 Corinthians 5:19-20
• Colossians 3:15-17

• Colossians 4:2-6
• 1 Thessalonians 1:2-10
• 2 Timothy 2:20-21
• Titus 2:7-8
• Titus 2:11-14
• 1 Peter 2:11-12
• 1 Peter 2:13-17
• 1 Peter 4:1-2
• 2 Peter 1:3-4

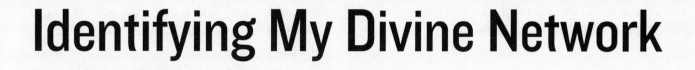

Identifying My Divine Network

> **Read the information about a divine network in the body of Christ and in your workplace. As God brings to mind Christ-followers who can help you with your mission assignment, record their names on the rules provided at the end of each section.**

A DIVINE NETWORK IN THE BODY OF CHRIST

God will place you in connection with other Christ-followers in a divine network. He often works through this network to accomplish things that no individual could accomplish alone. You gain peace and confidence in knowing that you are not alone in God's work. You are part of a team, the body of Christ. Its members bring a variety of gifts and assignments to the task of accomplishing God's purposes.

Members in the body of Christ can—

- pray for you and your concerns at work;
- give you godly and biblical counsel about work issues or decisions;
- help you discern what God wants to do in your workplace and your part in that work;
- encourage you when the going gets tough;
- correct you if you stray from Christlike behavior;
- provide a place for you to share testimonies about what God is doing in the mission field of your workplace;
- rejoice with you when God wins a victory through you;
- help you lead people to faith in Christ;
- help you make disciples of those who are born again.

In *Concentric Circles of Concern* Oscar Thompson tells the story of a couple named Alice and John. Alice was a Christian and a church member, but John was not. Oscar had a group of men he called his SWAT team—Spiritual Weapons and Tactics. This group targeted John. They prayed for him, took him to lunch, and played tennis with him. Soon John began attending church with his wife. Over a period of time, after hearing God's Word preached and experiencing the love of this group of men, John came to radical faith in Christ.

Every church needs SWAT teams, by whatever name they are called. We need to be intentional in reaching out to others for the cause of Christ. In some cases this may be a team of people who sense God's special calling to the target group. In other cases this team may be an existing group that gives part of its attention to outreach and witness. You may be the one who needs a network to help you. You may need people who are called to network with you at work, in your neighborhood, or with some of the people in your circles of influence.

If God called them out, what kind of people would you like to network with to help you obey the Great Commission? Check any that apply.

- ❏ A prayer warrior/intercessor who will pray specifically for me and my most wanted
- ❏ Someone who is gifted at building relationships and showing God's love
- ❏ Someone who is gifted at sharing the plan of salvation and leading a person to faith in Christ
- ❏ Someone who will partner with me in outreach by visiting together, praying together, or working in an outreach project together
- ❏ Someone who can help a new believer grow in faith and discipleship

Record the names of members of the body of Christ who could help with your mission assignment.

_____

_____

_____

_____

_____

_____

_____

_____

_____

A DIVINE NETWORK IN YOUR WORKPLACE

A divine network in your workplace can do things that a network in your church cannot do because its members are on site in the mission field of your workplace. This network may include not only coworkers but also people connected to your work, such as vendors, customers, and contract workers. As you gather with other Christ-followers in your workplace, you can share and pray with insight and knowledge.

Christ-followers in your workplace can—

- pray for those in authority over you;
- pray for specific individuals who need to know Christ;
- take specific problems to the Lord in prayer to seek God's direction;

- share evidence of God's activity that, when shared, sometimes reveals a clear plan that an individual could not see;
- discuss the application of Scripture to work practices, issues, problems, or decisions;
- confess sin to the Lord in behalf of your company and seek God's direction for seeking change in a God-honoring way;
- unite in prayer to seek God's work strategy;
- pray for one another and specific work concerns—relationships, decisions, problems, and so forth;
- pray together for work-related breakthroughs that will bring attention to the God you serve, like events in the lives of Joseph and Daniel.

Record the names of Christ-followers in your workplace who could be on mission with you.

_____

_____

_____

_____

_____

_____

_____

_____

_____

_____

_____

_____

——

Adapted from Claude V. King, _Final Command Action Manual_ (Murfreesboro, TN: Final Command Resources, 2001), 78–81. Used by permission.

Leader Guide

God created us and placed us in the body of Christ so that we could work together with other Christ-followers to see God's kingdom come on earth as it is in heaven. We are interdependent with one another. We cannot function as we ought without the rest of the body. *Made to Count Life Planner* guides Christ-followers to help one another discover, accept, and fulfill their God-given missions in a way that will make a difference in their world.

If you have not already done so, read "Using the *Life Planner*" on pages 6–7 before you continue this guide.

A SMALL-GROUP STUDY

Made to Count Life Planner was designed for self-paced, interactive learning. This means that individuals can read and study at their own pace to complete the daily assignments in the workbook. The content is designed to interact with readers. A segment of content is presented. Then a learning activity calls readers to respond. If correct answers can be identified, the content following a learning activity helps readers check their answers.

The individual study, however, is not complete without weekly small-group sessions to process learning and to help participants with application. This small-group process will take from 10 to 13 weeks. Typically, the first small-group meeting will be an introductory session or a retreat in which the message of the study will be introduced and workbooks will be distributed (see the ideas on p. 211). Members will begin their individual study following that session or retreat. However, the introductory session or retreat may be omitted. If so, distribute workbooks a week in advance of session 1 so that members can complete week 1 before meeting to discuss what they have studied.

Small groups will meet once each week for 10 weeks to discuss the content of the workbook. Your group may choose to end the study after session 10. Or you can expand the study to 13 weeks by conducting an optional Great Commission workshop (see p. 212) and adding a night to watch *Chariots of Fire* (see p. 222) or to catch up, review, or share testimonies.

> **Made to Count** Study Plan
> • Introductory session/retreat (optional)
> • 10 small-group sessions
> • Great Commission workshop (optional)
> • Night at the movies or session to catch up, review, or share testimonies (optional)

These options will help if you are coordinating your study with a Sunday School or church-school calendar based on 13-week quarters. Of course, some small groups may choose to continue meeting for prayer and support beyond the designated study period.

FORMING A SMALL GROUP

Although this message applies to home and church life, primary emphasis will be placed on application to participants' professions and workplaces. Therefore, the ideal small group for this study will be coworkers at a common workplace or workers in the same profession. As Christ-followers in the same workplace gather to share and pray, they will be able to deal with specific concerns and issues that are unique to their workplace. People from the same occupation or profession will be able to deal with common professional issues that they all confront. Ask God to guide you to enlist the people He wants in the group.

Your small group could consist of—
• coworkers in your immediate workplace;
• coworkers in your company;
• Christ-followers from your line of work or a similar line of work (for example, accountants, assembly-line workers, lawyers, nurses, schoolteachers, truck drivers, bankers, salespersons, and so forth);

- business persons who meet in a central location like a downtown church, restaurant, civic club, community center, or athletic club;
- fellow church members;
- a discipleship-training group;
- a home cell group or house church;
- retirees with common interests.

The sharing, discussion, and prayer that will take place in the small-group sessions need to be personal and in-depth. If a group is too large, some people will feel left out or frustrated if they don't have adequate opportunities to share, and shy people will not be challenged to participate fully. For this reason we suggest that you form groups of 6 to 8 people, with a maximum of 10. If more than 10 people want to participate, form multiple groups of 6 or 8. If several groups are meeting in the same workplace, profession, or church, you may want to schedule a couple of joint sessions so that people can share what God is teaching them.

This topic of this course provides a great opportunity to include people who have not yet accepted Christ. Be sensitive to the way God moves among the unsaved members of the group and give them appropriate opportunities to accept Christ. The activities following week 3 will assume that the participant is in a relationship with Christ.

SCHEDULE

Each week's group study, involving about one hour of sharing and praying, could be scheduled during a lunch hour, before or after work, on a Saturday morning, on a Sunday afternoon or evening, or at another convenient time. Some groups may wish to meet twice during the week for briefer periods. Consult participants to determine the optimal time for group sessions. If the sessions are held at work, do not allow them to extend into work time.

RESOURCES

Each participant will need a copy of *Made to Count Life Planner.* Because each person will need to give individual responses to the learning activities, a married couple will need to have two workbooks instead of sharing one copy. Order copies in advance (item 1-4158-2819-9) by writing

to LifeWay Church Resources Customer Service; One LifeWay Plaza; Nashville, TN 37234-0113; faxing (615) 251-5933; phoning toll free (800) 458-2772; e-mailing *customerservice@lifeway.com;* ordering online at *www.lifeway.com;* or visiting a LifeWay Christian Store.

The companion book *Made to Count,* though not required for your study of the Life Planner, is a valuable supplementary resource. You can purchase the book (item 0-8499-1819-7) at your local Christian bookstore or order online at *www.madetocount.com.*

Some Christian employers may want to provide this study as training and development for employees, in which case the cost of workbooks would be covered by the employer. Churches that coordinate small groups may want to cover some or all of the cost of the workbooks. In other cases participants will be expected to buy their own workbooks. Announce the cost as you enlist participants so that they will be prepared to pay for them at the introductory session or at another designated time. Be sensitive to people who may need financial assistance. In those cases you may want to subsidize the cost of the book or provide a scholarship.

YOUR ROLE AS A SMALL-GROUP LEADER

One small-group leader can be enlisted for the entire study, or participants may rotate the responsibility each week. As the small-group leader, you do not have to be a content expert. You will not be required to master the material and teach or lecture on the weekly topics. Team members will have already studied and started applying the content before coming to each group session. You will guide discussion, sharing, and prayer related to the content that members will have studied during the week. One of your primary roles is to guide participants to seek the Lord and His counsel about His mission assignments for their lives and workplaces.

Following this introduction you will find plans for conducting 10 small-group sessions. Each session provides suggestions for team building, responses to activities in the workbook, questions for content review, discussion questions, an optional special assignment for a volunteer, and a closing time of prayer.

SMALL-GROUP SESSION PLAN

- Team building
- Activity responses
- Content review
- Discussion questions
- Special assignment
- Prayer

Turn to page 213 and examine the session plan for group session 1.

The suggested session plans are not intended to be a rigid outline for the group sessions. They primarily guide you to the week's topics that might be most helpful to review and discuss. Feel free to adapt the suggestions and questions for discussion to meet the specific needs of your small group. Also add your own discussion questions or activities to customize the meeting to the unique character of your group.

For each group session determine an optimal time allotment for each segment of the session plan. Adjust these time allotments from week to week to best meet the needs of your group. Items in **bold type** indicate our suggestions for the most meaningful or significant topics for consideration.

One tendency will be to spend so much time in discussion that little time is left for prayer. Work diligently to avoid that temptation. Prayer, as you will learn, needs to be a major part of your work strategy. This may be the time God gives specific directions or answers to participants that no amount of discussion could achieve. Ask members to help you reserve time for the closing prayer period. If necessary, set an alarm or a timer to announce the close of discussion.

The special assignments in each session may require more than one week's preparation. Therefore, you may want to make these assignments several weeks in advance.

Spend time in prayer for yourself and the group so that you will be spiritually prepared for the session.

IDEAS FOR AN INTRODUCTORY SESSION OR RETREAT

An introductory session or retreat gives you an opportunity to introduce the message and format of *Made to Count Life Planner,* to communicate expectations, to encourage participation, to distribute copies of the workbook, and to set the spiritual tone for the study. Use some of the following ideas to plan this session.

1. Invite several participants in advance to share a testimony about the joy or challenge of living their faith in their workplaces or professions. If you have participants who have already studied the *Life Planner,* ask them to share testimonies about what God did during the study to make an impact on their life and work.

2. Distribute copies of the workbook and introduce *Made to Count Life Planner* by presenting the content of pages 6–7. Show members that each chapter is divided into five daily segments of reading and activities that they are expected to complete.

3. Consider asking participants to complete some or all of "My Faith at Work Assessment" (pp. 190–93). Allow time to complete the assigned items; then invite volunteers to share responses to some of the items (for instance, activities 6–8, 12–13, 16, 20–22, 25). If you have a large group (more than 10), divide into smaller groups of five to eight participants each for the sharing time so that more people can participate.

4. Present the group-study process that will be followed in each session and answer questions.

5. Take time to pray for the study.

6. Secure commitments from participants. Announce the date and time of the first group session and encourage participants to complete week 1 before coming to the session.

GREAT COMMISSION WORKSHOP

Consider conducting a Great Commission workshop between sessions 5 and 6 to help participants prepare to share the gospel of Jesus Christ through their relationships and to the ends of the earth. Or work with the small group to develop a Great Commission workshop for others in your church following the completion of your study of the *Life Planner*.

Before the workshop secure copies of some of the sample resources listed on page 204, adding others available from your denomination or local Christian bookstore.

Follow this process to conduct the workshop.

1. Use the content of week 6, the group-session plans for session 6, and the following items in the *Made to Count* Tool Kit to encourage and equip the body of Christ to obey the Great Commission.
   - "My Circles of Influence" (pp. 196–99)
   - "God's Activity Watch List" (p. 200)
   - "Praying for Those Yet to Believe" (p. 201)
   - "Preparing My Story" (pp. 202–3)
   - "Introducing Jesus Christ" (pp. 204–5)
   - "Identifying My Divine Network" (pp. 207–8)
2. Provide guidance and time for participants to complete the following activities.
   - Page 104, activities 4–5
   - Page 106, activities 2–4
   - Page 109, activities 8–9
   - Pages 202–3, "Preparing My Story"
   - Overview and model through role playing the various methods for introducing Jesus Christ on pages 204–5. Provide sample resources (such as tracts, books, marked New Testaments, and movies) for participants to examine.
   - Pages 115–19
   - Page 178, activity 1
3. Spend ample time praying for one another and for those who have not yet believed.
4. Discuss ways God may want your small group to become a SWAT team (see p. 207).

SESSION 1

A Life That Counts

TEAM BUILDING

What was it like growing up in your hometown?
What did you do for your first paying job?

ACTIVITY RESPONSES

1. Page 13, activity 3
2. **Page 16, activity 2**
3. Page 18, activity 2
4. Page 20, activity 4
5. **Page 22, activity 3**

WEEK 1 REVIEW

1. What are some ways Paul made a difference in his world (p. 13)?
2. What are the eight principles for a life that counts (p. 15)?
3. What are the three stages in God's process of making your life count? Which stage are you in now (p. 17)?
4. What are the characteristics of a mission or ministry that makes a difference (p. 20)?
5. What are some arenas in which God may give assignments for ministry (p. 22)?
6. **Which Scripture, illustration, idea, statement, or activity in week 1 was most meaningful to you? Why?**

DISCUSSION QUESTIONS

1. Read Philippians 2:13 (p. 11). What difference is present in Christ-followers that is not present in others because God lives in us and guides us to choose and do what pleases Him?
2. Do you agree or disagree with the following statement? Why or why not? "Every believer's vocation should be the result of a call by God" (p. 11).
3. Besides those who serve in full-time church-related positions like pastors or missionaries, who are some Christ-followers who have made a difference in their world? What have they done to influence others and to bring about change for good? These may be people you know or people you have only heard about.
4. **What do you think churches and pastors could do to better help lay people understand and more effectively live a calling for Christ in their daily lives?**
5. What are some of the greatest challenges in our society that hinder Christ-followers from living their faith more publicly?
6. What characteristics of God encourage you to believe that He can help you make a difference through your life?

SPECIAL ASSIGNMENT

Ask one or more volunteers to read the supplementary-reading assignments from *Made to Count* that are suggested at the beginning of each week in order to contribute additional illustrations or insights to the small-group discussions.

PRAYER

Invite volunteers to share what they want or need to get from this study of *Made to Count Life Planner*. Allow several members to lead the group in prayer that God will work in each of your lives during the coming weeks to make a difference in your world. *Optional in quads (groups of four):* Ask, How may we pray for you? Then pray for members one at a time.

SESSION 2

God's Unique Plan

PRINCIPLE I
God prepared a unique plan and calling for your
life even before you were born.

TEAM BUILDING

Why and how did you choose your current career and/or job?

ACTIVITY RESPONSES

1. Page 33, activity 4
2. Page 34, activity 2
3. Page 44, activity 4

WEEK 2 REVIEW

1. What is principle 1 for a life that counts?
2. Based on Ephesians 2:10, what did God create us for? What are examples of the purpose for which God created us (p. 30)?
3. What are some ways God worked through John the Baptist that made his life count (pp. 31–33)?
4. What makes a job or career sacred (p. 35, activity 3)?
5. What kinds of careers are represented by the people listed in Hebrews 11—the faith hall of fame (p. 36)?
6. What was the key to Joseph's success? What effect did that have on his masters (pp. 39–40)?
7. **Which Scripture, illustration, idea, statement, or activity in week 2 was most meaningful to you? Why?**

DISCUSSION QUESTIONS

1. **What is the traditional understanding of the differences between sacred and secular callings? How would you define *sacred calling* after reading this week's material?**
2. Does God's calling for your life guarantee success in the world's thinking? Why or why not (p. 43)?
3. What attributes or characteristics of God would lead you to agree that He planned for your life and calling before you are born?
4. How have you perceived God's calling for your life until now? Or have you?
5. If you were an outside observer of the lives of Rick Husband, astronaut (p. 24); Jay Sekulow, lawyer (pp. 26–27); or Peggy Wehmeyer, news correspondent (p. 37), what do you think you would observe in their work because they are Christ-followers that would be different if they were not Christ-followers?
6. What would be different about the church's impact on our culture if every Christ-follower understood and lived according to God's unique plan and calling for his or her life?

SPECIAL ASSIGNMENT

Ask a volunteer to secure a copy of *The Marketplace Annotated Bibliography: A Christian Guide to Books on Work, Business, and Vocation* by Pete Hammond, R. Paul Stevens, and Todd Svanoe (Downers Grove: InterVarsity Press, 2002) and to briefly review it in session 3. This book is the largest and most complete resource of annotated reviews on the subject of integrating faith and work.

PRAYER

Conversational prayer (members take turns praying, usually about one topic at a time): Pray for one another and for your church or churches that God will reveal His mission and calling to everyone and that His influence will increasingly be present in your community. *Optional in quads:* Ask, How may we pray for you? Then pray for members one at a time.

SESSION 3

Called to a Relationship

> **PRINCIPLE 2**
> God calls you to a life-changing relationship with Him through Jesus Christ.

TEAM BUILDING

Quads: When and how did you come to know Jesus Christ in a personal way? What difference has Christ made in your life?

ACTIVITY RESPONSES

1. Pages 50–51, activity 7
2. **Pages 54–55, activity 2**
3. Page 55, activity 4
4. Pages 61–62, activity 2

WEEK 3 REVIEW

1. What is principle 2 for a life that counts (p. 48)?
2. What are two things to which God calls you (p. 49, activity 4)?
3. What are some characteristics of the old, sinful nature and the new creation (p. 52)?
4. What are some lessons we need to learn from the parable of the Vine and the branches (pp. 58–59)?
5. What are some ways we can abide in Christ (p. 60)?
6. What are three purposes of a prayer relationship (pp. 62–63)?
7. **Which Scripture, illustration, idea, statement, or activity in week 3 was most meaningful to you? Why?**

DISCUSSION QUESTIONS

1. God used William Wilberforce (pp. 46–47) to bring an end to slavery. If God raised up people to accomplish the task, what are some of the evils in our society that need to be removed or changed?
2. **What is the difference between practicing religion and having a personal relationship with Jesus Christ (p. 54)?**
3. What are some ways you have experienced a life-changing relationship with Jesus Christ? What difference has Christ made in your life?
4. How do you think God could use your relationship with Him to make a difference in the lives of others in your home or your workplace?
5. What differences would occur in your prayer life if you approached prayer as a relationship with a Person rather than a religious duty you must perform?
6. **What have you experienced this week in prayer or in unhurried time with God that has been refreshing or meaningful?**
7. What changes would you like to make in your prayer relationship with God?
8. What are some appropriate ways and times your personal relationship with Jesus Christ can be reflected in your life in a way that touches others?

SPECIAL ASSIGNMENT

1. Call on the member who volunteered to review *The Marketplace Annotated Bibliography: A Christian Guide to Books on Work, Business, and Vocation.*
2. Ask a volunteer to investigate the content and resources of InterVarsity's Ministry in Daily Life Web site (*www.ivmdl.org*) and to briefly report in session 4.

PRAYER

Conversational prayer: Pray about your personal relationships with God, your prayer lives, and your abiding in Christ. *Optional in quads:* Ask, How may we pray for you? Then pray for members one at a time.

SESSION 4
Called to a Mission

> **PRINCIPLE 3**
> God calls you to partner with Him in a mission that is bigger than you are.

TEAM BUILDING

What is the greatest challenge or difficulty you face in living your faith on the job? *Or:* What is the greatest joy you have experienced in living your faith on the job?

ACTIVITY RESPONSES

1. Pages 69–70, activity 4
2. Page 76, activity 6. If you use this one, take time to pray for one another after responses are made.
3. **Page 82, activity 2**

WEEK 4 REVIEW

1. What is principle 3 for a life that counts (p. 66)?
2. What are the two parts of God's twofold call (p. 67)?
3. Why should Christ-followers devote themselves to doing what is good (p. 70, activity 5)?
4. What are some ways Christ-followers should live that are "profitable for everyone" (Titus 3:8, p. 71)?
5. What are types of mission assignments God may give you (pp. 79–80)?
6. What are seven arenas in which God may give a mission assignment? Can you think of others? What are they (pp. 80–81)?
7. **Which Scripture, illustration, idea, statement, or activity in week 4 was most meaningful to you? Why?**

DISCUSSION QUESTIONS

1. What would the difference be in quality and fruitfulness if God were the primary planner for my mission rather than me?
2. What are the responsibilities that come with salvation (p. 68)?
3. If Christ-followers lived and worked as Paul instructed in the Book of Titus, what differences would be evident in your workplace?
4. Do you agree or disagree with the following statement? Why or why not? "You are most Christlike when you forgive" (p. 75).
5. How is your life like a PVC pipe? What, if anything, did you learn from this parable? What, if anything, do you need to do as a response to this understanding about your life (pp. 74–75)?
6. **From the guidelines to consider for mission assignments (pp. 77–78), what thoughts or insights were most meaningful or applicable to your life? Why?**
7. Consider separately each arena listed on pages 80–81 as you answer: What are some ways God might use a Christ-follower to make a difference in this arena?
8. If a person is not hearing from God about an assignment, what might the reason be? What should he or she do about it (p. 82)?

SPECIAL ASSIGNMENT

1. Call on the member who volunteered to investigate and report on the content and resources of InterVarsity's Ministry in Daily Life Web site.
2. Ask a volunteer to investigate the content and resources of Youth with a Mission's Marketplace Mission Web site (*www.scruples.org*) and to briefly report in session 5.

PRAYER

Conversational prayer: Pray that God will prepare you for the mission assignments He has for you and that He will make the assignments clear. *Optional in quads:* Ask, How may we pray for you? Then pray for members one at a time.

SESSION 5

Called Now

> **PRINCIPLE 4**
> God calls you to be on mission with Him right where you are—starting now.
>
> **TOOL KIT**
> My Faith at Work Assessment (pp. 190–93)
> My Personal Prayer Guide (pp. 194–95)

TEAM BUILDING

If you could go anywhere and work at any job for one year, where would you go, and what would you do?

ACTIVITY RESPONSES

1. Page 88, activity 8
2. Page 92, activity 5
3. Page 95, activity 3
4. **Page 96, activity 2. Review responses to "My Faith at Work Assessment" in pairs or as a team.**
5. Page 97, activity 4

WEEK 5 REVIEW

1. What is principle 4 for a life that counts (p. 86)?
2. What are three types of career assignments that God may give (p. 88)?
3. In what ways did Aquila and Priscilla make a difference in their world (pp. 89–91)?
4. What are some ways God may work through a person to make an impact on his or her world (pp. 93–95)?
5. What are five different arenas in which God may focus His primary mission assignment for you (p. 96)?
6. What question can you use to open an opportunity to minister to hurting or needy people through prayer (p. 99, activity 5)?
7. **Which Scripture, illustration, idea, statement, or activity in week 5 was most meaningful to you? Why?**

DISCUSSION QUESTIONS

1. What are some advantages and disadvantages for lay people to host churches in their homes?
2. How could church planting by lay people in their homes, workplaces, or community facilities make a difference in your community, city, or region?
3. **What are some ways you have experienced God working through you to influence the lives of others (pp. 93–95)? In what ways have you missed God's work by not knowing His ways?**
4. What are some ways Christ-followers can have the greatest influence on their work or workplace?
5. In what way do you sense that God may be guiding you to be a partner with Him in your work or workplace?
6. What changes would you most like to take place in your profession or workplace to make it a more Christ-like activity or environment ("My Faith at Work Assessment," activity 17)?
7. What questions would you like to have answered about living your faith in your workplace or profession ("My Faith at Work Assessment," activity 25)?

SPECIAL ASSIGNMENT

1. Call on the member who volunteered to investigate and report on the content and resources of Youth with a Mission's Marketplace Mission Web site.
2. Ask a volunteer to check with your church or visit a local or online Christian bookstore and secure copies of evangelistic tracts, a marked New Testament, and other witnessing tools for participants to review in session 6. Refer the volunteer to the list of resources on page 204.

PRAYER

Conversational prayer and suggestions from "My Personal Prayer Guide": Pray that God will work through each of you to make a difference right now where you are.

SESSION 6

Called to a Great Commission

TOOL KIT

My Circles of Influence (pp. 196–99)
God's Activity Watch List (p. 200)
Praying for Those Yet to Believe (p. 201)
Preparing My Story (pp. 202–3)
Introducing Jesus Christ (pp. 204–5)

TEAM BUILDING

Who had the greatest influence on your coming to faith in Christ? *Or:* Who is the Christian business person or layperson you admire most for his walk with Christ? Why?

ACTIVITY RESPONSES

1. Page 102, activities 1–2
2. Page 104, activity 5. Why?
3. Page 106, activities 2–3
4. Page 108, activity 7
5. Page 109, activity 9
6. Page 113, activity 4
7. Page 116, activity 2
8. Page 117, activity 4
9. Page 119, activities 6–7

WEEK 6 REVIEW

1. How does the Great Commission relate to the eight principles for a life that counts (pp. 102–3)?
2. In Acts 1:8 what were the areas where Jesus' first disciples were to be His witnesses? What corresponds to those areas for you and your church (p. 103)?
3. What are some ways a person can cultivate relationships in order to build bridges to others (p. 109)?
4. What are some ways you can introduce Jesus Christ to those who need to know Him (pp. 111–14)? Ask the special-assignment volunteer to display samples of tracts and other evangelistic tools he or she has located.

5. Which Scripture, illustration, idea, statement, or activity in week 6 was most meaningful to you? Why?

DISCUSSION QUESTIONS

1. What was Paul's primary strategy for building redemptive relationships (p. 107, activity 3)? In your experience which of these responses is more typical? Or is not building redemptive relationships more typical?
2. **How can you help one another reach out evangelistically to those in your circles of influence?**
3. What is a time or a way you have introduced someone to Jesus Christ? Briefly describe it and the person's response.
4. What are some meaningful ways we can pray for those who need to believe?
5. Read John 4:34-38. What do you think Jesus would say about the harvest around you?
6. What would be different in your community if Christ-followers began to obey Jesus' final command—the Great Commission?
7. How has God worked through you or your church to touch the ends of the earth? What do you sense that He wants to do?

SPECIAL ASSIGNMENT

Ask a volunteer to investigate and prepare an information-and-contact list of local chapters of Christian business and professional groups or ministries (Christian Medical Dental Society, CBMC, Christ@Work [FCCI], Priority Associates, Executive Ministries, Nurses Christian Fellowship, and so forth). This volunteer should be prepared to distribute copies of the list in session 7.

PRAYER

Pray for one person in each of your circles of influence who needs Christ. Pray for guidance and boldness to witness to these people.

SESSION 7

God Reveals His Mission, Part I

PRINCIPLE 5

God reveals His mission through His Word, His Spirit, wise counsel, and His work in circumstances around you.

TOOL KIT

God's Word on Work (p. 206)

TEAM BUILDING

If you could change one thing about your work environment to make it more pleasant, what would you change?

ACTIVITY RESPONSES

1. Page 130, activity 10
2. Page 131, activity 3
3. Page 133, activity 3
4. Page 134, activity 4
5. Page 135, activity 5

WEEK 7 REVIEW

1. What is principle 5 for a life that counts (p. 122)?
2. What are four means through which God reveals His mission (p. 122)?
3. What are six specific aspects of the assignments God may give (pp. 124–25)?
4. What are the benefits or values that come from applying Scripture to your life (p. 127, activity 5)?
5. What are some ways you can know that God is speaking (pp. 129–30, activity 9)? Take time to discuss participants' questions.
6. **Which Scripture, illustration, idea, statement, or activity in week 7 was most meaningful to you? Why?**

DISCUSSION QUESTIONS

1. What is the importance of a willingness to obey even before God gives an assignment (p. 125)?
2. How can group prayer put together the pieces of God's vision (p. 134)? How have you experienced God revealing His mission or plan during group prayer?
3. **Which suggestions for prayer on pages 136–37 were most meaningful to you? Why?**
4. Why do you need to be careful about giving God deadlines when you pray and seek His will (p. 137)?
5. If others have given you a deadline and God has not answered, how should you respond (p. 137)?
6. How have you experienced God revealing His mission to you through His Word or through His Spirit?
7. As you recall the previous weeks of this study, what do you sense that God has been saying to you about your relationship with Him and His mission for you?

SPECIAL ASSIGNMENT

1. Call on the member who volunteered to investigate and distribute lists of local chapters of Christian business and professional groups or ministries.
2. Ask a volunteer to utilize *The Marketplace Annotated Bibliography*, your church library, the bibliography in *Made to Count*, and/or Internet research to prepare a list of biographies of Christians who have made contributions in non–church-related fields. The volunteer should be prepared to distribute copies of the list in session 8.

PRAYER

Conversational prayer: Pray that members will learn to hear God's voice. Ask the Lord to speak as you pray together. *Optional in quads:* Ask, How may we pray for you? Then pray for members one at a time.

SESSION 8

God Reveals His Mission, Part 2

> **PRINCIPLE 5**
> God reveals His mission through His Word, His Spirit, wise counsel, and His work in circumstances around you.

TEAM BUILDING

Quads: Briefly describe ways you sense that God has guided your work history to bring you to where you are today.

ACTIVITY RESPONSES

1. Page 144, activity 3
2. Page 145, activity 6
3. Page 150, activity 3
4. Page 151, activity 4
5. **Pages 154–55, activity 3**

WEEK 8 REVIEW

1. What is principle 5 for a life that counts (p. 140)?
2. **What does Proverbs 29:18 mean by "a vision" (p. 140)?**
3. When you sense that God has given you direction, what steps can you can take to test your impression (p. 142)?
4. What are some good questions to ask a mentor (p. 144)?
5. What are some questions to ask a spiritual counselor to clarify God's calling or mission assignment (p. 145)?
6. **What are some ways God uses circumstances to reveal His mission (pp. 152–54)?**
7. **Which Scripture, illustration, idea, statement, or activity in week 8 was most meaningful to you? Why?**

DISCUSSION QUESTIONS

1. How have you experienced God's presence at work this week? When and how?

2. What are the differences between a vision that a person creates and a divine revelation that God gives?
3. How did God guide Philip to the mission assignment with an Ethiopian official? What lesson(s) can we learn?
4. How did God guide Paul through wise counsel and circumstances? What lessons can we learn from him?
5. What is the difference between a mentor and a spiritual counselor? When would you use each?
6. Review in day 5 (pp. 152–54) the ways God may work through circumstances around you to reveal His mission. Which insights were most meaningful or helpful? What questions do you still have?
7. **What are some ways, if any, God has revealed Himself, His mission, or His ways to you during the past few weeks? How did He reveal these things to you?**
8. How best can our small group help one another know God's will and calling for our lives and work?

SPECIAL ASSIGNMENT

1. Call on the member who volunteered to prepare and distribute lists of biographies of Christians who have made contributions in non–church-related fields.
2. Ask a volunteer to contact other local churches to identify those that have groups or provide special ministries to Christians in their workplaces, such as seminars, conferences, workshops, or retreats. The volunteer should collect contact information and be prepared to distribute lists of this information in session 9.

PRAYER

Conversational prayer: Pray for one another and for God's wisdom and revelation of His mission for your lives and work. *Optional in quads:* Ask, How may we pray for you? Then pray for members one at a time.

SESSION 9

God Forges, Guides, and Provides

PRINCIPLES 6-7

6. God repeatedly brings you to a crossroads of choice as He forges you for His mission.
7. God guides and provides for your mission one step at a time.

TEAM BUILDING

What gift, resource, or opportunity has God given you for which you believe He expects the greatest accountability?

ACTIVITY RESPONSES

1. Pages 158–59, activity 2. Why?
2. **Pages 159–60, activity 3**
3. **Page 160, activity 4**
4. Pages 163–64, activity 6
5. Page 174, activity 3

WEEK 9 REVIEW

1. What are three stages in God's process of making your life count (p. 158)?
2. What is principle 6 for a life that counts (p. 161)?
3. **What are some choices you may be required to make at the crossroads in life (p. 167)?**
4. What is principle 7 for a life that counts (p. 169)?
5. If your faith is weak, what are four truths about faith that should encourage you (pp. 174–75)?
6. **Which Scripture, illustration, idea, statement, or activity in week 9 was most meaningful to you? Why?**

DISCUSSION QUESTIONS

1. In what ways does God use crossroads choices to guide and forge (shape) us for His service? Give examples.

2. **How can a wrong choice at a crossroads affect your future usefulness for Christ? Give examples.**
3. What are scriptural examples when God gave someone a second chance and when He did not?
4. What are some difficult choices in your workplace that may be crossroads choices? *Or:* What are some typical choices people have to make in their workplaces?
5. **What is the difference between a spiritual gift and the Gift (p. 173)? How are these gifts related?**
6. What are some of the resources God may provide to help you fulfill your mission?
7. **Suppose God calls you to a mission assignment, and you don't see how you can do it with your resources and skills. How should you respond?**
8. A presumptuous sin is one in which a person presumes on God to do something or presumes that he or she knows what God would say or desire when God has not revealed this information. What are some examples of presumptuous sins? What is the difference between presumption and faith?

SPECIAL ASSIGNMENT

1. Call on the member who volunteered to identify and distribute lists of other churches that have groups or provide ministries to Christians in their workplaces.
2. Ask a volunteer to investigate and report on resources and training opportunities on workplace ministry that are provided by your church's denomination or para-church associations. The volunteer should be prepared to distribute lists with this information in session 10.

PRAYER

Quads: Ask, How may we pray for you? Then pray for members one at a time.

SESSION 10

God Makes Your Life Count

PRINCIPLE 8
When you answer God's call, you experience His pleasure and change your world.

TOOL KIT
Identifying My Divine Network (pp. 207–8)

TEAM BUILDING

What has God said or done during the past two or three months that has been the most meaningful or life-changing?

ACTIVITY RESPONSES

1. Pages 207–8, all activities
2. Page 181, activity 4. Why?
3. Page 183, activity 4
4. Page 185, activity 4
5. Page 188, activity 3

WEEK 10 REVIEW

1. What is principle 8 for a life that counts (p. 180)?
2. What are some things Scripture identifies that are pleasing and not pleasing to God (p. 183, activity 3)?
3. Would our small group like to meet to watch *Chariots of Fire*? Shall we bring our families (p. 184, activity 5)?
4. Which Scripture, illustration, idea, statement, or activity in week 10 was most meaningful to you? Why? Which one in the entire study has been most meaningful?

DISCUSSION QUESTIONS

1. What are some ways your church could facilitate and support your work in your mission fields? What are some ways it already provides support (p. 179)?

2. How could you share your thoughts with your pastor and church in a way that is not critical but constructive?
3. What should we learn from the way Jesus constantly pointed to the Father as His source of words and power (p. 184, activity 1, and p. 185, activity 3)?
4. What do you sense that you (we) need to do next to follow God's calling on our lives (p. 189, activity 4)?
5. What has God done in or through our lives during our study of *Made to Count Life Planner* that deserves our praise and thanks?
6. Shall we meet again, perhaps over a meal, to catch up, review, or share testimonies (see p. 209)?

SPECIAL ASSIGNMENT

1. Call on the member who volunteered to investigate and distribute lists of resources and training opportunities on workplace ministry that are provided by your church's denomination or parachurch associations.
2. Call for reports from anyone who has been on special assignment and has not yet reported to the group.
3. Ask volunteers to write brief testimonials of ways God has used *Made to Count Life Planner* to encourage, strengthen, and equip them for their unique callings. Mail to Leadership and Adult Publishing; LifeWay Church Resources; One LifeWay Plaza; Nashville, TN 37234-0175.
4. Announce any plans for a Great Commission workshop (see p. 212).

PRAYER

Consider having a commissioning time for each person to fulfill his or her mission as God reveals it. ***Quads (or as a team, if time allows):* Ask one person at a time, How may we pray for you about your sense of God's mission for you or His plans for your work life? Then pray for that person before asking the next person.**